Beer 101 North

Beer 101 North

*Craft Breweries and Brewpubs
of the Washington and Oregon Coasts*

JON C. STOTT

McFarland & Company, Inc., Publishers
Jefferson, North Carolina

LIBRARY OF CONGRESS CATALOGUING-IN-PUBLICATION DATA

Names: Stott, Jon C., author.
Title: Beer 101 North : craft breweries and brewpubs of the Washington and Oregon coasts / Jon C. Stott.
Description: Jefferson, North Carolina : McFarland & Company, Inc., Publishers, 2017. | Includes bibliographical references and index.
Identifiers: LCCN 2017031154 | ISBN 9781476665672 (softcover : acid free paper) ∞
Subjects: LCSH: Microbreweries—Washington (State)—Guidebooks. | Microbreweries—Oregon—Guidebooks. | Beer—Washington (State) | Beer—Oregon.
Classification: LCC TP573.U5 S76 2017 | DDC 663/.309797—dc23
LC record available at https://lccn.loc.gov/2017031154

BRITISH LIBRARY CATALOGUING DATA ARE AVAILABLE

ISBN (print) 978-1-4766-6567-2
ISBN (ebook) 978-1-4766-2945-2

Front cover photographs © 2017 iStock

Printed in the United States of America

McFarland & Company, Inc., Publishers
 Box 611, Jefferson, North Carolina 28640
  www.mcfarlandpub.com

To my daughter Clare,
in gratitude for all her support

Acknowledgments

Although this book bears my name on the cover, it could not have been written without the assistance of many people. I am grateful to all the brewery and brewpub owners and brewers who graciously took time to share their stories and their beer. To the writers of the many fine beer books and magazine articles which I consulted during my research and writing, thank you. Finally, to my daughter Clare, thank you as usual for your support and for helping me with the tasting notes for many of the beers we sampled.

Table of Contents

Preface

Since 2010, the number of craft breweries and brewpubs operating in the United States has increased enormously. According to the Brewers Association, 4,656 were doing business in the middle of 2016. Washington and Oregon, two states that have been leaders in the modern craft beer movement that began in the early 1980s, have seen the numbers of breweries and brewpubs increase, from 2011 to 2015, by 105 percent. Much of this growth has taken place in the large metropolitan areas of Portland and Seattle and in such fairly large cities as Eugene and Salem, Oregon, and Spokane and Tacoma, Washington. What is surprising, however, is the fact that so many breweries and brewpubs have opened in villages, towns, and smaller cities.

Such is the case along U.S. Highway 101, from Tumwater, Washington, to Harbor, Oregon, just north of the California border. At the beginning of 2016, twenty-one villages, towns, and small cities, ranging in population from 690 (Yachats, Oregon) to 46,478 (Olympia, Washington), hosted 36 breweries and brewpubs.

Beer 101 North is an examination of the craft breweries and brewpubs along Highway 101 in Washington and Oregon and presents the back stories of the breweries, explores the relationships between these breweries and the communities in which they operate, profiles owners and brewers, and offers tasting notes about many of the beers each place offers. The book provides an in-depth examination of breweries and brewpubs of a specific area that both reflect the area in which they are located and serve as examples of some of the current trends in craft brewing. The Introduction gives a summary of trends in American brewing during the twentieth century and an overview of the craft beer movement since the early 1980s, with particular emphasis on Washington and Oregon. Parts I, II, III, and IV are a narrative of what might be called a beer lover's odyssey I made early in 2016 along Highway 101 from Thurston County, Washington, to the Oregon-California border. In the Conclusion, I offer hypotheses about why nearly all of the breweries and brewpubs I stopped at have been so successful, even those operating in very small towns, and I consider the future of the craft brewing boom along Washington and Oregon's "Wet" Coast.

1

Appendices provide information for visitors who might wish to include in their itineraries stops at the breweries along Highway 101 in Oregon and Washington. Appendix A, "A Directory of Breweries," includes basic facts (addresses, phone numbers, web sites, names of owners and brewers), details about the brewing operations (brewhouse sizes, annual production, regularly brewed beers, Great American Beer Festival awards), information about food service, policies on admitting children and dogs, and handicapped accessibility. There are also notes about special events each brewery hosts as well as its involvement in community and charitable activities.

Appendix B, "A Guide to Beer Styles," gives brief descriptions of several dozen styles of craft beer, along with examples of each style from the breweries I visited. Appendix C is a glossary of beer and brewing terms, while Appendix D, "From Grain to Glass," is an essay dealing with the basic ingredients of beers, the brewing process, and the packaging and drinking of beer.

While the technical terms found in this book are defined in the glossary, the meanings of six of the most frequently used are given here:

ales: one of the two major categories of beers, ales are brewed at relatively warm temperatures using top fermenting yeast and are generally darker in color, more full-bodied, and more robust in flavor than lagers. Examples include India pale ale, Porter and Stout.

lagers: the other major category, lagers are brewed at very cool temperatures using bottom fermenting yeast and are generally lighter in color, lighter-bodied and more delicate in flavor. Examples include the Pale American Lagers produced by the megabrewers, Pilsners, Helles, and Vienna Lagers. Bocks are darker, heavier styles of lager.

ABV: alcohol by volume, expressed as a percentage, which ranges from around 4 percent to over 10 percent. When available, the ABV of a specific beer is included in the text.

IBUs: International Bitterness Units, which indicate the bitterness, created by the hops, of the beer. The IBUs of lighter lagers may be around 15, while those of some IPAs can reach or even exceed 100. When available, the IBUs in a specific beer are included in the text.

Barrel: a standard unit for measuring beer by volume. A barrel is 31 U.S. gallons—that's just over 330 12-ounce cans or bottles of beer.

GABF: Acronym for the annual Great American Beer Festival, at which gold, silver, and bronze medals are awarded for the best beers in nearly 100 style categories.

One final note: Brewing is a fluid industry. Breweries open, close, or move. Owners and brewers change; certain styles are dropped and others added; tap-room hours and services can be altered. If you're planning on including visits to the breweries along Oregon and Washington's Highway 101, be sure to check brewery websites and/or Chambers of Commerce before you go.

Introduction

In December 2015, while doing preliminary research for my beer travels along Highway 101, I came across two press releases, the contents of which provided insights into the recent history, contemporary status and future directions of the American brewing industry. On December 2, 2015, the Brewers Association, the organization representing the craft beer industry, announced that there were now more operating breweries in the United States than ever before.[1] The number, 4,144, exceeded by 13 the previous high, which had been set in 1873, over 140 years earlier. Twenty days later, Anheuser-Busch, the nation's largest brewery, part of an international conglomerate, announced that it had purchased Breckenridge Brewery of Colorado, a medium-sized regional brewery that had been founded in 1990.[2] It was the fourth smaller American craft brewery that St. Louis based behemoth had purchased in 2015.

In 1873, brewing in America was a local industry. Beer did not travel well; most beer was consumed at or purchased for home consumption from a nearby brewery. It was not until the development of refrigeration, extended railway systems, and later, highway systems, that beer production became increasingly regional. After World War II, most local breweries disappeared and such regional companies as Miller, Schlitz, Coors, Stroh Brewery Company, Olympia, and Anheuser-Busch strove to become national brewers, their products available in all states. By the end of the twentieth century, Miller, Coors, and Anheuser-Busch achieved their goals. Most of the other regionals had either disappeared or had their brands purchased by Pabst, which had become a holding company that had such beers as Rainier, Olympia, Lone Star, and Stroh's contract brewed at, ironically, Miller plants and sold in the nostalgia market.

In 1978, the number of operating breweries reached its low point, 89, most of them plants owned by the emerging national companies and a six-pack or so of their soon-to-be-defeated regional competitors. But two years earlier, a small brewery had opened in Sonoma, California, that would mark the unheralded beginning of what has now become known as the craft beer movement. Jack McAuliffe's New Albion Brewing Company sold its products in the San Francisco Bay area to a small, but growing number of beer aficionados, people who welcomed beverages that had robust flavors, that featured creative and imaginative use of hops and malts, and that brewed such relatively unknown styles as India pale ales and stouts—in short, beers that were a marked contrast to the bland, highly carbonated pale lagers of the large regional and national companies.

McAuliffe's venture lasted only six years, but by the end of the 1980s the number of operating breweries had risen to 284. At the beginning of the twenty-first century it had reached 1,560, and at the beginning of 2015, 3702. What is interesting about the figure of 4,114 contained in the Brewers Association press release is that 680 breweries and brewpubs had opened in the first eleven months of 2015. Moreover, the Association expected the number to increase at a rate of at least two a day.[3]

Twenty-two of the breweries were giant complexes run by MillerCoors and Anheuser-Busch. A few were owned by such regional giants as Sierra Nevada, New Belgium, Yuengling, and Boston Brewing, companies that each produced over one million barrels annually. But what is surprising is that close to five hundred of the 4,114 brewed less than 100 barrels annually. While the two brewing giants had become international and many companies that had started serving a local area of perhaps a state or two had become regional and national, a considerable number were basically local.

The Anheuser-Busch press release signaled to some observers a disturbing trend in the American brewing industry. Many successful craft breweries, which had started relatively locally and had achieved their success in large part because of their creation of beers vastly different from the relatively indistinguishable offerings of MillerCoors and Budweiser, were being purchased by large brewing corporations. Many beer drinkers worried that the beers created after the smaller companies had been taken over would be inferior in quality. Others feared that, should the buying trend continue, many microbreweries might be forced out of business because they could not compete with the financial resources and powerful distribution networks the recently purchased breweries could now draw upon.

Certainly, however, the takeovers, along with the increasing number of new breweries and brewpubs, indicate that craft beer has become increasingly popular, a worthwhile alternative to the pale American lagers of the megabrewers. The owners and brewers of these new breweries developed a sense of community, both in relationship to the people in the towns and cities in which they operated and among each other. Much of the beer many of the modern craft brewers created was consumed within a few miles from the places where it was brewed. Breweries were once again becoming local businesses and the British term "the Local," referring to the neighborhood public house, could be applied to many of the new brewpubs and taprooms. And, in towns where there was more than one place brewing beer, brewers helped each other, loaning supplies to one another and encouraging each other to create imaginative new beers. There was competition among brewers, each wanting to create as good a beer as possible, but the competition was strongly flavored with cooperation.

Although the modern craft brewing movement had its beginnings in California in the late 1970s, many important microbreweries and brewpubs opened in Oregon and Washington in the 1980s. At a time when such large regional brewers as Blitz-Weinhard (Portland), Lucky Lager (Vancouver, Washington), Olympia (Tumwater, Washington) and Rainier (Seattle) were struggling, unsuccessfully, either to grow into national breweries or to survive being purchased by larger breweries, several relatively unnoticed events that would later be considered milestones in craft brewing history took place in the Northwest.

In 1982, Bert Grant opened Yakima Brewing and Malting in central Washington, selling much of the beer he made in his brewpub, the first one in America since Prohibition. In the same year, Red Hook Brewery opened in Seattle. Red Hook would later join with Portland's Widmer Brothers Brewing and Kona Brewing to form the Craft Brew Alliance, the ninth largest craft beer producer in the country. In 1995, Anheuser-Busch bought a third of the Alliance which, as part of the deal, joined the giant brewers' distribution network, thus becoming nationally available.

Cartwright Brewing Company was Oregon's first craft brewery, operating in Portland from 1979 to 1982. However, it wasn't until 1984 that the craft brewing movement really began in Oregon. Kurt and Rob Widmer opened Widmer Brothers Brewing and Dick and Nancy Ponzi began BridgePort Brewing (Oregon's longest continuously operating brewery). Both breweries have grown and prospered, although each has been absorbed into larger brewing organizations. These four people joined with Mike and Brian McMenamin, owners of a Portland pub, to successfully lobby the Oregon Legislature to allow breweries to sell their own beer in their own brewpubs. In 1985, the McMenamin brothers opened Hillside Brewery and Public House in Portland, the first of what became their highly successful chain of brewpubs in Oregon and neighboring Washington.

The number of breweries and brewpubs increased steadily in the two Pacific Northwest states during the 1990s and 2000s, and, in the first half of second decade of the twenty-first century, when the craft industry was enjoying its second boom period, the increase was far more rapid. In 2011, there were 124 breweries operating in Oregon; by the end of 2015 there were 228, fourth highest in the United States. During the same period, the numbers in Washington rose from 135 to 306, second highest. Oregon's 7.7 breweries per 100,000 people was second highest in the United States, and Washington's 5.9 per 100,000 people was sixth. Statistics released by the Brewers Association in May 2015 listed four Washington and Oregon breweries among the 34 regional breweries producing over 100,000 barrels in 2014; four brewpubs among the 13 producing over 5,000 barrels; and seven microbreweries (producing under 15,000 barrels annually) among the 46 that had brewed over 10,000 barrels.

Not only did Oregon and Washington's craft breweries produce considerable amounts of beer, they produced very good beer. In the four years up to and including 2015, Oregon breweries won a total of 89 medals at the Great American Beer Festival annual competition, considered one of the most important in the United States; during the same period, Washington breweries took home 33.

As I began assembling information about the breweries and brewpubs I planned to visit during my March journey, I noticed that in many ways the beer scene along Highway 101 was both similar to that of the Pacific Northwest generally and dissimilar in important ways. Like the rest of Oregon and Washington, there had been an explosion in the number of breweries in the last five years. Of the 42 I planned to stop at, only 12 were in operation before 2011. Two of the breweries were categorized as regionals producing over 15,000 barrels annually, a proportion in line with breweries across the country. But, 13 of the breweries turned out less than one hundred barrels a year, and 22 were brewpubs, both figures significantly above the national average. Moreover, all but four were located in towns of less than ten thousand. Once I left Thurston County, Washington, where the cities of Olympia, Lacey, and Tumwater were situated, I'd be visiting a large number of small breweries located in quite small population centers. Many of these breweries were family affairs, owned and run by a husband and wife, with some help from siblings, children, and friends. And large or small, the breweries and brewpubs along Highway 101 made very good beer: seven had won medals at the Great American Beer Festival annual competition.

As I prepared to begin my journey, I realized that I wouldn't just be experiencing a fairly representative microcosm of the craft beer movement as it was in early 2016, I'd also be experiencing a beer culture that was very local, its uniqueness created by the physical and cultural environments in which it had grown.

Part I

Thurston County's Craft Beer Boom

During the first two decades of the twenty-first century, several small towns or clusters of towns have emerged as craft beer centers, hosting several breweries and brewpubs. Marquette County, Michigan; Humboldt County, California; Santa Fe, New Mexico; and Billings, Montana, are but four.

In the last few years, Thurston County, Washington, located at the southern end of Puget Sound, has become one as well. For all of the twentieth century, the very large Olympia Brewing Company plant produced beer in Tumwater. But when it closed in 2003, only 10-year-old Fish Brewing Company was in operation. But by the end of 2016, the county's three cities, state capital Olympia (population 46,478), Lacey (population 42,393), and Tumwater (population 17,371) would be home to nine breweries, all but two of which had begun production in 2014 or later. Another brewery was scheduled to open in Olympia in 2017.

1. It's the Water
(Under the Bridge):
Starting in Tumwater

Olympia Brewing Company (Tumwater),
McMenamins Spar Café (Olympia)

My beer odyssey began on a misty, moist March morning on a footbridge that crossed the Deschutes River just above the Middle Tumwater Falls. A few hundred yards to the northwest, Highway 101—which runs through Washington, Oregon, and California from Olympia to the Mexican border—began. It was the first time I'd visited the spot, but I'd been seeing pictures of the bridge and the Falls for over forty years on bottles or cans of Olympia beer.

For nearly all of the twentieth century, Olympia had been brewed in buildings I could see as I looked northward downstream and then eastward, up the bank.[1] The Old Brewery (as it is still affectionately called by area residents) was visible through the bare branches of trees lining the banks. It had opened in 1906 and operated until the onset of Prohibition, which arrived in Washington State in 1916. Now it stands abandoned, its windows broken, tarps covering holes in the roof, mossy streaks decorating the walls. There's a chain link fence around it, but that hasn't prevented adventurous climbers from scaling the fence and then the walls to mark the brick facing with graffiti. Although deserted, dilapidated, and defaced, it is not forgotten. It's the principal concern of "The Old Brewhouse Foundation," which seeks to preserve a structure that is on both the National and Washington State Registers of Historic Places. The Foundation hopes to have the building renovated so that it can become a tourist attraction.

The New Brewery, at the top of the bank to the east, began producing and selling beer in January 1934, only months after the repeal of the 19th Amendment, and operated continuously until 2003. Wheat (or perhaps pale American lager) colored, it is an enormous complex of buildings—offices, brewery, warehouses—that also stands empty and is surrounded by chain link fences, although

"The Old Brewery," as it is affectionately called by residents of Thurston County, produced Olympia beer until Prohibition. It now stands abandoned, in disrepair and marked by graffiti. Plans are underway to renovate it so that it is safe for historical tours.

it is not in the dilapidated state of its predecessor. No graffiti mar the walls; the only sign I saw said "For Sale." As I was to learn, government and citizen groups had plans for it, not as an historical artifact to be preserved from the ravages of time, nature, and graffiti artists, but as a functioning building that would form the center for a revitalized section of Tumwater.

The story of Olympia Brewing Company (originally it was Capital Brewery; the name was changed in 1902) is, in many ways, typical of most American breweries that were founded in the late nineteenth century, fell on hard times later in the twentieth century, and ceased operating early in the twenty-first century. Its founder, like the founders of such breweries as Schlitz, Miller, Stroh, Pabst, and Henry Weinhard, was a German who immigrated to the United States in the mid–nineteenth century and later amassed a huge fortune selling beer to workers in boom towns and rapidly expanding cities. But, unlike these other newcomers, Leopold Schmidt was not a trained brewer. He left his homeland to seek adventure as a sailor on the high seas and, when he first came to the United States, it was to work on the ships plying the Great Lakes. Only after moving to Butte, Montana, to prospect for gold did he open his first brewery, discovering greater prosperity in dispensing liquid gold than in panning in streams for the solid kind.

Schmidt soon became a successful and influential citizen in Montana and became a member of the legislature. It was on a government organized trip to the Puget Sound area that he discovered the area's soon to become famous artesian well water, proclaimed that it was perfect for brewing, moved to the coast and in 1896 founded a new brewery. Cites around the Puget Sound were booming in the years before the outbreak of World War I, and Schmidt's pale lager, which bore the slogan "It's the Water" on bottle labels, became very popular. The brewery became a major employer in Tumwater and adjacent areas of Thurston County and the business that supplied materials and support services saw their employment rolls grow. The family itself became a highly respected part of the community, donating a fire truck for the city of Tumwater, underwriting much of the cost of constructing a street lighting system, and supporting philanthropic causes.

Leopold ran Olympia Brewing Company until his death in 1914. His son Peter assumed control, and during the early years of Prohibition the plant brewed soft drinks. The business was not profitable and the brewery was sold to a paper making company. When the "Great Experiment" ended in 1933, the younger Schmidt oversaw the building of the new plant, which began selling beer in January 1934. The family remained in control of Olympia Brewing until 1983.

Sales grew steadily and then rapidly in the boom years after World War II, and "Oly" was one of the most widely consumed beers in the West Coast and Mountain states. The glory days for the company came in the 1960s and 1970s. At the time, many regional breweries in the country sought to become national to complete head-to-head with Miller and Anheuser-Busch. The strategy involved buying smaller breweries in areas their own products were underrepresented and then using the distribution networks of the smaller companies. Olympia purchased Theodore Hamm's Brewing, which was very popular in Minnesota, the "Land of Sky Blue Waters," in 1975 and Lone Star Brewery, producers of what was called the "National Beer of Texas," a year later. By the later part of the 1970s, Olympia was employing more than 1,000 people and producing over three million barrels of beer a year; their product was available in more than 30 states.

And then disaster occurred. Olympia and the other aspiring regionals were "light struck." Miller, and soon after Anheuser-Busch, introduced light beer and spent millions of dollars advertising the new lower-alcohol product in national magazines and network television. The regionals could not complete;

they had not developed their own versions of the new beer style and they did not have the massive advertising budgets of the two enormous Midwestern companies. Olympia Brewing attempted valiantly to rally sales at the beginning of the 1980s with a series of creative and amusing commercials about a series of subterranean creatures called artesians who supplied the famous water used in the brewing—but to no avail. In 1983, the company, after 87 years of family ownership, was sold to one of the largest regionals, Pabst Brewing Company, which was still fighting (ultimately unsuccessfully) to become national. The Milwaukee-based company lost out in its struggle to become national. In 1996 it stopped brewing its products at its Milwaukee plant and contract brewed the various regional brands it had acquired (including Schlitz, Old Style, Rainier, Stroh's, and Ballantine) at various Miller plants around the country. Two of the brands it had acquired, Blitz-Weinhard and Hamm's, were sold to Miller in 1999. Miller promptly closed the Blitz-Weinhard plant in Portland and began brewing that product at the Olympia brewery which it had just purchased from Pabst. Olympia and Rainier, which Pabst owned, were also brewed at the plant. Ironically, Rainier and Blitz-Weinhard, which had been Olympia's largest regional competitors, won awards at the Great American Beer Festival in 1999, 2000, and 2001 for beverages made at the home of their long-time arch-rival.

The Miller stay in Tumwater was short—only four years. The Olympia facility was older and smaller than the others and it was considered outdated. In 2002, Miller was purchased by the international brewing giant South African Breweries (SAB) and a new era of "efficiency" was ushered in. At the end of June 2003, the Tumwater plant closed, leaving 300 employees jobless and seriously hurting many supporting businesses. "It left a huge hole in the city," remarked Heidi Behrends Cerniwey, Assistant City Administrator for Tumwater.[2] "The brewery and the Schmidt family had been part of the heart and soul of Tumwater for over a century." And, to make matters worse, when it departed, Miller placed a deed restriction on the property, prohibiting the use of the site for the production of alcohol.

It wasn't until 2013, after Miller SAB lifted the covenant, that interest in the property revived and grew. In 2014, it appeared that a development company who wanted to transform the buildings into a multi-use facility that included a small brewpub had successfully purchased the new brewery and grounds. However, the deal fell through, and in October 2015, the property, which had been divided into four pieces, was put up for auction. But all the bids were far below market value and were rejected. Then, in December 2015, local news media announced that the property had been purchased for four million dollars by a company called Tumwater Development LLC. For the price, it acquired 300 brewing tanks, two warehouses, and a bottling house. A spokesman for the company spoke of having a hotel, convention center, and brewpub, among other businesses, at the site.

The news was greeted enthusiastically in Thurston County, which was experiencing a brewing renaissance. McMenamins Spar Café and Fish Brewing had been operating for several years, and six new breweries had opened in Thurston County in 2014 and 2015, bringing the total to eight. Plans were afoot to create in the county a "Center of Excellence" for craft brewing and craft distilling. "Brewing has been a major part of this community for over a century," Cerniwey stated. "The craft brewing and distilling industries are growing rapidly in Washington. The center would foster research, training not only in brewing and distilling but also business aspects, and the dispersal of information to the public. The Center of Excellence would bring together groups of people from diverse backgrounds, all interested in making our area a hub for the state's brewing and distilling industries. It would have a tremendous influence on the economy of the area and would create many, many jobs," Cerniway enthusiastically remarked.

I had three specific memories of drinking Oly. The first was in the early 1960s when, as an underage drinker, I'd borrowed someone's ID (they didn't have pictures on them then) so that I could join a group of University of British Columbia students planning a trip to the Breakers, a dance club in the tiny border town of Point Roberts, Washington. They had Oly on draft, and forbidden and exotic (it was from a foreign country!) fruit (i.e., beer) had never tasted so good. The second comes from the late 1970s, when my family and I were visiting relatives in Blaine, Washington. My brother-in-law had bought a twelve pack of Oly (in cans now) as a break from the generic "BEER" that used to come in eleven ounce brown glass bottles (with a rebus under each cap). In comparison to that really cheap stuff, the Oly tasted like nectar from the gods. The third memory comes from the mid–1980s, when there was a prolonged brewers' strike in Alberta, Canada. After a couple of weeks, the Alberta Liquor Control Board decided to come to the rescue of distraught beer drinkers by importing Olympia beer into the province. The price seemed exorbitant, over fourteen dollars a case when the local stuff (before the strike) sold for just over ten. But we paid it. I was just becoming a beer snob at the time, but I quickly learned the truth of the saying "The worst beer is no beer." Oly was to the suffering beer lovers of Alberta like water found at an oasis in the middle of the desert.

The artesians, stars of those 1980s television commercials, disappeared long ago. But there's still artesian water in Thurston County and beer brewed with it. That evening, I sampled some of the water at a drinking fountain just inside the entrance to McMenamins Spar Café in downtown Olympia. It's connected to a well supposedly located below the men's washroom. But I hadn't come for the water, but to try the Spartesian Ale, brewed from that water, and the food, art, and ambience at the pub, one of 65 operated by McMenamins in Washington and Oregon.[3]

There are four things a visitor can expect at any one of the McMenamins locations: four standard beers, a core list of menu selections, art work that has been called "historical surrealism," and, in nearly every case, a carefully restored historic property. The McMenamins chain is certainly not made up of "cookie cutter" establishments. Among the historic buildings are schools, churches, theatres, farm buildings, and a ball room. Twenty-five of the pubs house their own breweries, where each brewer has the freedom to create his own recipes for the beers that supplement the core list. The food menus often offer items created from locally sourced ingredients. The artwork is specific to each building, frequently offering whimsical depictions of the place and its history.

By 1985, the McMenamin brothers, Brian and Mike, had spent many years

McMenamins Spar Café and Bar, located in downtown Olympia, has been decorated to recapture the spirit of its earlier existence in the 1930s. An artesian well under the building is used to brew "Spartesian Ale."

in the restaurant and pub business in the greater Portland area and had made sure that they had many taps dispensing top quality imported beers. The few craft breweries in Oregon at the time couldn't sell their beer where it was brewed. Mike and Brian teamed up with two other Oregon brewing families, Nick and Nancy Ponzi of BridgePort Brewing, and Kurt and Rob Widmer of Widmer Brothers Brewing, to lobby the Oregon legislature for the right serve beer made on the premises with their food. Late in 1985, Oregon State Bill 813 passed, and the modern brewpub movement began in Oregon.

"When we started, we couldn't afford to buy new shiny places," Brian told *Northwest Travel Magazine.* "So we bought old ones. These places always come with stories so we build on that."[4] With each old property they bought, they began a process of restoration. As Michael McMenamin noted, "It's not a renovation, it's a rejuvenation." Each building had long been part of a community and they wished it to remain that way, a place where people could get together and feel the importance of the history of the place as they enjoyed food and beer.

So important is the history of each property that the McMenamins employ a professional historian, Tim Hills, who is responsible for the essays that appear on the web pages of each pub and restaurant, detailing the past that is such an important aspect of the establishment's character. The building I had just entered, having finished my slurp of artesian water, had been known as the Spar since it was built in 1935. The Art Moderne-styled restaurant had been for many years a blue-collar establishment, frequented by loggers, longshoremen, and union laborers, who not only ate but also drank, played cards, smoked cigars, and placed bets on sporting events. On the wall at the back of each of the booths were paintings depicting these and other activities. Over the years, some pretty famous people had dropped in: Marlon Brando, Joan Crawford, Joe Louis, Sandy Koufax, and Dick Gregory, whose faces appeared on some of the characters in the paintings.

When the waitress arrived, I asked for a Spartesian, only to be told that the house's flagship India pale ale was not in stock. The small and, as I discovered later when I walked to the back of the restaurant to look at it, very old brewing system was broken and wouldn't be operational until a very hard-to-find part arrived. Around the aging equipment were scattered empty kegs that had contained other McMenamin brews shipped in from one of their other locations. The mash tun and brew kettle were decorated with funky McMenamins art.

As I scanned the menu's beer list, I noted below the names of their own beers, which sold for $5.75 a pint, Olympia, available for two dollars a can. I ordered one. I had to ask for a glass and after I'd poured the beer into a glass,

I studied the can. It looked just as I remembered it. But then, when I scanned the small print, I noted that it had been made for Pabst at a plant in Irwindale, California, one of the MillerSAB plants that contract brewed many of the brands Pabst had acquired. The slogan was still there: "It's the Water." But it certainly wasn't water that came from the famous wells Leopold Schmidt had been so impressed with over a century ago.

2. An Olympia Circ-Ale Tour

Cascadia Homebrew, Fish Brewing, Three Magnets Brewing (Olympia)

The morning after I'd sipped my artesian water and my California-made Oly, the rainclouds had moved on. In the bright sunlight, I began a tour of Olympia's three downtown breweries, each of them only a few minutes' walk from each other. My first stop, Cascadia Homebrew and Brewing Company, a supply store, U-brew on premises, and nanobrewery with taproom,was across the street from Spar Café and a block east along 4th Avenue. When I entered, I noticed a large flag and a poster dominating the wall to my left. The flag, which had three vertical stripes—blue, white, and green—along with the silhouette of an evergreen (probably a Douglas fir), was the emblem of the Republic of Cascadia, a cultural, ecological, and economic region that included British Columbia, Washington State, and Oregon. "There have been groups that wanted to make Cascadia a political entity," said owner/brewer Chris Emerson. "I chose the name because it embodied a sense of place and community. There's so much happening in this area in the craft beer culture. When I brew," he added, "I try to use as many local ingredients as possible."

Mounted next to the flag was a poster of Captain Homebrew, a fictional character who was certainly a super hero to most of the nation's growing number of homebrewers. Chris, a native of Seattle, had become interested in the hobby through his brother, among whose interesting creations had been a jalapeño stout. He'd attended Central Washington University with the goal of becoming a teacher, but shortly after graduation realized that he could combine both the profession he had trained for and his hobby by opening, in 2015, what at first was a supply and U-brew shop in the state capital. The idea of introducing a nanobrewery soon followed. "Having examples of the beer I was teaching people to homebrew would give them a sense of what the end product would be. The beers would showcase the ingredients they would be using for their own beers."

Chris Emerson originally began Cascadia Homebrew and Brewery as a homebrew supply store. He now brews and serves a variety of standard, as well as sometimes unusual, ales.

We sat on stools at the bar which separates the instruction area at the front of Cascadia from the supply shelves to the side and the small brewhouse at the back. Chris described his beers as being both classic styles and familiar styles with a twist. He explained that he didn't have a core list, but rotated his offerings. "Some are around more often than others," he noted and went on to explain that, one month away from Cascadia's first anniversary, he'd brewed 55 different recipes. His first beer, Speakeasy SMASH (an acronym for Single Malt and Single Hop) was designed to showcase Northwest pale malt (purchased from nearby maltsters) and Warrior hops (from Yakima). He used a yeast he'd propagated especially for this recipe. "Speakeasy was the first of a series," he explained. "I've done others that illustrate the characteristics of different types of malts and different hop varieties."

"Whale of a Pale" is an example of a familiar style with a twist: a 6.6 percent ABV, 37 IBU brew that uses familiar ingredients and then adds wheat and spelt, an Old World grain that adds earthy and spicy notes. He has a wheat beer that includes frozen pie cherries. It's called "Wheat's my cherry pie." And then there's one that uses nutmeg, a popular ingredient in pumpkin beer (an autumn favorite), but replaces the popular fruit with butternut squash. "I added 50 pounds of local squash, which I roasted for 16 hours. It's seasoned with nutmeg, vanilla, and ginger," all of them, he hastened to add, delicately used. He's also made a green tea saison, a lavandula (lavender) chocolate porter, a brambleberry vanilla stout, two gluten-free beers, and beers using elderberry, yarrow, and chanterelle mushrooms. Perhaps his most interesting "twist" is a root gruit, based on a style brewed before the widespread use of hops, which introduced herbs and roots as flavoring and bittering agents. His includes sarsaparilla, sassafras, and licorice roots, vanilla, and oats. It's a full-bodied 8.5 percent brew that's given a creamy texture by the oats.

Chris emphasized that his beers, unusual though they are, are meant to be shared. "I love my contact with the people who come here to learn to brew or just to enjoy the beer. I'm very happy to share my recipes with the community. It gets people excited about craft beer and brewing. I want this to be a place for people to meet and talk about beer, a place to promote brewing in the community. I'd be really pleased if someone who learned to brew here went on to open their own brewery."

Wishing Chris Emerson a happy first anniversary next month, I resumed my tour. The next stop was Artesian Commons, a two-tenths of an acre urban park, the site of music events, three-on-three basketball contests, and the home of a public artesian well which gushes 10 gallons of water each minute. A couple of joggers stopped to replenish their water jugs and someone else got out of a car, opened the trunk, and took out two one gallon milk jugs to fill and take home. The water, which is regularly tested to ensure its purity (and it never fails), is also important to the city's home brewers. Chris Emerson reported that several of his students stop there after classes to take some of it home for brewing liquor. It was also the initial meeting place of two men who, a couple of years ago, had become professional brewers. When he was a homebrewer, Rob Horn, now owner of Triceratops Brewing, used to head to the well for this essential brewing ingredient. There he frequently encountered Patrick Jansen, later the head brewer at Three Magnets Brewing but then a letter carrier, who would renew his supply of drinking water before continuing his rounds. This acquaintance has now become a strong professional and personal friendship, and the two of them frequently assist each other in their brewing activities.

It wasn't difficult to spot my next stop. On a building on the east side of the Jefferson Street a painted wall showed blue fish swimming through a sea of ripe grain. Above the mountains in the background was the name of the occupant: Fish Brewing Company. The brewery was the third largest and third oldest that I'd visit.

The year 2015 had been a highly successful one for Fish Brewing. It had

The water from the artesian well in a downtown Olympia park is frequently used by homebrewers.

produced over 12,000 barrels of beer, which had been distributed in seven West Coast and Rocky Mountain states. At the 2015 Washington State Beer Awards, it had been named "Large Brewery of the Year" and had garnered three gold medals and a silver at the annual state competition. It had also won a bronze medal at the Great American Beer Festival. But best of all, at the World Beer Awards, its Beyond the Pale Ale had been acclaimed the best beer in the world, better than the rest of the nearly 1,000 beers entered in the competition.

But success hadn't come easily, and, in fact, there were times during the ten years after its founding in 1993 when it seemed that Fish Brewing wouldn't survive. The journey to success was as difficult as that made by salmon navigating the fish ladders on the Deschutes River near the old Olympia brewery. There were small gains, frequent setbacks, and many times when the possibility of reaching the goal seemed impossible

Crayne and Mary Horton had the idea for opening a craft brewery in the early 1990s, shortly after they had returned to the United States from Japan, after Crayne had finished a stint teaching Political Science at a university there.

A very proficient homebrewer, he was ready for a career change. Olympia seemed the ideal place for a brewpub: there were no craft breweries between Seattle to the north and Kalama to the south, and Olympia, located beside Interstate 5, the north-south freeway, was easily accessible to distributors should the brewery decide to sell its product beyond the capital city area. Moreover, Olympia had the right demographics to make a taproom or brewpub quickly profitable. "Our target customers would be just like us—liberal, environmentally inclined, gracefully aging Deadheads living in the environmentally beautiful Pacific Northwest," he humorously explained in a piece he wrote for *Grist*, an online journal.[1]

Under the direction of Lisa Vatske, who would become general manager and financial officer for the brewery/brewpub, the new company developed a business plan, sought investors, and gave the enterprise a name. Some 75 people put money in the firm: relatives, friends, neighbors, Japanese colleagues, and others who believed in the viability of a craft brewery at the south end of Puget Sound. They decided to name their new brewery Fish Brewing. "It was appropriate for the area," Crayne Horton explained, and then confessed that one of his favorite bands had been The Radiators, who made use of fish motifs on their album covers and whose fans were referred to as "Fishheads."[2]

The brewery opened early in 1993, with Crayne taking on the roles of President and Head Brewer, Mary running a small kitchen, and Lisa overseeing the business end of the operation. "We decided to go for hoppy English style ales," Crayne remembers. "Our first beer wasn't a gentle, cross-over one." Fish Tale Pale Ale was a robust beer, hopped with Cascade hops.

For three years, business went well. The brewpub was very successful, and the beer was being shipped around Washington State and to Idaho, Montana, Alaska, and Oregon. The 15 barrel brewhouse could not keep up with the demand, and so, in 1996, Fish Brewing decided to expand. Equipment was purchased from Red Hook Brewery, who was also expanding and updating its equipment; the brewhouse moved across the street to its present location and a bottling line was installed. A full kitchen was built in the space vacated by the brewery equipment and the place became Fish Tale Brew Pub.

And then the problems began. A stock offering that was to provide funds to pay for the expansion sold very poorly. At the same time that craft brewing industry, after a decade of boom years, hit a mild depression. It was touch-and-go at Fish Brewing. The company could barely pay monthly bills and staff morale plummeted. Things became so bad that at the end of 1998, when the Washington State minimum wage was about to increase by eighty cents, Lisa Vatske had to let 10 of the company's 30 employees go. "We need to retrench. We need to make the brewery viable," she explained.[3]

Fish Brewing did survive. Years later, Horton gave the credit to Lisa Vatske, who managed to keep creditors happy and to initiate belt-tightening measures, and Lyle Morse, a shareholder and successful local businessman who replaced Horton as president and developed a highly effective business plan. Horton initiated two important developments at the brewhouse. First he decided the company should offer a mild beer in addition to the highly-hopped ales it had been brewing, thus broadening the market for the product. The result was Wild Salmon Pale Ale. Second, he decided to offer beers brewed with organic ingredients. "It was expensive," Vatske remembered. "At first we had to get our hops from New Zealand. But it gave us a special niche in the craft beer market."[4] Olympia, both she and Horton noted, was a great place from which to market the new beer, as it had a very ecologically conscious population. The first of Fish's organic beers was an amber ale.

Early in this century, Fish made two purchases that greatly increased the financial strength of the company. In 2001, it purchased Leavenworth Brewery, an award-winning brewer of German-style beers, located in the Cascade Mountains town of the same name. Then, in 2004, it purchased Spire Mountain Ciders from Washington Wine and Beverage Company, located in Woodinville, just north of Seattle. "Sal Leone, the president of the company, wanted to unload his cider line and he also wanted to purchase stock in Fish," Horton remembered. "We acquired a good product line and some much needed cash."

Both Vatske and Horton left Fish shortly after these purchases, and in 2008 Leone became the majority stockholder and president of the company. Production and areas of distribution increased and Fish soon became sought after in places where Pacific salmon had never spawned. An event telecast on the Food Network on February 11, 2013, spread the reputation of Fish Ales far beyond its distribution area. Guy Fieri brought his popular TV show *Diners, Drive-ins and Dives* to Olympia and featured Fish Tale Brewpub's chef Kerin Lewis preparing crab-stuffed cannelloni and a traditional pub meal, bangers and mash.

I walked through an undecorated door under the blue fish and golden grain into the brewery and met Jada Peters, a filtration officer. As she led me to the office of head brewer Paul Pearson, we passed a room filled with wooden barrels, over 50 of them, she said. They had been containers for Jack Daniels bourbon and wines from Fish's sister company, Washington Wine and Beverage, and were now used to age porters, stouts, and saisons, each barrel contributing subtle tastes of the previous beverages to the beer now stored in it. The space looked a lot different than it must have several decades ago, when it housed a knitting factory, or even more recently, when it was a performance space for rock bands.

Head brewer at Fish since 2012, Paul Pearson had first become interested in craft beer while studying finance and business administration at Colorado State University in Fort Collins, long considered by beer aficionados one of the best craft beer towns in America. "I got the homebrewing bug from one of my roommates. And then I became really interested when Jeff Lebesch, one of the founders of New Belgium Brewing Company, talked to our class."

Pearson began his professional brewing career on the Oregon coast in his home town of Florence. Wakonda Brewing Company was a small operation producing only a few hundred barrels annually, and Paul did nearly all of the production jobs, from ordering supplies to kegging the finished product. After three years, he moved up the coast to Newport, where he began working under the supervision of John Maier, the legendary brewmaster of Rogue Ales. "The first couple of days, I filtered more beer than I'd made in all my time at Wakonda. I really learned about the business of large commercial brewing." There followed a stay in the town of Hood River, Oregon, where Paul worked at Wyeast, a leading supplier of yeast products for the craft brewing industry. "I spent a

The entry to Fish Tale Brew Pub, a part of Fish Brewing Company, is fancily decorated, as is the front of the production brewery, which is located just across Jefferson Street in downtown Olympia.

lot of time in the lab, learning about yeast cultures and quality control." In 2012, when Fish began searching for a new head brewer to run their rapidly growing brewing operations, Pearson had both the practical experience and technical training they needed.

Paul talked about Fish Brewing's three lines of beer, as well as about some unusual creations. The highlights of the Fish Tale ales, which the web site emphasizes are "Brewed in the Republic of Cascadia," are the organic beers. Referred to on the web site as "The First Ale of the Republic," Organic Amber (5.0 percent ABV, 22 IBUs) has a malty sweetness which is balanced by the crisp cleanness of the Hallertau hops, while Wild Salmon Pale Ale (5.0 percent, 32 IBUs) features a complex balance between hops and malts. The Organic India Pale Ale (6.7 percent, 42 IBUs) is a medium-bodied Northwest version of the style with a firm malt body. None of these beers is very hop forward; the words Paul used most frequently to describe them were "sessionable" and "easy drinking." The two other regulars are Mudshark Porter (5 percent, 24 IBUs) and Beyond the Pale Ale (5.0 percent, 35 IBUs). The first is creamy with cocoa notes; the second, which Pearson talks about with enthusiasm and pride, is the award-winning Beyond the Pale, a Northwest-style pale ale that uses Maris Otter malt, a British variety that provides rich, bready flavors. Whole leaf dried Mosaic hops create a firm, but not assertive hop presence.

The second line is called "Reel Ales," a name which continues the fish theme and combines it with a punning reference to the British campaign for "Real Ales." Swordfish Double Cascadian Dark Ale (also known as American Dark Ale and Black India Pale Ale) is a 7.4 percent ABV, 64 IBU interpretation of a fairly new, but popular variation on the IPA style. Monkfish Belgian Style Tripel weighs in at 9.0 percent ABV, but is less bitter at 32 IBUs, while Starfish Imperial Red, which uses four varieties of hops and seven malts, is 7.5 percent ABV, with 63 IBUs. The champion of these strong, robust ales is the highly-hopped Barley Wine Ale, which is 10 percent ABV, with 100 IBUs.

The Leavenworth Biers line offers a German counterpart to the largely British emphasis of Fish's other beers. Boulder Bend Dunkelweizen (4.7 percent, 25 IBUs), winner of gold and silver medals at the GABF, is a dark hefe-weizen, with caramel, chocolate, and toffee notes. A hybrid of German and American versions of the style, it used to be called "Blind Pig," something that wasn't great to look at, but tasted great. Whistling Pig Hefeweizen (5.4 percent, 22 IBUs), winner of a GABF bronze medal, has banana notes, and true to the style, has yeast suspended in its bronze liquid. Premium Lager (5 percent, 23 IBUs) is a light to medium-bodied beer with a malty sweetness. When I tasted them, I found that each was clean and relatively light-bodied with little hop presence.

Paul and his colleagues have had fun producing beers linked to two very popular movies: *The Battle of the Five Armies* (the third in *The Hobbit* trilogy) and *Christmas Vacation*. In collaboration with its distributor, BevLink, which had been approached by MGM about creating a series of beers themed to the movies, Fish released Gollum Precious Imperial Pilsner, Smaug Imperial Stout (both new recipes) and Blog Belgium Style Tripel (a renaming of an existing release) in 2014. A year later, the brewery followed up with a trio of beers to celebrate the release of *Christmas Vacation: Cousin Eddie's RV*, an imperial brown; Yule Crackup, a gingerbread stout; and Family Wagon Imperial IPA.

Asked about the most unusual beer he's created, Pearson quickly replied: "Royster Stout." It's a beer he devised for SLURP 2015, the Shellfish Lovers Ultimate Rejuvenation Party. During the boiling phase of making a 7 percent stout, he added oysters in the shell, giving the resulting liquid a slight taste of brine and oyster. "And," he adds with a chuckle, "the oysters sure tasted great when we removed them from the kettle."

Passing back under the fish swimming through amber fields of grain, I headed down Jefferson, turned right onto Legion and walked toward Three Magnets Brewing, owned by Nate and Sara Reilly, one of many "brewery own-ing couples" I would meet during my journey along Highway 101. Three Mag-nets is in a building where, long ago when it had been a Sears warehouse, Sara's grandfather had served as manager. It's also the home to Darby's Café, which Sara has owned and operated elsewhere for over a decade and which moved to the present location at the beginning of 2016.

When I'd made the appointment to talk with Nate, he'd said that he might not be available, as his wife was expecting their second child. The baby hadn't arrived (Frieda Inez would be born a few days later), but Nate would be tied up in a meeting for a few minutes. Sitting at one of the picnic style tables, I looked around. Along one wall was a giant television screen, flanked by a large Seattle Sounders (soccer team) scarf and a Seattle Seahawks (football team) banner. "We aren't a sports bar at all," Nathan later emphasized. "But we love soccer, and we have a special menu when the team's on television. And this is Seahawks territory; we'd never get away with not showing their games." On the wall above the bar stretched a long stained glass triptych. At one end was a depiction of mountains and forest, at the other the sea. In the middle was a representation of the Olympia Beer logo, with horseshoe, bridge, and water-fall.

When Nate joined me, he recounted the history of the centerpiece of stained glass. It had long ago been commissioned by Olympia Brewery, who gifted it to Merchant Café in Seattle's Pioneer Square. Late in the twentieth century it was returned to Olympia and, when Three Magnets was preparing to open, its present owner, stained glass artist Bill Hillman, donated it to the new brewery, explaining that he wanted to share it with the community. It introduced a theme I'd encounter again and again during my trip: the importance of the relationship between a brewery or brewpub and the local community.

A few years ago, Nate and Sara, who'd always stocked Darby's with unusual and, as much as possible, area beers, discussed the fact that there was room in Olympia for a second local brewpub (the other being Fish Tale—McMenamins, as part of a chain, didn't really meet the criteria). Patrick Jansen, the one-time letter carrier, soon joined the conversation. He'd met the Reillys at a farmer's market/indie rock concert gathering and shared with them some of his homebrew, with which they were very impressed; he became their brewer. They decided to establish the brewpub downtown, a good location for people working at nearby businesses, state government employees, and students and professors from Evergreen State College, not to mention other beer lovers in Thurston County and the increasing number of beer tourists.

Even the name of the new brewpub would tie into the concept of "localness" and "community." "Three Magnets" was a phrase developed by Sir Ebenezer Howard, a late nineteenth century British philosopher/theorist/town planner who was appalled by the proliferation of enormous, sprawling industrial and commercial centers in England. As a way to counteract urban blight, he envisioned the construction of "Garden Cities," moderately sized population centers where people lived not too far from rural and agricultural areas or from business and industrial centers. The urban center, agricultural areas, and residential areas represented the three magnets. Large cities would be only a short train-ride away. Olympia, Nate explained, with its population of just under fifty thousand, its concentration of local businesses in the city center, and the growing number of nearby small farms, many of them organic, was the kind of place envisioned by Howard. And, for people longing for the big city lights, Seattle and Portland were each a two to three hour drive away. Three Magnets Brewery would enhance the sense of community, giving people the chance to gather to enjoy good food and drink, along with good conversation and, of course, Sounders and Seahawks games.

"Our plan was to create a place that had good food, a good atmosphere, and solid beer," Nathan said. The food, as much of it as possible locally sourced, would be prepared under the direction of chef Kyle Knuk and would be available on three different menus. Darby's breakfast and lunch menu, available from 8 a.m. to 3 p.m., offers standard, vegetarian, and vegan items, and provides its items with such interesting names as "Apple of My Eye," a Granny Smith, sharp white cheddar and cinnamon spiced omelet, and "Crustafarian," which features chicken-fried oysters. The brewpub has two menus, the "Sammich" menu from 11 to 4 o'clock. From four o'clock on, the "Pub House" menu is available. When Sounders or Seahawks games are on, "The Ultimate Gameday Experience" has beer specials, game day snacks, and raffles (if you're wearing team attire)—available from an hour before game time to the end of the contest.

If the food and the games on TV are two of the three attracting magnets for the brewpub, the other is the beer, which, although the pull of all the magnets is supposed to create a kind of equilibrium, is the most important. It is created by Patrick Jansen and his assistant Jeff Stokes, in consultation with Nat Reilly. Patrick credited Anchor Steam Beer, Sierra Nevada Pale Ale, Alaskan Amber, and Sierra Nevada's Celebration (Christmas) Ale with inspiring his home brewing, most notably his love of hops. "During our first year [2014]," he noted, "we wanted to brew a creative array of styles and clean beer. We didn't want to start off doing crazy things; we wanted to learn the rules creatively."

Three Magnets Brewing co-owner Nathan Reilly (left) and brewers Jeff Stokes (center) and Patrick Jansen stand beneath the stained glass mural, which includes the Olympia logo. The logo had been created for Olympia Brewing, donated to a Seattle area business, and then returned to Olympia, where it was purchased by a stained glass artist who donated it to Three Magnets.

They started with a session (lower alcohol) IPA and "Hoppy Small Saison." These were followed by a Russian Imperial stout, a barley wine and, this being the Pacific Northwest, stronger IPAs.

Within the first year, Three Magnets had not just brewed what Reilly had called "solid beer," they had created a beer that created national attention; Old Shook, their barley wine, won a GABF bronze medal. The award-winning beer was the result of an accident. "We were using Jeff's recipe," Patrick recalled, "and discovered that we didn't have enough crystal malt. So we ad-libbed, adding amber and Maris Otter malts." As he described the 11.0 percent ABV, 50 IBU ale, Pat used such terms as caramel, toasty, floral, hop-delicate, biscuity, and fruity. That night, after I'd enjoyed a bottle that he'd given me, I added the terms vanilla-y, chocolate-y, and plum-y. It was a really good barley wine.

As is the case with most Pacific Northwest brewers, Three Magnets' flagship beers are IPAs. The four of them—3 Mag Rain, 3 Mag Sun, Big Juice IPA, and Little Juice IPA—allow Patrick and Jeff to express creatively their love of hops. They range in ABV from 6.4 percent (Sun) to 8.5 percent (Big Rain) and from 60 IBUs (Rain) to 100 (Big Juice) and they include interesting combinations of hops, among them Magnum, Cascade, Centennial, Citra, Amarillo, Chinook, Mosaic, Simcoe, Galaxy, and Topaz. Rain is both citrusy and earthy, while Sun is piney and citrusy with a crisp mouth feel. Big Juice is the bitterest of the group, but the high level of hoppiness is prevented from becoming too edgy by the caramel malts. Little Juice has apricot and grapefruit notes, with the unfiltered version, Little Juice Smoothie, having a thicker body. For those who like very big IPAs, Rain, Rain, Rain weighs in at 12.5 percent ABV.

During their short history, the people at Three Magnets have created 57 different beers, many of them only once. The most unusual of these is one called "JustBEETit"—the name suggests the unusual additive. Jeff Stokes designed the recipe and, he noted, "Some people loved it and some hated it." The tasting notes remarked on its purple color and its very vegetable and earthy notes.

Patrick Jansen noted that Three Magnets, late in 2016, would be brewing many of their core beers at Matchless Brewing, a new contract brewery that he and friend Grant Bolt would own and operate in Tumwater. That would provide more opportunity for the Three Magnets brewing system to be used for specialty and one-off beers. Jeff Stokes would run the in-house brewery. Could there be a beer called BeetRepeat in the not too distant future?

3. Beyond the Capital: Brewing in Lacey and Tumwater

O-Town Brewing and Top Rung Brewing (Lacey),
Triceratops Brewing Company (Tumwater)

A dozen of the breweries I visited along Highway 101 were, or had begun as, garage breweries, where former homebrewers made the first steps toward creating commercial beers on small systems housed in very noncommercial settings. The first of these that I encountered was in Lacey, a town of nearly 45,000 just east of Olympia. After travelling east along Interstate 5 a few miles and then down the College Street thoroughfare to Montclair Drive, I passed a number of large houses with wide driveways on which were parked two or three cars and the occasional recreational vehicle, until I came to 4414, the street number of O-Town Brewing. When I knocked on the front door, a young boy and a barking but tail-wagging old black lab appeared. I was told to go through the gate to the side of the house, past the patio, to a pole barn at the back of the lot. There, Neil Meyer, Matt Smith, and Bryan Trunnell ushered me into O-Town Brewing. In addition to the two-barrel brewing system, the room contained a small bar with stools, a place for cleaning and then storing empty kegs, and a cold room. The walls were decorated with beer paraphernalia that would have made a collector of breweriana envious: decorative tap handles, banners, coasters, bottles and other delights, all collected by Trunnell, in whose pole barn the brewery was located.

Each came from different occupations: Meyer was an architect, Smith had been in construction and now managed a bar, Trunnell was retired from the military (as was a fourth partner, Jason Stenzel, who couldn't make our meeting). Each had been a homebrewer and each recalled drinking a beer that had changed their perceptions of what the beverage could be. For Neil, who started as an Olympia drinker, it was Widmer Brothers' Hefeweizen; for Bryan,

Former homebrewers (from left) Bryan Trunnell, Matt Smith, and Neil Meyer joined together (along with Jason Stenzel) to form O-Town Brewing, which operates in a pole barn behind the Lacey, Washington, home of Trunnell.

the German beers he'd discovered when his father was stationed in Germany. Matt's game changers were more local; he remembered enjoying the English-style ales of Fish Brewing.

A few years ago Matt and Neil had started S and M Brewing, while Bryan had formed Kastellan Braueri, creating such German styles as Oktoberfest, Keller-bier, and Altbier. It was after the three of them had made a trip to the 2014 Great American Beer Festival that they decided to combine their energies, talents, and finances to form O-Town Brewing, using Bryan's pole barn and brewing system.

O-Town's first beer, Brewtarsky (6.6 percent ABV, 38 IBUs)—an indirect reference to a character in the movie *Animal House*—was labeled a German IPA. "It was a style that didn't exist," Meyer said. "We used German malts and Northwest hops. It was clean and hoppy." As Matt Smith explained, this inaugural offering set the tone for the brewery's later creations. "We do specialty beers. People have become too IPA centric. We are German style with a North-west twist. We take beer that would fit a certain style and give it a twist. Beer doesn't have to be made to fit a category; it should be made to be enjoyed."

"And we like variety," Neil added. "In our first year we brewed nearly 20 different styles. That's the beauty of having a small brewing system. We can try out small batches, see what people think of them, and then, if they aren't just right, we can start over or forget about the recipe. We won't have wasted a lot of beer or money." Among these 20 beers were such well-known styles as stouts, IPAs, blondes, browns, porters, bocks, and American dark ales—along with variations of these and with inclusion of a variety of additives to achieve the twist.

One of the best examples of a brew with a twist is O-Town's best-selling beer, Sails 'n' Gunpowder (8.7 percent, 51 IBUs). "We asked ourselves, what if Caribbean pirates in the 1700s made an IPA," Smith said, a smile on his face, "So we brewed an English strong ale and added raw sugar, molasses, vanilla and coconut. Then we aged it two months, simulating barrel aging by using oak staves soaked in rum. Whenever we brew a batch, it sells out pretty quickly. People are always asking us when we're going to make more."

This adding of unusual ingredients is also seen in Alki-Chai Milk Stout (5.5 percent, 20 IBUs), Mt. St. Helles Bock (6.5 percent), and Mount Olympus Lahar (5.7 percent, 34 IBUs), each beer named after a Pacific Northwest landmark. The stout includes vanilla bean and Indian chai sauce, the bock—which is more of a German-style helles—has Anaheim and Serrano peppers, while Lahar is a brown ale which, when the trio was unhappy with initial results, was infused with espresso coffee and a hint of rye. I tried each of the "beers with a twist," noticing that the additives weren't overwhelming, that there were hints of flavors that did, indeed, give interesting variations to familiar styles. In the few weeks after my visit, O-Town came up with more interesting combinations. South Sound Saison (6.3 percent, 40 IBUs) contained heather which, the description stated, "accentuates the natural spicy notes of the yeast." The obvious extra in Night Stalker Coffee Cascadian Dark Ale (5.5 percent) made the black ale even, if it's possible, blacker.

Even though O-Town's reputation has been built in part because of its beers with a twist, it's worth noting the group makes several brews that are more conventional. Among these are O'Town Irish Stout (5.7 percent), Priest Point Porter (6.5 percent, 21 IBUs), Oly IPA (6.5 percent, 97 IBUs)—which uses hops grown by partner Jason Stenzel—and Burfoot Easy Blonde (4.5 percent, 23 IBUs), which uses an interesting mixture of both Northwest and German hops.

Talking about the future of O-Town in a county where craft brewing has enjoyed two years of very rapid expansion, Meyer noted, "We—if you count Kastellan—are the second oldest brewery in Thurston County. We would like to expand, and if we do we'll need a larger facility. But we want to make sure we've created a solid foundation and built a good reputation before we grow.

We've been in the black since we started, and we want to keep it that way." He didn't see the area's beer boom ending soon, remarking "there's room here for maybe two or three larger breweries." Bryan added that he believed that Olympia was about to become the next Washington beer destination, attracting tourists who would come for the variety and quality of beer offered by several breweries. To which Matt added: "I'd like to see Olympia to become the next Bend." He was referring to the central Oregon city that is home to over two dozen breweries and brewpubs, many of which had achieved national and international recognition.

Before I began driving to Top Rung Brewery, which was five miles away, I checked my phone and found a message from owner Casey Sobol that he might be a few minutes late, as he had to pick up his daughters at school and bring them with him. He didn't need to worry; I got lost in spite of very clear directions, and, when I arrived, his daughters Morgan and Brooke met me at the door. In addition to being co-owner and brewer's assistant to partner Jason Stoltz, Casey is a very active father and a captain in the McLane/Black Lake Fire Department, where Jason also works.

The brewery/taproom wasn't open that day, so the girls had the run of the place. But even if it had been open, they'd have been welcome. "This is a place for families," Casey explained. "There's a play area with games for the kids. It's a community gathering place; people bring their own food or order from the food truck when it's parked outside. We do have snacks, though—hot pretzels. However, we decided to focus on providing good beer and a place where people can enjoy it."

On one wall, there was a giant screen TV and beside it a Seahawks banner. "We have the TV on during the Seahawks games, but we don't turn the sound on. And nobody seems to mind. They can watch and still talk with each other." If patrons need something else to distract them, they can look at the back of building where the 10-barrel system is open to view and get a sense of how close they are to where the brews they are enjoying have been made.

Both Sobol and Stoltz grew up in the South Sound area, Jason in Tacoma and Casey in Olympia. As Sobol talked about his home town, his love of the dearly departed brewery in Tumwater was very evident. "The smell of hops always reminds me of the Olympia brewery tours our family made whenever we had out-of-towners visiting. At the end of the tour, they always served root beer to the kids—that was the best part. When I started to drink beer, it was nearly always Oly. Once in a while I'd have a Rainier—but it was always local beer. Our Lacey Dark Lager (5.2 percent ABV, 27 IBUs) is meant to be a tribute to Oly dark."

Casey and Jason met when the two were working on the same shift at the

When firemen Casey Sobol (pictured here with his daughters Morgan, left, and Brooke) and Jason Stoltz decided to open Top Rung Brewing, they wanted a place that would be family friendly. Like most Washington State brewpubs and taprooms, Top Rung displays its loyalty to the Seattle Seahawks. Patrons can watch the games, but the sound is turned off, so that people who want to converse can do so without shouting.

fire department and soon discovered that they shared a love of homebrewing. They began making beer together, one of which, Hosechaser Blonde, was so good that it won the "Beer for a Cure" contest, a cancer research fundraising project sponsored by a brewery in nearby Centralia. "That got us thinking about starting our own brewery. Fish was the only one in the county and there was room for another. So, we started hanging around our mentor, Dick [Young, a Centralia brewer], learning everything we could about running a commercial brewery." They opened Top Rung in Tumwater in 2014.

The name Casey and Jason chose for their brewery reflected their profession: fire fighting. Top Rung represented not only the high goals they set for the beer they brewed, but the highest rung on a ladder. The brewery's logo is shaped like a fireman's shield and has a ladder in the center and hops around the edges. Inside the taproom, there's a small ladder hanging from the ceiling and a child's size fire engine. The tools of their profession provide names for some of the beers, among them Prying Irons and Heavy Irons. "We wanted to celebrate the work of fire fighters, but subtly. We wanted people to buy the beers because of their high quality, not because we're fire fighters."

The first beer they brewed professionally was their award winner, Hosechaser Blonde. "It's bready and biscuity, with a low hop presence. It's easy drinking and ideal for someone who isn't used to the more robust flavors of craft beer." He mentioned that some of the customers who started with this 4.5 percent ABV, 25 IBUs beer have graduated to darker and hoppier styles. Among the dark beers is My Dog Scout Stout (6.0 percent, 30 IBUs), named the best stout in Washington State in 2015. Named after Jason's Labrador, it uses eight malts and is noted for its coffee and chocolate notes. Pyrolysis Imperial Stout is a stronger version of the style at 9.7 percent, 57 IBUs. When I asked about the name, Casey gave a fireman's answer: "It's the thermo-chemical breakdown of organic material at elevated temperatures in the absence of oxygen." I could only say: "Oh!" There are both bourbon barrel and red wine barrel-aged versions of Pyrolysis.

This being the Pacific Northwest, Top Rung offers three different India pale ales. Prying Irons IPA (6.7 percent, 60 IBUs) is a grapefruity and citrusy tasting beer that uses Falconer's Flight, Willamette, Nugget, and Cascade hops. Casey remarks that Cascade hops, first used in the 1970s, "changed everything in the brewing world." Heavy Irons, a Double IPA that weighs in at 8.2 percent ABV and a whopping 105 IBUs, is available only in the winter. Shift Trade IPA, available all year, is the mildest of the three: 6.2 percent and 50 IBUs. The Mosaic and Cascade hops used in the recipe contribute to the tropical fruit notes. Each fall, Top Rung releases a wet hop pale ale, which uses newly harvested hops they've grown themselves.

Two of Top Rung's regular offerings are a tribute to Olympia and the area's long history as lager drinking territory. In addition to Lacey Dark, people who fondly remember Oly can enjoy Lacey Lager (4.5 percent, 24 IBUs). The web site describes it as "crisp and clean with a nice finish.... A true blue collar beer." The name may well be an echo of "Lucky Lager," a popular post–World War II beer brewed in Vancouver, Washington.

Like so many new and successful craft brewing operations, Top Rung is growing, installing larger equipment, contracting the services of a mobile bottling company, and hiring a sales person. "We hope to grow to 5,000 barrels a year and to be available in more places. But," he paused, and then continued, "we really rely on the locals. It's their brewery."

The next morning, I visited Hoh River Brewery, the first Tumwater brewery to open since 2003, when SABMiller closed the Tumwater plant, claiming that it was too small to be operated profitably. The Oly plant could turn out well over a million barrels annually; Hoh River, with its two-barrel system, was lucky if it could reach yearly production in the low three figures. That's less than the amount that one of the megabrewing facilities spills in five minutes. John Christopherson, the owner/brewer of the new nanobrewery, had originally planned to open a brewpub in downtown Olympia, but when he discovered that it would cost over forty thousand dollars to make the building he chose handicapped accessible, he decided to open up in the Tumwater building that houses his Christopherson Wood Floors business. In the summer of 2015, he received his brewing license. By the end of 2016, his brewery could be one of three operating in Tumwater, and, if planning for a brewing center of excellence came to fruition, the number could rise to four.

An Olympia native, John Christopherson grew up drinking what he called the "usual fizzy stuff," until he discovered such craft beers as Sierra Nevada Pale Ale and Full Sail IPA. "Then I asked myself, how did I ever drink that other stuff?" It wasn't until five or six years ago that he began homebrewing. He confessed that he, like his father, was a workaholic—in addition to becoming increasingly more involved over the years in the family flooring business, he'd qualified for a pilot's license and operated charter flights and an air taxi between Seattle Tacoma International Airport and Olympia. "One day, my wife, Lynette, told me that I needed a hobby, something to get me away from working all the time. And for Christmas she bought me a 'Mr. Beer' kit." He quickly became hooked. "Within three months, I bought an all-grain homebrewing system and in the first year I made two hundred gallons of beer. I think that's more than you're allowed to. All the beers were very hoppy. I'm a hop maniac, I love hoppy beers."

I asked John why, when he decided to open a professional brewery, he

John Christopherson wanted his tiny taproom for Hoh River Brewing to be family friendly. In order for that to happen, he had to have food available. The canister of Twizzlers on the counter fulfills that requirement.

chose the name Hoh River. After all, that river never came close to Olympia and flowed into the Pacific Ocean. "It's a tribute to my wife's family heritage. Her grandmother was a member of the Hoh River tribe. And as well, we loved to take the kids hiking and camping along the Hoh. We even used to bring some jugs of water back here for homebrewing." One of the brewery's slogans states that the product is "Made from Rain Forest Rainwater." However, he acknowledged that he was going to drop the slogan. "We're not using that water anymore; Olympia has great brewing water; with a little tweaking, it's perfect for all the beers we make."

Hoh River Brewing occupies each end of the Christopherson Wood Floors building, with the brewhouse to the south and the taproom to the north. As we sat in the brewhouse, John talked about the early months of his new part-time career as a professional brewer. "We sold kegs and growlers to employees and friends and supplied beer for special functions. My first professional beer was Fast and Hoppy Hoh Double IPA. It was 10 percent ABV and used Amarillo, Citra, Mosaic and Simcoe hops. But I had to remember that while most of my friends and I liked really hoppy IPAs, not everyone did. So I developed a variety of styles."

These included High Divide Bohemian Pilsner, which at 32 IBUs was well-hopped for the style, but not overpowering. "It's a really refreshing drink," he commented. Hawk Ale, named after Lynette's mother Loretta Hawk, "a Native American—a true American," is a hefeweizen. "It's for people who aren't really into craft beer. It's an entry level beer for the tag along friends of my friends. It's less yeasty than German versions." Pacific Beach Pale Ale is, Christopherson says, not that hoppy. "Sometimes when I'm at home, I'll mix it half and half with my IPA." He went on to note that the Pale and Hefe were slow sellers.

We moved through the building into the taproom, a 12-foot by 14-foot space marked by duct tape in the other business's woodworking shop. On the counter in front of the beer fridge were packages of strawberry licorice, granola bars, and peanuts. "In order for children to be allowed in this area, I have to have food to sell. And these," he remarked gesturing at the packages before him, "are considered food by government authorities." I sampled his Happy Hoh IPA and Fat and Hoppy Hoh Double IPA—and they were hoppy. I turned down an offer of some strawberry licorice whips—it was just too early in the day for such sweet stuff.

Later in the morning, John would make his first sale to a licensed bar. Oly Taproom agreed to put his High Divide Bohemian Pilsner on tap. "It will be a good next step," he said, with a happy smile. "I'm not out to be huge. Not everyone has to be on a fast track to be a major craft brewer. I just want to make beer for people to enjoy and if it takes off, that's OK. I want to make styles that I like; I won't change my styles for profit."

I headed back to Olympia and Three Magnets where I was to meet with Rob Horn, who, two years ago, had founded Triceratops Brewing Company in his garage in suburban Olympia, but was in the early stages of enlarging his brewery and moving it to Tumwater. He was combining his interview with me and a meeting with Patrick Jansen, who was also planning his move to Tumwater.

Until a few days before our meeting, Rob, like Casey Sobol and Jason Stoltz, was a full-time fireman and part-time professional brewer. A native of New Jersey, he'd studied park management, which included a course in forest fire fighting. "I loved it," he remembered, and for 10 years he had been a volunteer fireman. He worked for three months in a Philadelphia area fire department and, when he moved to the West Coast, joined the Fort Lewis Air Base Fire Department. "We had a lot of down time so I took some on-line brewing courses from the Siebel Institute in Chicago. We used to talk a lot about craft beer. When we were off duty, we'd try out different beers."

That was a continuation of an activity he'd started in high school. "A bunch of us would get together and exchange beers we'd bought. We were educating our palate. I remember once I'd gone to the supermarket to buy a six pack for our meeting and when I got to the checkout stand, the guy working there was my old high school English teacher. I was lucky—he didn't recognize me." While at Fort Lewis, his beer education continued. His captain, Donald Wasson, became a mentor, taking him to homebrew shops, to Fish Brewing, and to various beer events in the South Puget Sound area. "I'd been home brewing. But I was using malt extract. The first beer I made was an ale with malt extract. It was terrible—tasted like motor oil." Wasson introduced him to all-grain brewing and the quality of Rob's beer increased steadily.

Rob's biggest supporter in his brewing career has been his wife Kelly, to whom he proposed while the two were hiking on Mount Baker (north of Seattle) during a vacation trip from the east. "She was the one who suggested that we get a license and start a brewery in our garage. Sammy, our oldest child was

Craft brewers frequently talk about the camaraderie and cooperation that exist among members of the profession. Here in the cramped quarters of Three Magnets, from left to right, Patrick Jansen (Three Magnets), Bryan Trunnell (O-Town), and Rob Horn (Triceratops) gather to talk shop.

starting school at the Olympia Waldorf School and the money we could make from a small brewery would help pay tuition fees." If family was one of the reasons Rob Horn started a small one-barrel brewery, family was also important in the name he gave to it. "I had three children, Sammy, Molly, and Ben—three little horns. That's why we decided on the name Triceratops." The children's names are also attached to three of the brewery's products: SAMMY IPA, MOLLY IPA, and BEN SMaSH. The dinosaur theme is found in Alamosaurous Amber, Bagaceratops Brown, and Megalosaurus Barleywine.

The brewery is in many ways, a family operation. Rob and Kelly cleaned and sliced over a dozen pounds of strawberries for the first beer they sold, Strawberry Blonde, which was purchased by Top Rung. "My dad loves brown ale, and when I brewed a batch for his birthday, Sammy helped me with the recipe and made the labels." His father-in-law Russell, better known as "Pappy," helps at events and does the company books. Molly likes hanging out in the garage when her father is brewing, and Ben has fun loading and unloading empty kegs—if he's paid twenty-five cents a keg. All the children have accompanied Rob on a trip to Yakima to get fresh hops.

Perhaps the biggest influence family had on Triceratops was on the decision to close the garage brewery, purchase larger equipment, and move to a Tumwater industrial park and into a building where space was being built to Rob's specifications. "As a fireman, I often had to work on holidays. I was missing important time with the children. It was time to move on. So I tendered my resignation, cashed in my 401Ks, and started the process of expanding and moving." He admitted that he'd be very busy, but now, with all the children in school and his wife teaching, he could be away during the day and still have time in the evening and on holidays to be with them.

When he'd been remembering his high school beer "education," Rob spoke of Sam Adams Scotch Ale, a very malty beer, as one of his favorites. His choice reflects his East Coast background, where one of the first major craft beers was Sam Adams Boston Lager, a very malt-forward beer. When he arrived in the Northwest, the land of hoppy beers, he worked at combining his malt-forward approach with the area's emphasis on well-hopped IPAs. "I think that making malty beers balanced with hops will be my niche in Olympia. One of the grains I particularly like experimenting with in my recipes is rye." Rhythm and Rye IPA, named after a local bar that has been very supportive of his work, he hopes to make his flagship beer after the move to larger quarters is complete. Craftsman Copper Ale and Hawthorne Coffee Milk Stout, brewed in conjunction with Hawthorne Coffee Roasters in Olympia, are two more examples of Triceratops' malt-forward brewing.

Even the IPAs feature a strong malt presence. On Rate Beer, a consumer evaluation site, one commentator on Triceratops Goat IPA remarked: "There is a good amount of malt flavor added to the hops to make this a good session IPA." Reviewers of Sammy IPA commented: "I liked the malt backing," and "[It has] a big malty sweet nose."

While we were talking, O-Town's Bryan Trunnell came by, delivering a keg of ale for Three Magnets. The two exchanged greetings. "You know," Rob observed, after his friend had gone into the brewhouse, "the craft brewing community here is like an extended family." He talked about how the people at O-Town, Top Rung, Fish, and Three Magnets had helped him when he was starting out and still help him now that he's expanding. In a few weeks, he and Patrick Jansen would be taking a collaboration beer, Big Dumb Face Session Triple IPA, to the Washington Beer Collaboration Festival. Five other area brewers had combined to create an India red lager for the event. After we'd finished our conversation, Rob headed inside to talk with Bryan and Trunnell, while I headed to the bar area to try a glass of Tricer Bock, a collaboration between Three Magnets and Triceratops. It had a rich taste of roasted malts and a clean finish.

My beverage finished, I stuck my head in the brewhouse to say goodbye to the three brewing amigos and to wish Patrick Jansen well with the brewery he was in the process of putting together in Tumwater. "Our first beer should be ready in a month," he told me. When I asked what it would be, he smiled and replied, "Why an IPA, of course!"

I had one more stop to make before turning onto Highway 101, a return to the bridge over the Deschutes River. The pictures I'd taken on the misty morning had turned out badly. Hopefully the spray from the swollen river would have lessened after a couple of rainless days and, with the sun shining brightly, I'd get an image that looked more like the Olympia beer label. The results were only slightly better.

On my way back to the parking lot, I decided to take a quick look at Schmidt House, once the home of the brewery's owner and now the headquarters for the Olympia-Tumwater Foundation. The building wasn't open for tours, but Don Trosper, Karen Johnson, and Dennis Larson, three members of the executive who had just finished a meeting, invited me in. On hearing of my project, Karen agreed to take a photograph of a reported beautiful piece of graffiti—a representation of the horseshoe, bridge, and falls—on one of the doors of the old brewery and send it to me. Dennis talked about his forthcoming book *The King of Hops*, a history of one of the area's first and most important hop growers. As I thanked them and prepared to take my leave, Don said he had one last thing he wanted me to see. He pointed to a picture hanging on the wall near the front door, walked over to it, and removed it from its hook. Behind

On the wall just inside the front door of Schmidt House, home of the founder of Olympia Beer, in Tumwater, Washington, is this fresco-style painting of the Olympia Beer logo.

it, painted in the plaster, was the Olympia beer logo. It had been commissioned by the Schmidts when the house was being built and only later became the brewery logo. Karen noted that the crest was very similar to one Schmidt had had created for his Montana brewery and that the horseshoe was part of the family crest back in Germany.

Part II

By the Shores of the Salish Sea and Beyond

As Highway 101 winds along the western shores of the Salish Sea (a collective term for Puget Sound, and the Straits of Juan de Fuca and Georgia), it passes through four towns that are home to six breweries or brewpubs. With a couple of exceptions, both the towns and breweries are small. The population of Port Angeles is just under twenty thousand; that of the others ranges from six hundred to below ten thousand. Only two breweries, Port Townsend Brewing and Propolis Brewing, produce over one thousand barrels annually and distribute beyond their local areas. Four brew under one hundred barrels each year, being content to serve locals and tourists in their (usually small) tasting rooms and/or in area bars. "Of course," one person, who referred to himself as a weekend brewer, remarked, tongue-in-cheek, "if Budweiser came along with a check for a million dollars, or even one hundred thousand, I'd certainly listen."

4. The Challenges
of Small Town Brewpubs:
Shelton and Quilcene

Grove Street Brewhouse (Shelton)
and 101 Brewery (Quilcene)

During the drive from Olympia, I noticed signs of approaching spring. Although the Olympic Mountains to my left were topped with fresh snow, the evergreens below them had sprouted light green tips and, on the branches of the maples and alders, buds were about to burst open. To the right, I caught occasional glances of inlets and bays of the Salish Sea, where the small waves sparkled in the bright sunshine. My first stop was Shelton, a town with a declining population of just under ten thousand. Once an important logging center, it had suffered from the decline of that industry. Now it boasted oyster cultivation and the harvesting of Christmas trees as important industries. As I walked around the small downtown area, I noticed several empty stores.

I had come to visit Grove Street Brewhouse, which had opened in 2009, proudly announcing that it was Mason County's first brewery. When I'd contacted the owners in February, Tessie Thompson had agreed to meet me, if, she said, "we're still open. We're going day-by-day." As I reached the entrance, I noticed a sign announcing that only cash was accepted at the establishment and that there was an ATM inside. I introduced myself to co-owner Jeff Thompson, who didn't seem to know I was coming and who told me that Tessie was taking care of the grandchildren. He apologized, stating, "We've got a lot on our plate just now," and agreed to talk with me in a few minutes. It was St. Patrick's Day, and he had to go back to the kitchen where he was preparing bangers and mash and corn beef and cabbage. I looked around the brewhouse while he finished his tasks. Three of the four conditioning tanks had signs reading "empty" pasted on them. The other still had some Old Pinchfister Ale in it.

His preparations over, Jeff talked about the founding of Grove Brewhouse

44

in 2009. He'd long admired the building on the corner of Grove and First Street. It had been an automobile dealership, a motorcycle- and then boat-repair shop. He purchased the property and decided to turn it into a brewpub. "We were going to convert Budweiser drinkers," he noted. "Before that we had to renovate most of the building. It had been built in 1945." They purchased a brewing system from a defunct Florida brewery and hired as their brewer Adam Orrick, a recent graduate of Siebel Institute in Chicago and its sister organization, Doemen's Academy of Munich, Germany. But 2009 was a challenging time to open a brewpub in a small town with declining revenue and a lot of Bud drinkers. "We had an investor, but he cut off his funding. We had to borrow big and carry on by ourselves."

While we were conversing, I noticed that there were only two or three people in the brewpub. Jeff remarked that Shelton is not a great supporter of local businesses and wondered if, because it was a small town, people didn't want to run into each other in a bar. In addition, the original investor was anxious to recoup the money he had put in and was hoping that the Thompsons could find a buyer for the place. "Things have been really tight this winter," Jeff explained. "A few months ago, a customer gave us enough money to brew a few batches of beer and that's kept us going until now. If we can hang on until the spring, we may be able to keep going. Spring, summer, and fall are great months for tourists, and they like craft beer."

When he returned to the kitchen to continue work on the St. Patrick's Day specials, Jeff's daughter Leah, who had been working at the bar, joined me. She'd also been the brewer for a couple of years. "I helped our first brewer, Adam Orrick. He left in 2011 and I also helped the brewers who followed him. Then, when we found ourselves without a brewer, I stepped in. Adam came back to give me a two-day crash course, and here I am." Now, with the tanks running dry, Grove Street had guest taps from Three Magnets and Fish Brewing.

With tonight being the occasion for St. Patrick's Day celebrations as well as Thursday night's regular open mike session, Leah and Jeff were hoping for a somewhat livelier, and so more profitable crowd. "We're family friendly, so on Thursday people often bring their children. The Open Mike starts at six o'clock; people can enjoy a meal, listen to some local musicians and then go home to get the kids to bed."

I wished Leah and Jeff good luck both for their St. Patrick's evening festivities and the upcoming weeks and months. When I left, the same three people were seated at the bar; no one else had come in. I thought of a line on Grove Street's Facebook page. It described Shelton as "a sleepy little drinking village with a logging problem." Perhaps the problem was that there weren't enough loggers still working nearby and there were too few drinkers of craft beer.

When I checked back a few weeks later, Leah said that they still hadn't resumed brewing. Then in the summer, I read this Facebook post: "Thank you, All! It's been a Grand Run. October 1, 2009–July 14, 2016. Beer, Tea, and Revelry!" A couple of months later, I learned that the restaurant and brewhouse wouldn't stay closed. I noticed in the Brewers Association directory breweries for Washington State that Keelhaul Brewery was listed as "in planning" for Shelton. When I called the number listed, Will Handly, who along with Eric McLemore was an owner/brewer, answered and told me that the two had taken over the space occupied by Grove Street. "We've got a lot of details to cover and a lot of physical work before us, but we hope to be open by the end of the year." Once again I realized that the craft brewing business is, figuratively as well as literally, very fluid.

I proceeded north for an hour passing stretches of the shoreline of Hood Canal, a narrow fjord extending south over fifty miles from its mouth near the northern entrance to Puget Sound. My next stop was the village of Quilcene (population 591), a one-time major but now small logging center, home of one of the largest oyster hatcheries on the Pacific Coast, and a starting point for hikers into the Olympic National Forest. It was also the home of 101 Brewery and Twana Roadhouse.

I wasn't scheduled to meet owner Melody Bacchus for an hour, so I decided to sample some beer and order dinner. Most of customers seemed to be locals, many of them wearing green t-shirts and one sporting dyed green hair. The exceptions were sitting in a corner at a large table in front of the fireplace and under West Coast Native-style decorations of orcas and salmon. Two played ukuleles and another a harmonica, and they were singing old time, "sing-along-with-Mitch" type tunes.

My taster of four house beers arrived. They ranged from light to dark, and each had a name related to the logging industry: Sidewinder White Wheat (4.8 percent ABV), Peckerpole Pale Ale (5.6 percent), Hook Tender Honey Brown Ale (5.6 percent), and Look Out Stout (6.0 percent). I more or less ascertained the meanings of three of the names, but had to ask what a peckerpole was. It was a long-ago logging term for a tree that was so spindly it really wasn't worth harvesting. The beers were non-threatening, middle of the road brews, with minimal hop presence. Non-craft beer drinkers could enjoy bottles of Corona, Rainier, and Coors Light. While I was sipping my Peckerpole Pale, I looked out the window to see a logging truck travelling down Highway 101. Its load seemed to be made up entirely of peckerpoles, the great first and second growth evergreens having been long ago cut down.

The menu, in addition to the corned beef and cabbage special, listed fairly standard pub fare—pizza, burgers, subs and grilled sandwiches. Under the

When Melody Bacchus, the owner of Twana Roadhouse in the village of Quilcene, became an empty nester, she considered selling the restaurant. Instead, she decided to teach herself how to brew beer and added the name 101 Brewery to the establishment.

"Fresh and Local" heading, were steamed clams and oysters on the half shell. My choice was the "Everything Burger"—it was very big and very tasty.

As I was finishing my French fries and draining the last of the taster glasses, Melody Bacchus, who'd been busy working in the kitchen, came over to my table. She told me how Twana Roadhouse, which she'd owned and operated for nearly 20 years, also become 101 Brewery. "A few years ago, my eldest daughter moved out. I was an empty nester and thought it was time to leave the business and move. I put the roadhouse on the market for a year, but I couldn't sell it. I wondered what I should do; so I decided to reinvent myself and the restaurant. I'd become a brewer and it would become a brewpub."

She explained that her son-in-law was a homebrewer and that the family often visited brewpubs during their vacation travels. "I was really interested in breweries and brewing, and I watched what he did and how the places we stopped at ran their businesses. I thought that installing a brewery here would be an interesting addition to the place. We'd be able to offer a variety of styles. And, with more and more of our customers, especially travelers, being interested in craft beers, it seemed the right time." She decided it would be doable if she installed a small system. Then, she went to the Internet, read everything she could about beer and brewing and trained herself how to brew on her newly acquired 15-gallon system.

She had to gut the garage behind the roadhouse and renovate it so that it could house the new system, and she had to get permission to open from officials of the nearby school, as well as meet the state and federal licensing requirements. That was both time-consuming and frustrating, but not so frustrating as her first attempts at brewing. "I had to throw out lots and lots of beer. I wasn't doing it right and it was sour, undrinkable." Finally, in 2012, the brewery opened for business.

While we were talking, Melody showed me the barroom, which was decorated with such old logging tools as a crosscut saw and double-bitted axe. Then we proceeded to the brewhouse, which seemed cramped in the renovated garage. "I don't work here anymore. My daughter and her husband, Mark McCrehin, moved back here a while after we'd opened. So he does the brewing now. The beer we make is popular with our customers, and the system is so small that he has to brew four or five times a week. It's really labor intensive. I'd really like a bigger system."

As we returned to the front of the restaurant, she talked about the future of craft brewing. "I really think that it's difficult for very small brewers. You have to have a restaurant, a place to offer your beer, or you have to distribute. Distribution is a real challenge; there's lots of competition for taps or shelf space if you bottle. In a restaurant like ours, it's not make or break selling our own beer. But it's a nice complement to our food. And the people who live around here are really happy that they can eat at a place where they can also drink local beer."

5. From Hop Diggidy to Golden Saison Spruce: Port Townsend

Port Townsend Brewing and Propolis Brewing

At the point where Highway 101 turns westward, I took a 12-mile side-trip along State Highway 20 to Port Townsend, a city of just under ten thousand that is noted for its historic Victorian style buildings, its thriving art community, and its many festivals, one of the most unusual of which takes place in January. At Strange Brewfest, brewers bring beers with such unlikely flavors as Almond Roca (a popular Northwest candy) and salami. The most popular concoction at the 2016 gathering was "Phuket, Let's Go to Strange Brew," a Thai inspired IPA that included cilantro, sriracha and gelled beer noodles.

Late in the nineteenth century, residents dreamed of a great future for the city. Situated where the Strait of Juan de Fuca meets Puget Sound, it was one of the major ports on the Pacific Northwest coast and forest products from the area were shipped from its docks to distant cities and lands. It was believed that, should the transcontinental railroad locate its western terminus there, Port Townsend would become the most important city north of San Francisco. However, when decisions were made to have the railroad terminus on the southern part of the Puget Sound, the dream died, and Port Townsend became a small, not enormously important city. It was during the 1970s that it became, as the Moon travel guide *The Olympic Peninsula* termed it, "a safe haven for artistic souls."[1]

Like most towns before Prohibition, Port Townsend had breweries. The first, Port Townsend Brewery, was founded in 1874 by William Goellert, who operated it for three years until he was convicted of selling alcohol to Indians. It continued operation under various owners and with various names until 1888. In 1905, a second Port Townsend Brewery opened with local owners; however it was taken over four years later by Leopold Schmidt, owner of

49

Olympia Brewery. Plagued with water problems that made the beer cloudy, something that wasn't a problem in Tumwater, the brewery didn't make it past Prohibition. In 1933, Peninsula Brewery opened. However, it operated for only two years, after which the town was without a brewery for over six decades. In 1997, the third brewery named Port Townsend Brewing opened. A year later, Maxwell's Brewery and Pub, later renamed Water Street Brewing, opened downtown. In 2010, when it was not granted a renewal of its lease, it shut down. Port Townsend Brewing is still in business, making it the longest operating brewery in the town's history.

On a bright March day, I visited the city's two breweries: Port Townsend, and Propolis, which had begun brewing in 2012. Both were in marked contrast to the brewpubs I'd visited in Shelton and Quilcene. Although each had a tap-room, neither served food. And the beers of each had achieved recognition (and a strong sales record) in places far distant from the breweries in which they were produced. While the breweries were located within a couple of blocks of each other, they produced very different beverages. Port Townsend offered a fairly familiar range of craft beers that included Chet's Golden Ale, Hop Dig-gidy IPA, and Reel Amber. Propolis Brewing offerings, which it defined as "Sea-sonal Herbal Ales," included Golden Saison Spruce, Archillea Dubbel and Wyrt Farmhouse Stout.

Port Townsend Brewing is located right next to the Boat Yard, a complex of maintenance, repair, construction, and storage buildings for boats ranging in size from canoe-length to 150 feet long. "This area is zoned for light industry, and that's what a production brewery is considered to be. That's why we are located here rather than in town," co-owner Kim Sands told me as she greeted me in the parking lot where I was standing, staring at the dozens of boats that had been pulled onto the land. She went on to say that the location wasn't a disadvantage. In fact, within a year of Port Townsend's opening in 1997, "we realized we'd have to expand. Nearly all our business was from sales at our tap room; but we wanted to distribute beyond the town and that meant we'd need more space for brewing equipment."

As we sat in the spacious taproom, on the walls of which were hung paint-ings by a local artist, Kim told us how Port Townsend's first brewery in over six decades had come into being. She and husband Guy had run a construction company in their hometown of San Diego, and, in the later 1990s, there was a slump in the industry. "But at the same time, there was a boom of smaller craft breweries in smaller cities," she noted. Port Townsend was experiencing a tourist boom, but it had no craft brewery, and the Sands decided to pull up stakes in California, move north and "go for broke"—that is, build a craft brew-ery. "We built the place on credit cards," Kim remembered. "In those days, banks didn't think small breweries were good risks." In 1996, they leased space in one third of the building in which we sat and which is now completely occupied by the brewery. "We were lucky to open in a year, there was so much paper work, so many hoops to jump through. But we were used to that from the construction industry, and so we just kept at it, one step at a time. When we opened, we were so tight for money that we had to use plastic cups instead of glass in the taproom."

Guy, who had been homebrewing for years, produced 600 barrels of beer the first year, most of it pale ale or porter. It wasn't too difficult to get residents and tourists to try their product. Craft beers from Seattle's Hales Ales were in several of the downtown bars and restaurants; the locals were familiar with the newer styles of beer. "We were so well received that on our first Fourth of July, we had forty customers jammed into our tiny tap room—along with musicians and two seven-barrel fermentation tanks, which were squeezed in behind the bar."

Kim Sands, right, co-owner of Port Townsend Brewing, and brewer Carter Camp stand in what was the original, very crowded taproom. The brewery initially occupied a small portion of the building; now it occupies the entire building and another across the parking lot.

Expansion proceeded steadily. In their second year of operation, the Sands added fermentation tanks; in their sixth, in order to place their ales in local supermarkets, they purchased a primitive bottler. It would fill six 22-ounce bottles at a time, but once full, the bottles had to be hand capped, one at a time. As distribution of the product widened, more tanks were added. More and more of the building was taken over. Near the end of the first decade of the new century, the present taproom was built at the end of the building.

At the time of my visit, Port Townsend Brewing occupied the entire structure. But that was not enough. More equipment was needed to create enough product to meet a demand that had increased greatly when Safeway and Quality Foods supermarkets in Seattle and points north began carrying Port Townsend ales. The building across the parking lot was acquired and housed a bottling machine that could fill and cap 100 cases a day, a cool room for filled bottles and kegs, a keg washing station, and storage space for empty kegs, bottles, and various pieces of equipment. That freed up space in the original building for an expansion of the brewery. A 15-barrel system was installed, with two 45 barrel fermenting tanks, four 60 barrel, and two of their old 30 barrel tanks. The brewhouse now has the capacity to produce 10,000 barrels annually.

While we were waiting for the arrival of head brewer Carter Camp, I remarked to Kim that there were no television sets adorning the walls of the taproom. "No," she said, "if people want to watch the Seahawks, they'll have to go to one of the bars downtown; if they want to drink our beer and watch the game, they can come here, buy a growler of beer and take it home." That doesn't mean that Seattle's very popular football team is forgotten at Port Townsend Brewing. The names of four of the ales refer to the Seahawks. "Beast Mode" Imperial IPA (8.9 percent ABV, 90 IBUs) is a reference to running back Marshawn Lynch, and Browner's Brown Ale (5.9 percent, 35 IBUs), to cornerback Brandon Browner; 43 to 8 Imperial IPA (8.5 percent, 85 IBUs) salutes the score by which the team defeated Denver in 2014 to win its first Super Bowl. And C-Hawk Imperial IPA (8.5 percent, 90 IBUs) deliberately "misspells" the nickname to indicate the recipe's inclusion of Chinook, Centennial, and Columbus hops.

Head brewer Carter Camp, having attended to some business in the brewhouse, joined us in the tap room. He'd begun homebrewing when he was a student at the University of Washington in Seattle. It was at this time that he discovered Sierra Nevada's Big Foot Barley Wine, a robust ale that made him understand how truly flavorful a beer could be. His first job was at Hale Ales where he was a bottler and where he began to learn the differences between kitchen stovetop and commercial brewing. From there he moved to Big Time Brewery and Ale House, Seattle's first brewpub, as an assistant brewer. A back injury prevented his doing the heavy lifting that is an essential chore in brewing and he missed the chance for a promotion to head brewer. But, three years later, he heard that Guy Sands of Port Townsend Brewing was looking for a new assistant and in January of 2008 began working here.

Port Townsend produces 13 year-round and seasonal beers, along with special one-offs (Camp estimates he's done close to 80 of these in the eight years he's been with Port Townsend). The regulars range from Chet's Gold Golden Ale, a crossover beer that's 4.7 percent ABV and 20 IBUs, to Barley Wine, which is 10.5 percent ABV and 95 IBUs, and is aged at least a year before serving. He remarked that early in his brewing career, he'd developed a love of big, hoppy beers and said that his "theme" is big IPAs, Imperial stouts and Imperial porters. It's not surprising, therefore, that sixteen of the beers described on Port Townsend's web site are over 7 percent ABV, and that 14 have IBUs of over 60. The beer he says that most realized what he intended is Drunken Sailor Bourbon Barrel Aged Imperial Brown, a 9.2 percent ABV offering.

Not all of the ales he creates are hop bombs. Reel Amber is 5.4 percent and 35 IBUs, the Porter is 5.5 percent and 25 IBUs, and, the most unusual of the beers he had concocted, Yoda Green Tea Gold, which adds Bancha, an organic green tea, to Chet's Gold, is, like its base beer, only 4.7 percent ABV and 20 IBUs. S.H.I.P. (the abbreviation for Single Hop Imagination Ale) is 5.25 percent ABV and a relatively mild 50 IBUs.

Asked to describe the house characteristic of Port Townsend's ales, Camp said: "We work to be true to style, to strike a balance between hops and malts, and to be consistent from batch to batch of the same style. Of course," he added, "we do give a slight edge to the hops." This can be seen in Chet's Gold, in which the Hallertau hops give a crisp, tangy bitterness not unlike that found in pilsners, but is especially evident in the IPAs. A list of the hops Camp uses in his various interpretations of the style reads like a page from a brewers' supply catalogue and includes: Simcoe, Citra, Sorachi Ace, Cascade, Columbus, Zythos, Amarillo, Centennial, and Chinook. It's appropriate that Port Townsend's most popular IPA, the label of which features a painting of Kim with a wreath of hop leaves in her hair, is called "Hop-Diggity."

After Carter Camp had returned to his brewing duties, Kim Sands and I walked through the building, from what might be called the new part of the building to the old. We passed the new fermenters and the two old ones that had survived the expansion project, and then came into the old taproom, tiny and cramped in comparison to the one we'd just left. On one of the walls was an advertisement for the early twentieth century Port Townsend Brewery. It proclaimed that its beer was available for purchase at five cents a glass—a far cry from the $4.00 to $4.50 a pint now charged. A look of quiet pride came over Kim's face. Perhaps she was remembering 1997, that first summer when the Fourth of July crowd seemed to reaffirm her and Guy's decision to pull up stakes in California and open a brewpub in this small city they now called home. "It's been quite a ride, these last 19 years," she admitted. When I asked what pleased her the most, she said that it was the fact that the brewery had become so much a part of Port Townsend. "The community welcomed us right from the start," she said. "And we've tried to give back. We've sponsored many community events, including festivals and music and drama presentations. We've probably given over five thousand dollars worth of beer just to the Wooden Boat Festival."

We walked outside from the back end of the old taproom onto a grassy area that serves as a beer garden. "Local musicians perform here on Sunday afternoons when it's warm and dry. And people can leave their dogs in an area just beyond the fence. The dogs seem to enjoy the music too. It's hard to imagine that this space used to be a lumber yard." The fence around the beer garden was covered with withered vines and leaves. "But in a few weeks, it will be very green." And what were the vines? Why hop bines, of course.

It was only a two-block walk from the parking lot in front of Port Townsend to the newly opened brewery and taproom of Propolis Brewing Company. The company had been started in 2014 by Robert Horner and Piper Corbett, who met at the Port Townsend taproom. Both were carrying cameras, began a conversation about photography, then discovered their mutual love of Belgian beers, and later in the evening enjoyed glasses of elderberry wine. "There's an old saying," Robert remarked, smiling happily, "that if you drink elderberry wine with someone when you first meet them, you'll end up being married within a year. We were."

A Midwesterner who had studied architecture at Ball State University in Indiana, Robert had been interested in teas made with herbs that possessed medicinal qualities. That interest was carried over into his research on early brewing history. When I asked what made him interested in long-ago beers, he corrected me. "Beers are made with hops, but ales were made with herbs before hops became widely used." Among these herbs were many of those he was familiar with. And he liked the idea that such subtle nuances of flavors could be created using simple brewing techniques that were hundreds of years old.

Piper was a Port Townsend girl who had grown up exploring the nearby forests and fields, learning about the properties of the trees and plants she encountered during her rambles. She'd discovered Belgian ales during a high school trip to Europe and the discovery stood her in good stead when she returned home. "We were at summer camp when the senior counselors raided our tent to check for beer, which, of course, was forbidden. When they discovered my stash of Belgian ale, I got off more lightly than the other girls, who probably had Budweiser. I guess they were impressed by my taste in beer." She attended UCLA, where she studied theatre and film arts and TV writing, and returned to the Olympic Peninsula, where she was involved in marketing and publicity for a local winery.

One of the things she had discovered over her glass of elderberry wine was that Robert wanted to start a brewery, not one that produced highly hopped IPAs, but one that used the subtle and varied bittering and flavoring herbs and other natural ingredients to create ales like the ones he and Piper had learned to appreciate. "I don't share the overblown excitement over hops," he remarked. They acquired space in a building that had once housed a book-bindery and set up a one-barrel brewing system. "There wasn't much room inside," Robert remarked. "And so we had to brew outside under an awning."

The name of their brewery, Propolis, is a term that not only refers to the substance bees create to coat the outside of their hives, but also symbolizes Robert and Piper's philosophy of brewing. The word "propolis" literally means "before the city," the material that is in front of the thriving, interdependent community of the bees. Moreover, it is made from what could be called "local, naturally sourced ingredients," material gathered by the bees from the buds of nearby trees. Like the bees, Robert and Piper would frequently roam the forests and fields collecting ingredients for their beer. Many scientists believe that the ingredients in propolis may be helpful for people suffering from cold sores and other similar diseases, just as the ingredients in the ales Robert and Pipe create can, consumed in moderation, be helpful. Finally, the meaning "before the city" can refer to a preindustrial, pre-urban era, a time when ales were made from natural ingredients by people living in rural, agrarian environments.

During their first year of operation, Robert and Piper brewed 150 batches of their ales, a total of 114 barrels. That quantity put them at number 1,361 on the microbrewery production list. But one of their creations, Beltane Elderflower Saison with Brett, won a gold medal at the 2014 Great American Beer Festival competition. Here's how the tasting notes on the brewery's website describe the ale: "Spring floral nose, citrus notes of tangerine; pineapple and tropical fruit; golden straw hue; light buttery-creamy body with rustic honey tartness; bright floral highlights, crisp and dry finish." The words used are not only descriptive, but adjectives like "spring" and "rustic" underscore the creators' belief in crafting ales that celebrate both the natural and pre-industrial worlds. "We were at a farmer's market selling our ales when we got the news" Piper remembered. "Suddenly our Twitter account went wild."

"It certainly created great brand awareness," Robert added. That awareness increased demand for Propolis Ales, and a second one-barrel system was added in the brewery's cramped quarters. By the middle of 2015, it became apparent that operations would have to be moved into larger quarters and a larger brewing system installed. By the time the taproom was open and the new 15-barrel system operational, distribution had expanded to most of Washington State, to Oregon, northern California, southern British Columbia, parts of Idaho, and even Chicago.

Regarding Propolis' production of what the website calls "Seasonal Herbal Beers," Robert remarked that "combining herbs and beer seemed natural. Herbs are all around you." He reemphasized that they were used in brewing before hops and stressed the link between the creation of beer and the earth from which the ingredients came. "The liquid you get after you've mashed the grains is called wort. And that's the same word that's used in the names of some of the herbs and roots traditionally used in brewing. I thought it was interesting that long ago people used to say of a really skillful ale-wife, 'She's got good wort cunning.'"

While Robert and I were chatting generally about the craft brewing explosion, Piper arrived in the taproom. He didn't call her his "ale wife," but it soon became apparent that she had "good wort cunning." She was involved in most of the brewing operations, particularly in the gathering of herbs and fruits and in the packaging of the final product. "Between the two of us," she said, "we handle every unit of product we send out: bottling, capping, waxing the necks of the bottles, pasting on the labels, and packing the bottles in cartons."

Piper offered me a glass of one of the ales currently on tap. I declined, explaining that I had a long and curvy road ahead of me that afternoon, but I did accept a craft soda, poured in a very elegant stemmed, tulip-shaped Propolis glass. She explained that the shape of a glass influenced the drinking experience; it enhanced the joy of contemplating the beer to be enjoyed. "We want people to enjoy the delicate, subtle, lyrical balance of what they're drinking. It can be an elegant, ceremonial experience. We ask people what they expect in a beer. When they talk about hops and hoppiness, we tell them that there are subtle flavors in herbs that you won't find in hops. In fact, we want our ales to showcase the herbs we use."

As Robert and Piper explained the processes of gathering and brewing, he again stressed that Propolis created "Herbal Seasonal Ales"—not beer. "We strive to be local, organic, and sustainable," he said, indicating that local materials are gathered during the seasons in which they are available and that the seeds of the plants harvested are returned to the land. The names of the beers celebrate the seasonal cycles, often using the titles for Pagan festivals that honored the land and the bounty it produced. Ostara Golden Saison refers to a

Co-owners Piper Corbett and Robert Horner founded Propolis Brewing in part to celebrate the local landscape, from which they gather many of the ingredients for their ales.

spring festival; Beltane, the name of the award-winning saison, is an observance that takes place in early May, at the time the elderflowers are ready for gathering. The ingredients for Litha Golden Saison are gathered around the Midsummer Solstice Festival, while Mabon, an observation of the autumn equinox, gives its name to an amber Pumpkin saison.

As we talked about the various ingredients, I thought frequently of the term "terroir," a word used to describe how soil and climate conditions in which grapes are grown influence the final product. The concept came up when we were discussing the evergreen tips (harvested in spring) that are used in the Spruce Golden Saison. "The flavor depends on the variety of spruce use; you find different spruce species from place to place. And even tips from the same species may be different from one location to another," Piper explained. She also remarked that the crop of the wild salmon berries used in the barrel-aged Salmon Golden Ale could be different from year to year, even if the fruit came from the same bushes. "Our ales age well and we often have different vintages of the same specific beer. We often offer customers vertical tastes—that is, they get to sample the same beer brewed in different years. They are quite surprised when they discover the difference among the vintages."

The Propolis ales are released in three categories: the Field-Crafted series, using ingredients from local farms; the Wild-Crafted series, in which the various herbs and fruits are foraged for in neighboring forests and in farm fields that have been reclaimed by nature; and the Barrel-Crafted series, in which both domestic and wild ingredients are used in the ales that are aged in wine or liquor barrels.

As my two hosts described the wild plants they harvested, I remarked that brewing had once been viewed as one of the activities that helped create civilization. In order to make both bread and beer, people had do give up hunting and gathering and settle down, developing farming communities. By ranging through wild fields and forests gathering ingredients, Piper and Robert were reverting to what some historians thought were primitive practices. They smiled and remarked that the end beverage was an elegant product that could be enjoyed, almost ceremoniously, by groups of people.

Piper continued on a more serious note. "You need to know the land if you're going to use these wild ingredients. When I was a kid, I got to know all the plants and trees around here. We need to rediscover the natural world in which we live. I hope by using local ingredients, it will help people reconnect with the land." Sipping Spruce Golden Saison (7.8 percent), which is vitamin rich, is, she says, "like drinking in the forest." When, after I had returned home, I shared a bottle of the Spruce Saison, I didn't feel like I'd been walking in the forest or, as had been the case with some spruce beers I'd sampled, that I'd had sampled a huge bunch of crushed evergreen needles soaked in a small glass of water. I wrote down in my tasting notes that there were understated spruce notes and that it was a delicate and nuanced ale—just as it should be.

Urtica (7.5 percent), a dubbel style ale that uses nettles, "is woodsy, foresty; you can taste the forest around you." Each spring, Robert taps the river birch trees growing wild in a farmer's field, collecting the sap to flavor another golden saison. Piper has a special fondness for the ingredients in Prunus (7.5 percent), a barrel-aged Flemish-style ale: "I picked the wild cherries from a tree that I used to love climbing in when I was a little kid." Among the other wild ingredients Propolis uses are huckleberries, blackberries, juniper berries, Oregon grapes, and wild heather.

It seems appropriate that the field-crafted series, which uses many locally grown ingredients, should include many saisons. That was a style that was developed in Belgium in pre–Industrial times and the brews are often called farmhouse ales. In late summer, field workers who were nurturing the crops in preparation for harvest would be supplied with tart, peppery saisons to quench their thirst. Among the local plants used in the brewing of the Propolis saisons are lavender, a bittering agent for Lithia; hyssop, which imparts menthol flavors to Erthe, chamomile, which provides apple-like notes to Erthe, pumpkins for Mobon Amber Saison, and strawberries and rhubarb in Pi (an appropriate pun), a golden Belgian-style ale.

Robert stressed, "The aging process is more important than the brewing process." That is because, after the mashing, boiling, and primary fermenting operations are complete, which usually only takes a matter of days, a lot more has to happen to the ales before they reach their full maturity. It's often said that the best beer should be less than three months old, but that's not the case with Propolis ales. The website description for each ale includes cellaring notes that suggest the beer should be allowed to age for at least a year, and sometimes over four years. In that way, new flavors, from added ingredients, added yeast that induces secondary fermentation, and the wine and liquor barrels in which some of the ales have been stored can become part of the mature product.

The addition of yeast into kegged beer to provide additional flavors is an important aspect of secondary fermentation. In recent years, many brewers have used *brettanomyces*, a wild yeast strain that was popular in nineteenth-century British ales and in Belgian lambics. Over the year or so that this yeast is active, it can create what have been variously called earthy, funky, horsey, and goaty notes, adding to the complexity of flavors already in the ale. Beltane, the elderflower saison that won the 2014 GABF gold medal in the American Brett category, had been aging for over a year. Eight additional Propolis ales use *brettanomyces* in the aging process. So, if you pick up a bottle at once of the specialty stores that carry them, don't plan on opening it when you get home. Put it in your beer cellar and instead try one of the craft beers that are best before they're three months old.

For certain ales, the vessel in which it is aged contributes to the final flavor. In recent years, increasing numbers of craft brewers have begun storing their beers in wooden (usually oak) barrels, a practice that is in a sense a return to long-ago methods of keeping beer (a kind of pro-polis storage system). But to this they have added a new wrinkle: they use barrels that have previously contained such flavorful alcoholic beverages as wine, rum and bourbon. As the beer comes in contact with the inside surfaces of the barrel it acquires traces of the alcohol or wine flavors that have soaked into the wood and sometimes the flavor of the wood itself. Fourteen Propolis ales, many from the Wild Crafted and Field Crafted series, have been part of the Barrel-Crafted series. Gardin (7.5 percent)—which includes sage, hyssop, and thyme and uses *brettanomyces* in secondary fermentation—is aged in cabernet barrels; Old Bruin and Quad-Folius mature in bourbon barrels; while Pi (strawberry/rhubarb), Huckleberry and Apricot-Ostara acquire hints of the syrah barrels in which they are stored.

Just before I departed to begin my drive along the Olympic Peninsula, Piper asked me which of their ales I'd like to take with me. My next stop would be on the beach that was just north of the town of Sequim and bordered the Strait of Juan de Fuca. I had read that, in 1792, explorer Captain George Vancouver had sent crew members from his ship *Discovery* to gather spruce buds from trees near the shore. They would be used to brew an ale that would fight scurvy—the first beer brewed by Europeans in the Pacific Northwest. And so I chose the Propolis Spruce Saison. When I sipped it from the tulip glass she also gave me, I'd think of those long-ago sailors and wonder if their ales tasted as good as this one.

6. Suds Along the Strait: Sequim and Port Angeles

Fathom and League Hop Yard Brewery (Sequim)
Barhop Brewery, Dungeness Brewing (Port Angeles)

European settlement of what is now Clallum County, which borders the Strait of Juan de Fuca from just west of Port Townsend to the Pacific Ocean, began after the middle of the nineteenth century. By the early twentieth century, Port Angeles, the county seat, had become a boom town. Large-scale logging had hit the Olympic Peninsula and lumber milled in the town was loaded onto vessels in the area's large, sheltered harbor and shipped to the growing metropolitan areas of the south Puget Sound and California.

Like most late nineteenth and early twentieth century boom towns, Port Angeles had a brewery. Angeles Brewing and Malting was founded in 1901 and the products created by brewer Adolph Otinger were consumed locally and shipped to Port Townsend and the Puget Sound area (where they faced stiff competition from Seattle beer) and even across the 18-mile-wide strait to the Canadian city of Victoria. After eight years of operation, the brewery experienced serious financial problems and, although it was sold in 1913 for $65,000 and renamed the Angeles Brewing Company, it struggled until the end of 1915, when Prohibition came into effect in Washington State. Although after the repeal of Prohibition plenty of beer was consumed in Clallum County, most of it undoubtedly Rainier and Olympia, residents wouldn't be able to enjoy locally produced beers until 2005.

That was the year that Ed and Wanda Smith, who'd operated a restaurant and pub in Port Angeles since 1999, began brewing their own beer under the name of Peaks Brewpub. Ed, who had discovered how good craft beer was when he met the legendary Bert Grant, founder of the United States' first brewpub since Prohibition, had been a Bud drinker. Now he set out to convert other Bud drinkers. "There are 19,000 people in this town," he told me when I talked to him in 2011, "and I'll bet I've educated half of them about really good beers."

It was near this beach north of Sequim, Washington, that eighteenth-century British explorer George Vancouver sent his men ashore to gather spruce tips to make scurvy-fighting ale. Many contemporary brewers in the Northwest, including Propolis of Port Townsend, use locally harvested tips as an important element in some of their beers.

Over the next decade, Port Angeles and the neighboring town of Sequim experienced a beer boom and, at the beginning of 2015, there were five local breweries serving the 94,000 people of Clallam County. In 2009, Tom Martin, a water control engineer and an award-winning homebrewer, opened Fathom and League Hop Yard Brewery in an outbuilding of his property in Sequim. A year later, Tim Curry, a transplanted California homebrewer, opened Barhop just outside Port Angeles. In 2012, another homebrewer, Mic Sager, opened Dungeness Brewing in an outbuilding on his property on the slopping hills south of Port Angeles, and Ed Smith sold Peaks and opened a small production brewery named Twin Peaks. Two years later, Josh Blue and Quinn Chalk opened The Hop Crew Brewing, another outbuilding brewery, this one in Sequim.

The rapid growth of craft breweries in the area was no doubt a result of the popularity of central Clallam County as a tourist destination. In addition to offering superb fishing, it was the northern gateway to the Olympic National

Park, one of the country's most popular wilderness areas. Port Angeles was also a stopping point for tourists taking the ferry to and from Victoria, B.C. However, it would probably be better to use the term "boomlet" rather than a boom to describe the increase in breweries. In 2014, the five operating breweries produced a total of 160 barrels—that's less than one percent of the 2014 production of Olympia's Fish Brewing. With the exception of Smith's Twin Peaks, four were nano-breweries, one-barrel affairs run by homebrewers turned weekend professionals, distributing their ales and lagers to a handful of outlets in the Port Angeles and Sequim areas. Unfortunately, as in the case of all booms, however small, there was a casualty. Citing health problems, Ed Smith announced early in 2015 that Twin Peaks was closing down. It's perhaps not insignificant that a 2014 posting on the brewery's Facebook page had commented on the costs of bottling beer and the increasingly narrow profit margins.

On a sunny March Saturday, I visited three of the area's four operating breweries. Unfortunately, Tom Martin, who after nearly seven years as owner-brewer of Fathom and League was the senior brewer of Clallum County, was not in town. However, a few days earlier, we talked on the telephone. He laughed when I began our conversation by remarking that water was one of the more important non-human elements of his life. He said that he had come to Sequim as a water engineer for the Clallum County Public Utilities Department. "I make water by day and beer by night," he said. Before he'd come to the Olympic Peninsula, he'd been a homebrewer for nearly a decade, using the Seattle area water to make beer in his kitchen, which he jokingly referred to as "Bucket and Pot Stovetop Brewing." His pilsner was twice named the best lager in the respected Puyallup Fair competition.

When it came time to open his commercial brewery and give it and some of his beers' names, the area's maritime history influenced him. The terms "fathom" and "league" are nautical measurements signifying the depth of the water over which a ship is sailing and the distance it has travelled across it. Discovery Imperial Stout is named after the vessel captained by late eighteenth century explorer George Vancouver, and Pumpkiness Lager makes a punning reference to Dungeness Spit, near which Vancouver dropped anchor. Tom turned his brewery professional on May 5, 2009, the 217th anniversary of the day on which the *Discovery*'s crew rowed ashore to gather spruce tips for making beer.

When Tom, Lisa, and their daughter Astrid were preparing to move to Sequim, they discovered a house in the Carlsborg district with a detached garage/shed and a pasture area beside it. "I thought, the shed can be my brewery and I can grow hop vines in the field," he remembered. A short while after, neighbor Gabriel Schuenemann, the owner of Alderwood Bistro, dropped by, tried Tom's Raingold Pilsner and announced, "I could sell your beer at my restaurant." And so, Fathom and League became Clallum County's second microbrewery.

"I set about to make balanced and healthy beers, using local ingredients as much as possible," Tom explained. OPA (Olympia Peninsula Ale), a year-around brew which uses home-grown hops, is a hoppier version of the English classic Extra Special Bitter (ESB). A neighbor smokes the oatmeal used in Alder Wood Smoked Oat Stout. Local names are given to several of the beers. Dark Edge, an American strong ale, refers to the edge of the nearby rainforest, while Mastadon Scotch Ale alludes to a 10,000-year-old skeleton discovered near town. Krabben Kolsh is sold at the annual crab festival held in nearby Port Angeles. "I'm putting the stamp of the Peninsula on my beer," he said.

Asked about future of the current craft beer boom, Martin remarked: "As long as people want their beer to be local and the local brewers make good beer, it will continue." Then he quoted the maxim of Charles Banford, well-known author and professor of brewing at the University of California, Davis: "Beer should be drunk as close as possible to the brewery where it's made."

When I arrived at the pole barn that is the unmarked home of The Hop Crew Brewing Company in Sequim, bright sun shone through the open front doors illuminating a one-barrel brewing system standing in the center of the large interior. Propane tanks were heating water that would be poured into the mash tun and a few yards away plastic fermenting tanks on wheels were lined up ready to receive the hopped wort that would be ready in a couple of hours. Josh Blue and Quinn Chalk, the brewery's co-owners and head brewer and assistant brewer/quality control director respectively, were preparing for their regular Saturday morning activity, making the beer that they would be distributing to central Clallum County restaurants and bars.

Josh and Quinn had met while both were working for ServPro, a fire and water damage repair and restoration company whose local franchise was owned by Quinn's family. Josh had tried a bottle of Sam Adams Winter Ale, a brew flavored with spruce tips, and discovered that beer could do more than give the brewer a buzz—it could taste good. Then, one day, when he was working at a house that had been water-damaged, he made a discovery. "I was taking boxes out of a cupboard and noticed that one of them was a homebrew kit. The lady said that it had belonged to her late husband and told me I could take it home if I wanted to." He did. The first batch was a disaster. "It really tasted terrible," he laughed. "But I bought copies of Charlie Papazian's *The Joy of Homebrewing*, both the first and second editions, and really studied them. Things got better, and my friends started telling me that my beer was pretty good." One of Josh's

Josh Blue (left) and Quinn Chalk, co-owners and brewers of The Hop Crew in Sequim, Washington, turned their weekend hobby into a business that supplied beer to local area bars and restaurants. They closed the brewery in late 2016.

buddies took some of the beer to a bar and invited the owner to try it. "He told my friend that if we were professional brewers, he'd buy it and serve it at his place—it was that good." That got Josh and his friend Quinn thinking. They decided to start a very small commercial brewery, borrowed ten thousand dollars and travelled to Portland to buy the system that now stood in the middle of the pole barn.

Like many people starting a new brewery, Josh wanted to find a name for it that was both creative and appropriate. His choice, The Hop Crew, was chosen after Josh had attended a Tragically Hip concert and noticed that the roadies wore T-shirts with the phrase "The Hip Crew" on them. The words and the name of his favorite brewing ingredient led to his choosing the name "The Hop Crew." The brewery released its first commercial beer early in March of 2014. It was an IPA made with Cascade, Simcoe, and Citra hops and was described on the web page as "a beer for the hop lover in all of us." Josh called it "Tragically Hopped IPA."

In just under 10 months of operation in 2014, The Hop Crew produced

52 barrels on its one-barrel system and acquired accounts in five restaurants or bars in Port Angeles and Sequim. I asked Josh if, considering the success of their first two years, he and Quinn had any expansion plans. Did they intend to buy a larger brewing system, increase production, and widen the distribution area? He paused and then replied: "We'd like to, but first we want to pay off the debts we acquired in starting up. And we want to make our beers better and better."

Late in the fall of 2015, another factor developed that caused a postponement of expansion plans. "In September, I was pouring at the Arts and Draughts Festival in Port Angeles and I offered a glass of our Fly by Night Stout to the owner of Barhop Brewing, which had a booth next to ours. Half an hour later, he came over and asked me if I'd like to become his brewer. I started there not long after and, in late November, it became a fulltime position. So, we'll have to wait and see." A few months after my visit, Josh and Quinn made a decision. Blue's job at Barhop started taking up more and more time. The Hop Crew was no longer working as a weekend brewery. The two partners closed the operation and sold the brewing equipment.

From Sequim, I headed to Port Angeles along Highway 101 and then turned south on Mount Angeles Road, which wound gradually uphill toward the Olympic Mountain Range and Olympic National Park. My destination was Dungeness Brewing, another weekend operation producing craft beers for area bars and restaurants. Like The Hop Crew headquarters, it occupied an unmarked pole barn a hundred or so yards from the residence of its owners, Mic and Kelly Sager. I parked next to the brewery beside dirt-filled barrels bearing the labels Chinook, Cascade, Nugget, and Centennial, the names of hops Mic used in making his beers (although the ones that would climb from these pots were purely ornamental, he later explained).

Mic came from his house to greet me, grinning either sheepishly or mischievously. "I forgot to let Kelly know that you were coming until just a few minutes ago. I'll tell her that you've arrived; she'd like to meet you." The two met several years ago when Kelly, who was looking for some craft beer for an Oktoberfest she was organizing, approached Mic, who'd been brewing for several years, ever since he'd been given a gift certificate to use at a brew-on-premises shop. "I'd been a Miller Genuine Draft drinker," he confessed. "But craft brewing showed me what beer could really be." Drawn together by their love of good craft beer, the two became brewing, as well as life, partners.

Dungeness is a production brewery and isn't licensed to sell beer to the public. However, while we were talking, two people showed up at the door. John and Carol Shervey were beer tourists, part of that growing breed of craft brewing enthusiasts who cannot pass a brewery, no matter how small or out of

Award-winning homebrewer and, with his wife Kelly, owner of Dungeness Brewing Company in Port Angeles, Mic Sager has actually used Dungeness crab legs in one of his specialty brews.

the way, without stopping and visiting. Mic offered them a glass of the Kelly's Stout we were sampling and they chatted for a few minutes before departing, telling us as they did that they were on a quest to visit Washington State's over 300 craft breweries.

The taproom had a bar with four stools in front of it, two taps behind it, and a large poster of a Dungeness crab with the brewery's name under it. A couple of couches were in the middle of the room. Along the end wall was a very large screen TV and an equally large Seahawks poster. "The taproom is really for ourselves and our friends," Mic explained. "When Seattle was in the Superbowl in 2014 and 2015, we had over 40 people in here. I made a special brew for the party." Hanging from wires strung from the ceiling, were over 130 growlers, the logos of various craft breweries on their brown glass sides. Mic had collected many during his travels; others had been donated by friends and fellow brewers he'd met at festivals. The Sherveys, shortly after they had left, returned with another one for him to add to the collection.

The Sagers decided to turn their hobby into a weekend profession when they won first place in a homebrewing competition. Kelly, who enjoyed creating recipes that duplicated the taste of beers she had enjoyed, "but with our own twist," had developed a recipe for the stout that now bears her name. The prize was the opportunity to brew a batch of the award winning beer on the one-barrel system used by Barhop, which had recently opened a taproom in downtown Port Angeles. When the owner tasted the stout, he told them that they should get a license, which they did. In mid–August 2012, they sold their first professionally produced beer, Agnew Amber, a robust ale that was Kelly's interpretation of Alaskan Brewing's Amber, perhaps the most popular non–IPA beer in the Pacific Northwest.

Sales were sufficiently brisk during the first year that, when Barhop decided to replace its one-barrel system with a three-barrel one, Mic and Kelly decided to replace their 10-gallon system with the one Barhop no longer needed. It sits in the middle of the brewhouse, which occupies one half of the outbuilding. Around it are fermenters on wheels and along one wall a storage space for kegs and a cold room. There is a lot of open space. But the Sagers do not intend to fill it with more equipment. They have no expansion plans. "We have day jobs that make it possible for us to enjoy brewing professionally on the weekends," Mic explained. He is an administrator in the health care business, she a mortgage loan officer. "And besides," he added with a chuckle. "We need time to enjoy our beer, and all the other good beer that's being made around here."

The beers the Sagers brew can be placed into three categories: the hoppy beers that Mic loves; the darker, maltier ones that are Kelly's favorites; and beers that are ... well, just off the wall. The hoppy beers include Trail 90 IPA (7.3 percent ABV), which is named after a Honda motorcycle, the (unusually long) number of minutes of the boil, and the number of international bitterness units; 3CsIPA (6.3 percent ABV), which uses Chinook, Centennial, and Cascade hops; along with a grapefruit and a jalapeño flavored IPA. In addition to Agnew Amber, the top selling Dungeness beer, the "dark-side" offerings include Southbound Train Porter, Kelly's Stout, and Hooch, a 10.3 percent stout aged in whiskey barrels. Each winter, the Sagers brew a hearty winter seasonal Woody Warmer, a 10.2 percent beer that includes pumpkin, ginger, cinnamon, and allspice.

The "off-the-wall" offerings deserve their own paragraph. Since Dungeness Brewing opened it has been a regular participant in Port Townsend's annual Strange Brewfest, and each year, the brewery's Facebook entries have reported that the beers they poured there were extremely popular and their supplies quickly exhausted. The base beers are their familiar favorites: IPAs, stouts, and, in one instance, a Scottish Wee Heavy. But there the familiarity ends. The IPA adds strawberries and rhubarb; the Wee Heavy, called "Wee Shroomie," based on a recipe developed by Mic's friend Denny Conn, includes chanterelle mushrooms. But the most unusual is Crab Stout. Six live crabs are dropped into the kettle during the last ten minutes of the boil, two crabs for each five gallons of finished beer. When I asked Mic what the beer tasted like, he remarked, "Unusual." Then he went on to say that he saved the cooked crab and that it certainly tasted delicious when he used it in dishes he prepared for his Super Bowl parties.

Our final stop on this busy Saturday was at the Port Angeles Esplanade, a newly created promenade along the shores of the Strait of Juan de Fuca. Barhop Brewing and Artisan Pizza was located across from the Esplanade. As we parked, I noticed people disembarking from the Black Ball Ferry, which had just arrived from Victoria and had docked a block away. In the summer, Port Angeles has become a destination for beer-loving day trippers from Victoria. Barhop can be either their first stop on arrival or their final one before departure.

Barhop, which had moved into its present location—its third—late in 2012, had been started in 2010 by Tom Curry, a non-medical worker in the health care industry. He'd been a homebrewer in northern California in his younger days and had developed a taste for such well hopped ales as Sierra Nevada Pale Ale and Russian River's Pliny the Elder. In 2010, Mr. Barhop, as he nicknamed himself in Facebook posts, decided to revive his love of brewing and to "ferment the rain," creating what the Barhop website describes as "aggressive California-style ales, with a Northwest twist, using fresh Northwest ingredients."

The first location for the brewery was in a small building in the Harbinger Winery just west of Port Angeles. His beers were served in the winery tasting room and at bars and restaurants in the Port Angeles/Sequim area. In 2011, he moved the taproom to downtown Port Angeles and, a year, later relocated both the taproom and brewery to its present site. Here he established regular Friday live music nights, enlarged his one-barrel brewery to a three-barrel system, and introduced a food menu which featured artisan pizzas. Then, in late 2015, Curry made a major change. Mr. Barhop, who had initially handled the brewing duties himself assisted by and later succeeded by his son and son-in-law, hired a professional brewer, Josh Blue.

The building that housed the taproom and brewery had been, among other things, a fruit packing plant, warehouse, and antique store, and had a rustic look and feel to it. On original wood floors sat old worn tables and old (but not rickety) happily mismatched chairs. The decorations almost seemed like they were survivors from the building's antique store life: an old safe, a railroad crossing sign, a ship's vent and porthole, a Texaco gasoline pump, and a crank telephone. There were foosball and pool tables, a large-screen TV, and the obligatory Seattle Seahawks poster. The three-barrel brewing system sat in the middle of a large back room—there would be plenty of room for expansion that, in Facebook posts, was frequently mentioned as coming soon.

Five Barhop Ales, all brewed by Josh Blue, were on tap. Redneck Logger and Patio Pale Ale (5.4 and 5.2 percent ABV respectively) were easy drinking, session-type pale ales, well rounded, with a slightly sweet malt base that balanced the hops. Hop Head Willie IPA (6.6 percent), Big Northern Wheat IPA (7 percent), Winterhop Imperial Stout (9 percent) were certainly stronger and hoppier. But the hops did not overwhelm. As Josh had said earlier in the day, he had created beers that let the hops taste like they should.

7. Black Beards
and Yellow Boots:
Westport and Seaview

Blackbeard's Brewing (Westport, WA),
and North Jetty Brewing (Seaview, WA)

The next morning, with rain clouds forming to the west, I began the longest stretch of my trip that didn't have a brewery to stop at along the way. From Port Angeles to Westport, on the southwest coast of the state, was a distance of 184 miles, a craft brewing wasteland. Highway 101 headed inland just west of Port Angeles, skirting Crescent Lake on the way to Forks. Moss-covered dead trees stood by the road, and in many cases clear-cut hillsides rose on both sides. There weren't any forest giants to be seen, only, when there was timber, acres and acres of third growth trees that barely deserved to be called pecker-poles. Just past the town of Forks, the highway began to run beside the Pacific Ocean, which I wouldn't be far from for the rest of my trip, and I encountered the first of many sea stacks, those rocky islands standing just offshore that had been formed when the land connecting them to the mainland had been eroded away by centuries of pounding waves.

I drove through Aberdeen, Washington, surprised that this small city of 17,000 didn't have a craft brewery and hadn't had a one since 1944. Aberdeen Brewing Company, which advertised that it made "the Beer that makes Milwaukee Jealous," operated from 1902 until the start of Prohibition. In the 1930s, the brewery was completely refurbished and under the name "Pioneer Brewing Company" produced lager beer, much of which was shipped to the California area, until 1944, when the wartime shortage of supplies forced it out of business. While in Olympia, I had heard rumors that a new brewpub might be in the works for the town of Hoquiam, just outside Aberdeen.

From Aberdeen, it was a 20-mile side trip along Highway 105, through the almost-hamlet of Oscota, briefly the home of Gray's Harbor Brewing in the late nineteenth century, to Westport. The cranberry capital of Washington State, it is also the home of an enormous commercial and charter fishing fleet. Although it has a year-round population of just over two thousand, the figure swells by several thousand more during the summer and on pleasant fall, winter, and spring weekends, as tourists arrive to enjoy the beaches, superb surfing, and wonderful fishing. That is probably why, when Blackbeard's Brewing opened in the summer of 2015, it was one of three small breweries in town. However, on Labor Day weekend, Westport Brewing, which was the first brewery ever to operate on Washington's Pacific Coast and which specialized in beers that had been infused with cranberry flavoring, announced that it was closed for the season. Shortly after that a "for sale" sign appeared on the small brewery building. It was still for sale when I drove by it. Then, just before Thanksgiving, Bog Water Brewing, also the home of Cranberry Road Winery, was completely destroyed by fire. When I drove by it, all that remained was the paved parking lot and an outdoor pizza oven. Now, Blackbeard's Brewing, owned by Ryan and Katy Montes de Oca, was the only brewery left.

Like other brewery owners I met along Highway 101, the Montes de Ocas moved from a larger inland city, in their case Puyallup, a city of 40,000 just south of Tacoma, to establish a business in a small coastal town. But their journey was much longer than the 100-mile drive from their suburban home to the shores of the Pacific and it began many years before they opened their brewery. Ryan had begun homebrewing while studying chemical engineering at the University of Nevada, Reno. When he met Katy, an elementary education graduate from University of Nevada, Las Vegas, and discovered she liked craft beer, he appointed her his official taster.

At the time, Ryan fantasized and dreamed about owning his own brewery. But he realized that startup costs were enormous and, should the chance arise to turn his dream into a reality, he didn't want to accumulate large debts. So he designed and had a friend build a 10 barrel brewing system: a mash tun, kettle, fermenter and bright tank. If the time came, he'd have the equipment (all paid for). His job as a flavor developer for M&M/Mars, the candy maker, took him from Nevada, to Mississippi, Pennsylvania, and then, when he became a senior member of the Starbucks flavor development team, to Washington State. Everywhere that Ryan, Katy, and soon their two sons went, the mash tun, kettle, fermenter and bright tank went too. That was one of the conditions of the transfers with M&M/Mars and the appointment with Starbucks. Ryan laughed when I asked if he'd considered creating business cards that read "Have Tun Will Travel."

It was in Westport that the equipment found a home and was first put to use. Both Ryan and Katy loved to fish and the boys loved the beach, and so the

Ryan Montes de Oca, brewer and, with wife Katy, co-owner of Blackbeard's Brewing in Westport, Washington, stands beside one of the brewing tanks he designed and had made many years before he began brewing professionally. When the Nevada native's employment took him to Mississippi, Pennsylvania, and then Washington, the 10-barrel brewing system followed. It now has (hopefully) a permanent home in Westport.

Montes de Oca family made frequent weekend and summer trips to the shores of the Pacific and wound up buying a second home there. Ryan met Chris Tiffany, the owner of Cranberry Road Winery, who was considering adding a brewery to his business. The two became equal partners in Bog Water Brewing; Ryan moved his tanks to Westport and, on the weekends would use his flavor development skills to create beer.

"The partnership didn't last," Ryan noted, "and we went our separate ways. But many of the local people kept asking me when I was going to start brewing again. They liked my beers and missed them. That's when I noted a vacant A-frame building on Ocean Avenue. It was only a couple of blocks away from the water, a perfect location to make and serve beer. The place had been a thrift store, a hair salon, a gift shop and an art gallery. We bought it, gutted it, renovated it, and opened on the 2015 Memorial Day weekend." The tun, kettle, and tanks had a new home, Blackbeard's Brewing, named to honor the very popular summer festival, Pirate Daze. Katy, who had moved from Puyallup with their sons when the business opened, managed the taproom/restaurant. Ryan came out on weekends to brew.

When I arrived at Blackbeard's just as the drizzle, which had begun as I passed through Aberdeen, turned into a steady rain, it was early afternoon. There were a few patrons: a table of locals celebrating a birthday, a few weekend tourists, and a couple of beer lovers who were planning on starting their own nanobrewery. The bar/dining room was cozy: a bar, a gift shop in the corner, and several sturdy tables with benches. A couple of shelves along a wall contained several dozen black mugs sporting bas relief pirates' skulls, each vessel the property of a patron who had joined the mug club. The kitchen behind taproom was cramped and the brewhouse back of it was claustrophobic. There wasn't much elbow room between the four original pieces of equipment and the new fermenters that had been purchased when the Monte de Ocas had decided to open their own business.

The movements of the employees seemed well coordinated, and nobody bumped into each other. But one could imagine how difficult things might become when crowds increased in the summer, especially now that Blackbeard's was the only brewery in town. I wasn't surprised when Katy told me that in November, only a few months after they'd opened, she and Ryan decided that they would expand and that more space would be ready for the upcoming summer.

The kitchen prepares appetizers, salads, and pizzas and I enjoyed a chicken Caesar before I sampled Blackbeard's five regular beers. Ryan explained that until expansion is completed, they simply don't have enough space for the tanks needed for more beer styles. I began with the Golden Ale (5.2 percent), a crisp, subtly hopped beer that had been added to the beer list when Katy suggested to her husband that they needed something light to serve as a crossover beer for patrons new to the craft beer scene. Next on tap was Strawberry Blonde (5.2 percent ABV), which had originally been called Dead Red after a legendary female pirate. "We wanted something a little different," Ryan said. "We use over 300 pounds of strawberries for each 10 barrel batch." It wasn't too sweet, which is sometimes a problem with berry beers, and had just a subtle hint of strawberry flavor. The tart finish provided just the right ending for each sip. Hop Fever IPA, the brewery's best seller, was a 6.5 percent, 60 IBU ale. The Cascade, Centennial, Chinook, and Simcoe hops provided a variety of subtle flavors, while the bitterness was balanced by an earthy, malty character. Ahoy! Amber, Katy's favorite, was heavier and hoppier than most versions of the style. At 6.5 percent, it was also stronger than many others. Puffin Porter (6 percent) an oatmeal chocolate porter, was a medium-bodied drink with a clean finish.

Ryan excused himself to meet with people involved in the construction of the expansion and then return to Puyallup and his Starbucks day job, which in a couple of weeks would take him to Switzerland. Katy invited me to inspect the new building that was taking shape on the other side of a muddy expanse that had served as a parking lot for construction workers' vehicles and equipment. "This will be a beer garden," she said of the open space. "Kids will be welcome here. They can drink the Rowdy Root Beer we make. In warm weather, we can also have music out here." The new 4,500 square foot building would house the soon-to-be-expanded brewery and a taproom. She pointed to a wall being built across part of the building: "There's going to be a winery on the other side of it. You can't have a brewery and a winery side-by-side. They have to be separated and have different entrances." With the well-travelled brewing equipment being out of the present building, the kitchen will be enlarged and menu options expanded.

On one of Blackbeard's early Facebook posts, Ryan Montes de Oca wrote: "20+ years of brewing, equipment that's been coast to coast, tells you a little something about my passions/dreams." Now they were being actualized, becoming realities that were better than what the dreamer had imagined.

The next morning I returned to Highway 101 and drove through the continuing rain to Seaview (an unincorporated part of Long Beach, Washington) to visit North Jetty Brewing Company, located just north of the protective wall that gives the brewery its name and is situated at the north side of the mouth of the Columbia River. Erik and Michelle Svendsen, co-owners and brewer and assistant brewer respectively, had just returned from Seaside, Oregon, where they'd participated at the Pour at the Coast Festival, one of the Northwest Coast's most popular beer celebrations. It had been the final event of two very busy weeks. On March 5, Michelle had hosted the Big Boots Collaboration brewing event, in which female brewers from the area created a beer, proceeds from the sale of which would go to toward the scholarship fund of the Pink Boots Society, the trade organization of women involved in the brewing business. In addition, she and Erik had just overseen the installation of a new 20-barrel fermenter and had concluded interviews for a new head brewer.

Like Katy and Ryan Montes de Oca, Michelle and Erik had bought a vacation home on the southwest Washington coast so that they'd have a place to escape from the pressures of city life. Erik, who had started homebrewing as a college student, was a CPA in Vancouver, Washington. Michelle, the mother of three children, grew up in Bend, Oregon, "before it was a great beer city," and hadn't originally liked beer. But she developed her interest in and taste for it when she met Erik and became not only his wife, but also his brewing apprentice. Later, Michelle taught what she'd learned about beer to her daughter

Taylor, now fifteen years old, who had become interested in brewing and is now the youngest member of the Pink Boots Society, an association of women in the brewing industry. "She can't legally do any brewing. But she's learning about the equipment, the ingredients, and the process," Michelle said.

In 2010, the family moved permanently to Seaview and "we've become busier than we ever were in Vancouver," Michelle admitted. Erik took a CPA job in Astoria, Oregon, eighteen miles away, while she ran a cleaning business and ran the household. Then, early in 2013, things got even busier. The owners of The Lost Roo, a local restaurant, who knew of Erik's homebrewing hobby and were thinking of adding in-house brewed beer to their menu, asked the Svendsens if they'd be interested in making beer for them. Within a few months, Erik and Michelle bought the restaurant, installed their own brewhouse, and opened in April 2014 as North Jetty. Erik, with Michelle's assistance, did the brewing; he kept the books and she was the marketer. Business was so brisk that they expanded from a 1.5-barrel to a 10-barrel system, added a new fermenting tank, began bottling their product, and hired Kirk Hurd from Astoria's Buoy Beer Company to assume the majority of the brewing duties.

To do all this, they went through the usual funding methods—savings, bank financing, and the like—and developed another source for raising money. They created a Founders program, in which individuals investing $225 would receive 20-ounce pours instead of the usual 16-ounce ones, special glassware, and two private catered parties. When the brewery needed a new tank, they sold tank sponsorships at $300 each.

Erik said that he strove to create beers that had a clean, crisp mouth feel and where hops and malts were in balance. When I tasted samples of several North Jetty ales, I told him he'd certainly achieved his goal. We started with North Jetty's top seller, Cape D IPA (6.2 percent ABV, 58 IBUs), which he described as "traditionally bitter." However, the IBUs were only 58; the Cascade, CTZ, and Centennial hops contributed citrus notes, didn't overwhelm, and were nicely balanced by the Pale, Crystal, and Munich malts. As the beer warmed a little, it acquired a malty mellowness. Leadbetter Red Scottish Ale (4.8 percent, 23 IBUs), the second best seller, used seven different malts, along with English hops. It was a malt-forward beer, with the sweetness held in check by the hops. Starvation Alley Weissbier (4.6 percent, 11 IBUs) was a Bavarian-style wheat beer flavored with bitter orange peel and locally produced organic cranberry juice. Discovery Coast Coffee Milk Stout (5.8 percent, 34 IBUs) used locally roasted coffee beans. First Crack Pale Ale, at 4.5 percent and 41 IBUs, was a very quaffable American-style pale ale.

Michelle spoke enthusiastically about the beers she'd been closely involved in developing and brewing. About North Jetty Autumn Blueberry Rye, she

Michelle and Erick Svendsen moved to the small community of Seaview, Washington, to escape the hectic pace of city life. But after they started the very popular North Jetty Brewing, they are, Michelle says, busier than they ever were in the city.

remarked: "I said to Erik, let's put these things together. It was a recipe by a committee—of two." She is very proud of Yellow Boots Kolsch, named for the colored footwear she slips on while brewing. Delicate and flavorful, it is given a crisp, clean finish through the use of Hallertau hops. Big Boots Rhuberry Blonde is a real beer by committee—a collaboration brew created on March 5 by four area brewers for Women's Collaboration Brew Day. The Pink Boots Society sends out general guidelines to all the collaborating groups, and then they use their creativity. "We used 50 pounds of strawberries and fifty of rhubarb and added five pounds of lemon zest. It's a wheat beer that uses kolsch yeast. The proceeds help fund the Pink Boots Society's scholarship fund." She invited me to try a glass, warning me that it hadn't completed the conditioning period. Nonetheless, it was well-balanced, with the fruit contributing very subtle notes, and the yeast giving it a lightness and crispness.

I asked Erik for his take on the craft beer boom, the increase in new breweries opening and the number of breweries, including new ones, expanding their production facilities. How long can it go on? How can all of these breweries be successful? He remarked that it is certainly going to be difficult to be the next Deschutes or Bells, naming two very successful and large craft breweries. "But if you can be content with being your local craft brewer and doing a good job of it, you can certainly be successful." The word "local" had come up frequently during our conversations. Michelle noted that they had both wanted to be active in local affairs, being part of the community, not just a company that brewed beer in Seaview.

"We give local names to our beers," she went on. "Cape D for our IPA. The D stands for Disappointment, the name of the cape, but we didn't think disappointment was a very positive word to be highlighted on the label. Leadbetter is the name of a state park; North Head IPA refers to the North Head Lighthouse." She went on to say that two of the ales use local ingredients: the roasted coffee beans in Discovery Coast Coffee Milk Stout and organic cranberry juice in Starvation Alley Weissbier. One North Jetty beer is created specifically to help a local organization. Teachers and staff from the local high school help Michelle and Erik in the brewing of Straight A Amber. Fifty cents from each pint is donated to the Long Beach Education Foundation.

Although their beers are distributed in eleven Washington and Oregon counties and tourists from such cities as Portland and Seattle enjoy coming to the brewery, the Svendsens like to consider that the taproom is "like Long Beach's living room." A local craftsman created the large mirror that hangs from one wall; the Cape Disappointment Coast Guard Station donated the marker flags that decorate other walls. Two weeks before Christmas, at a time when tourism is at its lowest, the North Jetty taproom is the site of a very popular community event: Holidays at the Jetty. Santa Claus is the featured attraction and families bring their children (who are always welcome at the taproom) to be photographed with him. "Local merchants and craftspeople bring things for sale and people get a chance to do some of their Christmas shopping. Street Side Tacos parks their truck right outside the building, or people can bring their own food." There are some out-of-towners who make the trip for the event, but it's mainly enjoyed by the locals. This is Long Beach's living room at its festive best.

As I prepared to go out into the rain, Erik summed up the joy he and Michelle experience during the arduous task of running a small brewery in a small town: "We're doing what we love, and it pays the bills."

Part III

Beaches and Brews on the North Oregon Coast

I crossed into Oregon on the Astoria-Megler Bridge, a four-mile span crossing the Columbia a few miles from where it enters the Pacific Ocean. As it nears the hillside city of Astoria, it rises sharply, reaching a height of nearly 200 feet, sufficient to allow passage of the oceangoing vessels that proceed upriver to Portland and beyond. Over the next four days, I'd be visiting nine breweries and brewpubs between Astoria and Pacific City. Had I travelled this route ten years ago, I'd have made only three stops, and if I were to travel it eight months from now, there would be three additional stops. This 89-mile stretch of Highway 101 had been caught up in the craft beer boom that was sweeping the country.

8. Astoria's Ale Trail

Wet Dog Café/Astoria Brewing;
Buoy Beer Company, Fort George Brewery
and Public House, Hondo's Brew and Cork

When I was an elementary school student in western Canada, Astoria was one of the few American cities we talked about during the history segments of our social studies classes. That was because the 1811 establishment of Fort Astoria by the fur trading magnate John Jacob Astor was seen as a threat to the Canadian trading companies the Hudson's Bay Company and the North West Company. In fact, during the War of 1812, the British took over the settlement, controlled it until 1818 and renamed it Fort George after the reigning king. "Who knows?" our teacher asked us. "If we hadn't taken over that fort, we might all be Americans now."

Astoria prospered during from the middle of the nineteenth century to the middle of the twentieth. It was an important port, ship building and trading center, and headquarters for the prosperous lumbering and fishing industries. It was also a packaging center, with over two dozen seafood canneries lining the Columbia River at one time. It might have challenged Seattle and Portland in importance had not two devastating fires, one in 1883 and another in 1922, all but destroyed the city. During the last half of the twentieth century, the logging and fishing industries, and with them lumbering and canning operations, declined drastically and population dropped from over 14,000 in 1920 to under 10,000 by the year 2000.

During the last quarter century, Astoria has become a tourist destination, with visitors contributing greatly to the economy. Charter fishing is very popular. A river walk and, in the warmer months, a trolley, run beside the Columbia River, passing restaurants, art galleries, and museums. Historical tours visit old Victorian homes and other landmarks of the city's past. Cruise ships stop regularly at the deep sea port. And, over the last two decades, a vibrant craft beer scene has developed. There are four breweries, with another one, Reach Break

Brewing, scheduled to open late in 2016, and a tap room for Rogue Ales, the very popular Newport, Oregon, brewer. Astoria is no longer just a place to stop briefly while travelling south to the resort beach towns of Seaside, Gearhart, and Cannon Beach.

When Astoria Brewing, part of the Wet Dog Café, opened as Pacific Rim Brewery in 1997, it was the first brewery to operate in Astoria since 1916. After the great fire of 1883, four breweries had operated in the city: Astoria Brewery, St. Louis Brewery, North Pacific Brewery, and something listed simply as Mrs. Theresa O'Brian's Hotel and Brewery. Only North Pacific made it into the twentieth century.

Wet Dog Café and Brewery, which had been named after the original owners' dog, who loved to swim in the river, was my first stop. I parked my car next to the trolley tracks, less than 100 yards from the river, and walked to the entrance, next to which was a bone-shaped neon sign proclaiming "open." Inside, to the right was a small brewhouse, to the left, the largest brewery gift shop I would see in my travels. The restaurant area was very large and, even though it was mid-afternoon, very crowded. I heard the hostess tell a group that had entered that they'd have to wait for half an hour if they wanted a seat by the windows (which opened onto a patio during warmer weather) and on which dogs on the leash were allowed. (For a dollar, patrons could order a cooked-to-order three-ounce meat patty for their canine companions.) Even standing near the entrance I could see, through the windows, several ships lying at anchor on the river, and beyond that, the rising hills along the Washington shore.

Co-owner Karen Allen arrived from her office and invited me to join her at the employees' table, one of only a couple that were vacant. I asked her to clarify for me the relationship between Wet Dog Café and Brewery and Astoria Brewing Company, which, on the website and in many beer guides are generally lumped together. "Wet Dog Café" was the original nightclub founded in 1995 that her husband, Steve, had taken over in 1997. Astoria Brewing, the brewhouse I'd seen while entering, was a separate entity making beer for the Café. When the demand for the beer became so great that the small system couldn't keep up, a new brewhouse, with much larger equipment, was built down the block. It opened in 2014 and the old brewing equipment became part of the renamed Wet Dog Café and Brewery. Astoria produced most of the beer for the café and several beers that were canned using the Wet Dog label. The old system was used as a test brewery and for making limited edition brews.

Steve Allen, a Certified Public Accountant, had become involved in the nightclub when the original owners, experiencing financial difficulties, needed a new partner. "But, he didn't want it to be a night club with a bar and some food," Karen explained. "He wanted it to be a family-friendly restaurant that made its own beer. You can see that families love it here. We have a kids' menu and activities for them." She met and married Steve after he'd bought Wet Dog and, as she talked about families proudly noted that all the members of their blended family—they have seven children between them—have worked at the restaurant. Son Andy is now a part-owner; daughter Kera manages the gift shop and son Mike is also involved in the business. "Even the employees are part of our family," Karen added, "they've been with us so long." She added that just before next Christmas, the restaurant would be closing down for a few days so that Karen and Steve could take family members and extended family members on a short cruise.

John Dalgren, the head brewer, joined us. "He began working with us as a line-cook," she told me as she introduced us. "I told him that he had a real chef's palate and that he should go to Portland to a culinary school. Then our brewer quit. John had been helping out in the brewery, so I said he should become a brewer. 'It's no different from being a chef,' I told him. 'It's like making soup.' I've got to show you the old brewery. It's got a story. John will tell it to you."

I was beginning to realize that, even though most of the equipment in most breweries looks quite similar, some brewing systems have unusual histories. Dalgren explained that shortly after he'd taken over as head brewer, there'd been a problem with the kettle. "I noticed that stamped into the metal were the words 'Elliot Bay' and a telephone number. So I called and the person who answered the phone said, 'Elliot Bay Correctional Facility.'" It turned out that some years ago a few of the inmates of the Seattle prison were allowed to make pieces of brewing equipment—using only manual tools. These were some of them.

But the story wasn't over. "A couple of years ago," John continued, "a customer asked if he could look at the brewing equipment. He was pretty big, rough looking guy, but he seemed really gentle. I brought him in here and he looked at the mash tun and kettle really carefully. Then he said, 'I think I made this equipment when I was in prison.' I poured him a beer, we talked for a few minutes, and then he left."

As we walked to the end of the block to an old building that had been extensively renovated to house the Astoria Brewery and Tap Room, Dalgren filled in the details of his beer biography. "I'd been drinking craft beer since I was 16 and had done some homebrewing before I came to the Wet Dog Café. On my days off from the kitchen, Chris Nemlowill [now co-owner of Fort George Brewery] let me help around the brewery—for free. I learned a lot, read a whole lot of books about brewing, and realized I wanted to become a

Karen Allen, co-owner of Astoria Brewing/Wet Dog Café, and brewer John Dalgren stand in front of brewing tanks that have an interesting back story. When one of the tanks needed fixing, Dalgren telephoned a number stamped on the side and reached Elliott Bay Correctional Facility in Seattle, Washington. The tanks had been made by inmates.

professional brewer. I even considered enrolling in the brewing program at the University of California, Davis. Then Chris left to start Fort George Brewing with Jack Harris. Steve and Karen Allen asked if I could help while they searched for a new brewer. They needed someone to keg the last of the beer Chris had brewed. I said, certainly. Then, a few days later, they asked if I'd like to brew. I was to do one batch, and if it turned out fine, I'd be hired as brewer for a 90 day probation period." The first beer John made was supposed to be an amber ale, but something happened. It tasted good, but it was too strong for an amber ale. So he called it an American Strong Ale. People liked it and he survived the 90 day probation period. That was a decade ago. "I'm still learning and Astoria's a great place for doing that. All the brewers around here help each other. There's a friendly competition that makes each of us work to be better. And you can learn from drinking each other's beer—I know I do."

The tap room wasn't open the day of my visit, so Dalgren unlocked the door, proudly showed me the new brewing system and led me to the bar area, which consisted of a balcony which wrapped around the four walls and looked down into the brewery. Patrons could sit at stools and see where the beer they sipped had been made. The layout was a creative response to a structural problem encountered during renovations. The building was too old to support heavy brewing equipment on the main floor, so some of the floor was removed so that the tanks could be lowered into the basement.

We sat at the small bar and John described the beers he poured from the nearby taps. First up was Lincoln Lager, a 4.9 percent ABV, 10 IBU beer that was initially named Low Tide Lager. "But," he explained, "the day I was kegging it, my son Lincoln was born, so we changed the name in honor of his birth." Light, crisp, and clean, it uses Saaz hops and Czech yeast, and so, not surprisingly, it tastes like a Bohemian pilsner. Old Red-Beard Amber (6.1 percent, 35 IBUs) also has a naming story; it celebrates owner Steve Allen, who's now-graying beard was once red. Dalgren describes the amber as a "not too hoppy, middle-of-the-road ale, with a solid malt presence." It was a rounded beer, with the caramel malts subtly balanced by the Cascade hops. Ichiban IPA (7.5 percent ABV, 75 IBUs) uses the Japanese word for "one" and was the first beer made on the new system. Clean and crisp, it showcases the Citra hops, the only varietal used, which give a crisp, citrusy finish. Our final sample was of the ambiguously titled Poop-Deck Porter (6.2 percent, 35 IBs). Was it a maritime reference or a link to the name of the café? Whatever the significance, it was a full-bodied, rich beverage, a dark-brown drink with a thick brown head.

Along with his comments about the beers we were tasting, John interspersed statements about his philosophy of brewing and how that influenced the styles of the beers he created. "I rely on the four traditional ingredients," he stated, noting that, even though he had made some fruit beers at the request of Karen Allen, he wouldn't make a Belgian Wit because he didn't want to use coriander and orange. Instead, he made a German wheat beer which he named Volksweissen (6.3 percent, 13 UBYs). "I like balance," he continued. "Except for IPAs, I don't think hops need to be center of the action. People want to taste the style of the beer, not the Yakima Valley [a major hop growing area]."

The beer that does emphasize hops, that is a real "hop bomb," is Bitter Bitch Imperial IPA. It's strong, 8.2 percent, and bitter, 134 IBUs, the most I've ever had in a beer. "When I started brewing, I tended to be intimidated by hops," he said. "I didn't know much about them, so I used a lot. But Bitter Bitch turned out fine and it's very popular." He gave me a can to take with me. The next evening I tried it. It came quite cold from the fridge and at first all I could taste was the bitterness. As it warmed up, some malt flavor crept in. Before I threw the can away, I read the description on the side. "This bitch has bite!" it concluded. It certainly did!

The next day, I visited Astoria's three other breweries, all of them a pleasant walking distance from each other—if the forecast rain showers held off. My first stop was Buoy Beer Company, two blocks west of Wet Dog Café. Founded in 2014, it had won a Great American Beer Festival silver medal just a few months after opening and had quickly become one of the faster-growing breweries in Oregon. Production increased from 975 barrels during the first 10.5 months of production to 3,125 in 2015. Jessyka Dart-Mclean from the marketing department led me from the business offices, across the trolley tracks to a large square building that extended out from the riverbank and was supported by large piles. We passed through the brewhouse with its 20-barrel system and seemingly countless fermentation tanks and through the restaurant to the taproom, which contained a 3-barrel pilot system. Along the way we walked over a large rectangle of clear material that gave a view of the pilings that supported the building, and of the river below. "Quite often, there'll be sea lions down there," she told me. (Later, while I was talking with members of the ownership group, the loud barks of a sea lion briefly interrupted our conversation.) In the taproom, which had picture windows looking out on the Columbia River, she introduced me to Luke Colvin, Andrew Bornstein, and Dan Hamilton, three of the owners, and Kevin Shaw, the head brewer.

When I asked the members of the group to describe the origins of Buoy Beer Company, Hamilton began by giving a succinct overview. "There was a group of people with overlapping skill sets and life experiences. Luke Colvin pulled it all together, creating a synergy that made the creation of the brewery possible." Luke, the owner of Arbor Care, a tree maintenance company, had realized that there was a limit to how much a service industry could grow in an area with a relatively small population. "I thought that starting a manufacturing business would be a great challenge." Then, one day, while dining with his family at Pelican Brewing in Pacific City, a two-hour drive to the south, he had the idea that starting a brewery would be the ideal manufacturing business. It would serve the local community and, if the product was good enough, sales could be expanded eastward toward and into Portland, one of the meccas for craft beer lovers. He discussed the idea with his brother-in-law David Kroening, who had a business degree and had worked for MillerCoors and later in digital marketing. The two created a business plan and then began raising funds. Much of the 2.2 million dollars raised came from Luke's customers in the tree care business.

One of those customers was Dan Hamilton, a teacher from California who had retired to Seaview, a few miles south of Astoria. "I'd been a wine drinker, but then, one of my university professors took me to his favorite pub and bought me an Anchor Steam Beer. That made me really interested in good beer, and I started homebrewing. I really liked making German lagers. One of my friends and I used to fantasize about owning a brewpub." When he moved north, he built a small brewing system in his home and served his beers to friends and the people who came to his house to do work. One of the latter was Luke Colvin, who invited Dan to become part of his planned venture. Hamilton became a partner and the major beer consultant and holds the title of "Founding Brewer."

The brewery would need to be in a building large enough to hold commercial brewing equipment, a restaurant and a taproom, and that would be in a location that would make it part of the community. That's where another of Luke's friends, Andrew Bornstein, came in. An owner, with his brothers, of the Bornstein Seafood Company, he had long wanted to find a new use for the ninety-year-old riverfront fish packing plant that had stood vacant since the company relocated its operations several years ago. "I had to give Luke and David flashlights when I took them to look at the place. It was a real train wreck. Junkies and homeless people were squatting in it. Part of the roof had blown off and raccoons were living in the walls." But it had what Luke, Dave, and Dan were looking for: size, a magnificent view, and the right location. The renovation/restoration was so successful that in 2014 it received an award in one of the Oregon Main Street Foundation categories: Best Adaptive Reuse of a Building.

Early in their discussions, Kroening and Hamilton came to two important and, it turned out, related decisions. First, they agreed that the brewery needed both a small pilot brewing system and a larger commercial one. Second, it should be run by a professional brewer with several years' experience in a production brewery. Kevin Shaw, head brewer at Portland's BridgePort Brewing Company, one of the largest craft brewers in the country, had become frustrated because the brewery did not have a small pilot system with which to develop new recipes, and he frequently had to make the hour-and-a-half drive to Corvallis to use the one in the Fermentation Sciences Department of Oregon State University. One day, when he was talking with the people at Portland Kettle Works, he learned that they were building a pilot system for Buoy Beer Company, which, they told him, was looking for a brewer.

Kevin had been aware of craft beers since he was a little boy. "When we'd go on driving trips, my father would look for microbreweries. He'd stop the car and go in while the kids sat in the car. When I turned 21, I started going in with him." It was while he was working as an elementary school teacher in Seattle that he really became interested in brewing. He and his housemates befriended the owner of a neighborhood brewpub and Kevin's girlfriend, seeing his enthusiasm, bought him a homebrew kit. The house became the location for its occupants' beer making experiments—and there were frequent disasters. "Lots of

Craft breweries have helped to revitalize Astoria's downtown, particularly along the Columbia River. One of these has been Buoy Beer Company, housed in what had been an abandoned fish processing plant. Three of the co-owners (from left), Dan Hamilton, Andrew Bornstein, and David Kroening, stand with head brewer Kevin Shaw in front of the smaller of the brewery's two brewhouses.

exploding bottles," Kevin confessed. "And once we filled a Party Pig (a porcine shaped plastic keg—push the snout and the beer comes out) and put it in the closet where we hung our jackets. Something happened and beer sprayed everywhere."

Deciding he wanted to turn professional, Shaw moved to Portland, where he began knocking on brewery and brewpub doors, finally landing a job working for Starr Brewing (now defunct) for a year. He then studied at Chicago's prestigious Siebel Institute before working for three years in Yakima, Washington, for the colorful (he often wore a kilt), outspoken, and now legendary Bert Grant, founder of the nation's first modern brewpub. Then it was on to Portland's BridgePort where he'd been for fourteen years when Buoy Beer found him. "At first," Luke said, "we didn't think we'd got him. He was just the person we wanted and when we phoned to offer him a job we couldn't reach him. We thought he'd lost interest." It turned out he was down in Corvallis trying out a recipe on the system there. When they finally contacted him and he realized that he could work at a new brewery with its own pilot system, he quickly accepted.

Luke and Andrew excused themselves to tend to tree and seafood businesses respectively. Kevin and Dan talked about the beers that had been created in Buoy's just over two years of existence. They grouped these in two categories: German-style lagers and Northwest ales. Their first beer, brewed on the pilot system and served when the brewpub opened on Valentine's Day of 2014, was intended to be a Helles, the name coming from the German word meaning "light" or "pale." "However," Kevin said, "it didn't quite turn out as we planned, so we just called it a North German lager." Since then, they have honed the recipe so that it fits the style guidelines. A 5.3 percent, 19 IBU medium-bodied pale beer, it is less bitter than most German pilsners, and maltier. Another German beer created in those early months was a dunkel, from the German word meaning "dark." "I hadn't had much experience with dunkels, so I followed Dan's recipe closely." Dan emphasized that it was "all about Munich malt, which provides toasty, slightly caramelized flavors." It is very slightly stronger (5.5 percent) and more bitter (20 IBUs) than most dunkels, and is a rounded, medium-bodied drink in which the chocolate, toffee, and caramel malt flavors are balanced by the crispness contributed by the Tettnang hops. The dunkel gave the new brewery national attention when it won a silver medal at the 2014 Great American Beer Festival.

Buoy's other lagers include a Czech-style pilsner, which at 6.2 percent ABV is a little stronger than most interpretations of the style. It has a little honey-like malt sweetness; however the Saaz hops take the edge off of this and contribute bitterness (35 IBUs). The Czech-style pilsner is one of the two Buoy products currently being bottled. Other lagers include IPL (Imperial Pale Lager) and Cascadia Dark Lager. Buoy Cream Ale is a lager-like ale designed to be a gateway beverage for those new to craft beers.

Given that Kevin Shaw worked for BridgePort, whose IPA was, around the turn of the century, one of the most popular of the American IPAs, it's not surprising that he has created several versions of the style. Buoy IPA, the other beer that is bottled, is strong (7.5 percent ABV) and quite bitter (70 IBUs), but it is a balanced beer with the piney and fruity notes offset by the malts. There have been several batches of single-hopped IPAs using, among others, Cascade, Centennial, Galaxy, or Columbus hops and each measuring 6.7 percent ABV. At the high extreme, Kettle Demon IPA is 9.5 percent, while at the lower, The Crop of Monte Crystal, a wet hopped ale, is a mere 4.9 percent. Other Northwest-style ales include Pale Ale and NW Red Ale. An oatmeal stout and a porter round out the regular offerings. Limited "editions" include Imperial Rainbow Petit Saison, Roggenbier (a German style smoked beer), and Raspberry Chocolate Stout.

I asked Kevin Shaw how, after so many years working with a very large craft brewery, he would describe his experience at Buoy over the last two years. "It's really something different; it's certainly not corporate like BridgePort. I have a very big say about the beers and, whether they succeed or fail, I'm the one who's ultimately responsible." After he had heard what Kevin said, Dan Hamilton smiled, looked over at the head brewer, and remarked: "And I get to watch really skilled brewer make really great beer."

Although there were nasty looking clouds in the west, it was sunny as I left Buoy and then walked four blocks south and uphill on 8th Street, then seven blocks east on Duane Street to Fort George Brewery and Public House. It was situated where Fort George, the British name for Fort Astoria, had stood and it occupied a one-time auto repair shop that had been built in 1924, but had been tenantless, except for birds that had flown through the many broken windows and built nests on beams, for several years before Jack Harris and Chris Newlowill opened their brewpub in 2007.

The place was packed with lunch goers, many of whom, judging by the names on the sweatshirts and ball caps they wore, were tourists. An overflow crowd sat outside at tables on the patio. Jack Harris, the co-owner and brewmaster, arrived from his office and suggested we go to the upstairs area, which was closed until later in the afternoon. "It's got a wonderful view, and we'll be able to hear each other," he explained. The view was spectacular, encompassing several miles of the river and the Washington shoreline. Long-ago occupants of the fort would not have had much difficulty spotting invaders—if they arrived by day and there was no fog.

Five weeks before my visit, the second floor area was packed, along with all the other public spaces in the brewery. On the Saturday of President's Day weekend, Fort George Brewery had hosted the Festival of the Dark Arts, a celebration featuring over 60 different stouts from different breweries, along with art displays, ice carving exhibitions, live music, and performances by, among others, local belly dancers. It wasn't just a celebration of a very popular dark ale, but also a celebration of Astoria, a growing arts center, a craft beer mecca, and tourist destination.

Jack's beer beginnings were, to say the least, inauspicious. "When I was in college, I drank Olde English 800. Nobody else would touch it. But I was poor, and it was a buck ninety-nine a quart." When his finances improved he graduated to Hamm's and his friends were glad to accept the occasional can he offered them. He worked at one of the McMenamins bars in the Portland area, "But I wasn't very good at it, so they moved me to the kitchen, where I was a bit better. One of my housemates who worked at another McMenamins as a brewer told me that he was leaving and that, if I wanted, I should apply for his job. I did and I discovered that brewing was what I really wanted to do." He was head brewer for McMenamins Lighthouse Brewery and Restaurant in Cannon City and then moved to Colorado, where, as head brewer for Mountain Sun, three of his beers won gold medals at the Great American Beer Festival.

But Jack was a West Coast boy, and, when he learned that a head brewer's job was opening up at Bill's Tavern in Cannon Beach, he applied. He was so anxious to get the job that when co-owner Jim Oyala arrived to open up the place, Jack and his dog were sitting on the steps outside, early for the interview. Harris's award-winning ways continued at Bill's: one gold and two bronze GABF medals. It was here that he met Chris Nemlowill, a homebrewer who had brought some samples of his beer for Harris to try, hoping that if they met with approval, he might work at Bill's, learning the techniques from a proven master. They did, and Chris worked as an assistant brewer before taking the position of head brewer at Astoria Brewing/Wet Dog Café.

"When Chris left Astoria Brewing, he decided he'd like to start his own brewpub and he came to me for advice," Jack Harris remembered. "I told him that I wasn't interested in being a consultant, but that I'd like to be a partner." The two of them joined forces and, when all the local banks showed no interest in them, the two borrowed from friends and family. "And we paid them off, two years before we had agreed to," Jack stated, noting that the brewery quickly became far more successful than they had dared to hope.

"But, when we were getting ready to open in 2007, we were down to $1,200 in the bank. But, the money thing wasn't the most scary." When I asked him what was, he said, "Come downstairs and I'll show you." He led me back down the spiral stairs and through the crowded restaurant to the brewhouse at the back. "That's 'Sweet Virginia,'" he said, pointing to the 8.5-barrel brewing system that had been relegated to secondary duty in 2010, when a new 30-barrel system had been installed in a building down the block. When they were putting their new brewery together, Chris and Jack had located a used brewing system in Virginia Beach, Virginia, hence the name. But Sweet Virginia almost didn't complete the journey from the Atlantic to the Pacific Coast. "It was abused and really dirty. But we dismantled it, had it loaded on a flat bed, and put the smaller parts in a U-Haul we'd rented. We were driving across Nebraska when we saw dark clouds out to the side and then heard an alert on the radio. There was a twister coming towards us. We had no insurance and all our money was in the brewing equipment on the truck. There was nothing to do but keep going. It touched down and there was mud and rain everywhere, but it missed us." In memory of the terrifying event, Fort George's flagship IPA is named Vortex.

"When we started, we were selling nearly all our beer in the brewpub,"

Jack Harris, co-owner and head brewer of Fort George Brewery and Public House, stands before another brewing tank with a story. "Sweet Virginia," as the system is affectionately named (after her earlier home in Virginia) was being shipped across the country on the back of a flatbed truck when a tornado touched down a few hundred feet from the highway. "If it had been any closer, we'd have lost everything," Harris remembers.

Jack continued. "But then we started getting local accounts and in a few years we'd expanded our distribution into Washington and the rest of Oregon. Now we're all over those states and in Idaho as well." Fort George Brewing had to expand, and it did, to the building at the end of the block. We walked through the patio, across a parking lot and into the Lowell Building, the one-time home of an automobile dealership and now the home of "Little Miss Texas," a 30-barrel brewing system from Houston, a canning line, and the rest of the production brewery's facilities. The taproom, which looks out on the many tanks of the brewhouse, is like an English pub, with dark walls, a cozy (albeit electric) fireplace, games such as chess, a foosball table, and books. There is a TV for people who want to watch sporting events. "It's really a place for people over 30," Jack says. "On weekends, when there is no brewing going on, we put tables out at the edge of the brewery area. It gives people a completely different experience."

Beyond the taproom, what used to be the automobile dealership's showroom has been transformed into an event space. It is the site of frequent weekday evening lectures and has been used for weddings and even wakes. "We make it available to education groups and local non-profit organizations. It's a way of giving back to the community. And," he smiles, "most of the people who come to events here enjoy having one of our beers, or maybe even two."

I finished my visit with Jack Harris by asking him about the house style of Fort George's beers. He remarked that his brewers weren't expected to slavishly follow style guidelines. "We have a kind of laissez faire attitude here; people have a free hand." He does like to use as many local ingredients as possible, including spruce tips harvested each year from the area's trees. "We take a day off in the spring, and most of the brewing crew goes out into the woods to gather the tips." The over 200 pound harvest forms one of only three ingredients added to water to make Spruce Bud Ale; the others are yeast and two-row barley malt. There are no hops.

That isn't to say that Jack doesn't like hops; he says that he loves them, although he objects to the overemphasis some brewers place on IBUs. "They don't describe the wonderful complexity of hops; I'd like to see people use words instead of numbers." Of the 144 beers listed by Rate Beer (78 of them brewed in 2014 or later), 24 are IPAs. The descriptions created for these beers indicate what Harris means by descriptive words rather than quantitative numbers. Overdub IPA, a 4.5 percent ABV session IPA, possesses "a sensory overload of mango and papaya hop aromas, dank grapefruit tones, and mellow citrus finishing notes." Vortex IPA, a 7.7 percent beverage, was designed "not to rip your taste buds off your tongue, but rather vigorously stimulate them and your palate into a lupulin-ecstasy of pleasure."

In addition to Vortex, Fort George offers two other year-round IPAs: Big Guns Session IPA (4.2 percent ABV) and The Optimist IPA (6.2 percent). Other beers include Cavatica Stout, a robust 8.8 percent ale that uses four malts along with Cascade hops; 1811 Lager (5.1 percent), a malty pre–Prohibition style lager named to honor Astoria's founding; Quick Wit (5.2 percent), a Belgian wheat beer that includes elderflowers and lemongrass in addition to the usual coriander; and Working Girl Porter (4.75 percent).

Cavatica, named after the kind of spider that was the heroine of *Charlotte's Web*, is not the only stout that has been brewed at Fort George. There have been 18 of them over the years and many of them have displayed the brewer's creative use of added ingredients, including cherries, walnuts, strawberries, pumpkins, oysters, and truffles. Specialty beers like these have long been a Jack Harris specialty. Mint and honey were among the additives in the gold medal beers he created at Mountain Sun and a blackberry beer was one of the Bill's Tavern medal winners. Two months after my visit Fort George would win a silver medal at the World Cup of Beer competition for a jalapeño beer.

As we walked back to the brewpub, I remarked on Fort George's rapid growth over the last four years: from 3,500 barrels annually to 13,700. I jokingly asked if the brewery had been contacted by Anheuser-Busch, which had recently taken over several craft breweries. He didn't answer my question, but smiled and then said: "Last year we made inquiries about buying them out." Fort George had issued a press release stating that the brewery was in the initial stages of gathering investors to purchase the brewing giant. Chris Nemlowill was quoted as saying that Fort George had no intentions of moving Anheuser-Busch's operations from St. Louis, while Jack Harris stated that Bud Light's Lime-a-Rita would definitely fill a niche for Fort George. A gofundme campaign was apparently being organized to raise the $250 billion necessary to complete the purchase. The announcement was made on April 1, 2015.

The clouds had moved closer as I walked down hill to Marine Drive and started east for my final visit of the day: Hondo's Brew and Cork. I was leaving the touristy section of town with its newly retro historic buildings and entering an area of low office buildings and automobile repair shops. Located in a small building tight against the hillside, Hondo's was the smallest of the four Astoria breweries I visited. Since 2013, when it became a nanobrewery, in addition to bottle shop, homebrew supply and brew-on-premises store and taproom, its three-year production totaled 43 barrels. In 2015, when production increased by nearly 30 percent, it ranked 2180th among microbreweries, with only 75 others producing less than 19 barrels.

The place was very quiet when I entered: one person sat at the small bar talking to the bartender and a woman sat at an old oak dinner table at the back of the room. The patron finished his beer and left, and the bartender greeted me. He was James Graham, bartender, manager, brewer, and homebrew instructor. The lady at the table was his wife, Shannon Lewis, who had helped Michelle Svendsen of North Jetty Brewing in Seaview in the brewing of the Pink Boots Collaboration beer.

James briefly outlined the history of Hondo's. It had been founded as a homebrew supply store in 2005, by R.J. Kiepke, a contractor and longtime homebrewer. A lover of craft beers, Kiepke had added the bottle shop and later taproom to provide Astorians and beer tourists with a wider variety of craft beer than was currently available in the area. "He had the guest taps, the homebrew supplies, and the brewing equipment. So it seemed logical that we should create our own beer," James explained. There was a kind of synergy created among the different branches of Hondo's. "People would try our beer and then some of them would buy supplies to take home so that they could try to make the same style themselves."

James showed me around the store-brewpub-taproom. First we visited the one-barrel brewery, which had been doubled in size since it was installed three years earlier. We walked past the homebrew supplies—bins of malt, packs of hops and yeasts, small pieces of homebrewing equipment—to the bottle shop area, a cooler that included many brands that would never be seen in a supermarket or even many larger bottle stores. Then we sat down in what someone had called "a living room of a brewpub." In addition to the oak table, on which was a chess board, and the dining chairs, there were very comfortable looking couches and behind them a foosball table. It was here that the local homebrew club met regularly to share with each other their various creations, many of them made from ingredients purchased just a few yards away.

"We've got a wider variety of ingredients than most bigger breweries—different malts, hops, yeasts—and so we can try out all kinds of different styles. And, because we're small, if we screw up, we haven't wasted a lot of time and materials." He estimated that, among the over 100 batches brewed since 2013, there have been over two dozen styles or style variations.

The names of the beers brewed at Hondo's reflect owner R.J. Kiepke's love of dogs. The brewery is named after one of his dogs, a drawing of whom graces the logo. Others include Dexter Joe's Doghouse IPA, Cresky Dog Czech Pils, Doberman Dunkel, Old Yeller Wit, Pugtail Pale, Hellhound Imperial Stout, and Schnauser BerlinerWiess.

Unfortunately, in late spring, Hondo's was experiencing dog days. After the first customer had left, no others had come in. Perhaps it was too early in the late afternoon for the locals to arrive and the taproom was relatively far away from the places the tourists visited. Just two weeks earlier, R.J. Kiepke had announced that he was putting the establishment up for sale. While he said that he would consider going into partnership with someone else, he was no longer interested in carrying the business by himself. Shortly after that James Graham moved on and R.J. resumed the roles of brewer and manager. Given the charm of Hondo's, it would be a "doggone" shame if he decided to close up shop and hang a "Dog Gone" sign on the door.

When I left Hondo's, it was raining cats and dogs.

9. Beach Town Breweries: Seaside and Cannon Beach

Seaside Brewery (Seaside), Bill's Tavern and Brewhouse (Cannon Beach)

When I arrived at Seaside Brewery, located beside Highway 101 at the edge of downtown Seaside and a few blocks from the ocean, the parking lot was empty. I was an hour early for my meeting with Jimmy Griffin, one of the co-owners, and so I walked down the main street. It was crowded as children and their parents, along with university students, wandered between the many shops, all of them catering to the tourist trade. Seaside, a town of 6,500 people, had, since the late nineteenth century, been one of the northern Oregon coast's most popular tourist destinations. At first, it had catered to summer vacationers and weekend visitors, but recently it had become a spring break destination, and in late March, according to the Moon travel guide, the population quadrupled. And this was spring break week.

By the time I returned to Seaside Brewery, the parking lot was nearly full and the vestibule was crowded with people waiting for a table. The square, two-story brick building that housed the brewpub had a story. The ground floor had been a jail, with one portion serving as a drunk tank, and the second floor had held the municipal offices. Griffin explained that when he and his partner Vince Berg had acquired the building, they wanted a place that did more than offer good food and drink; they wanted to create a place that captured the building's history. "We used repurposed materials, much of the wood and bricks from the original building," he said. The tiled floor at the main entrance has a 1920s retro look; the wall behind the bar, which at one time separated the drunk tank from the rest of the first floor, had window bars from the old jail set into it. The taps lining the wall were made of driftwood gathered a few blocks away and shaped in Jimmy's garage for their present use. "They are connected to serving tanks that are in the old drunk tank," he laughed. In the corner of one of the dining areas, a jail cell had been built, and parents took photographs

Not only does Seaside Brewing have an excellent location right next to Highway 101, it has an interesting story, having once housed the town jail. Here co-owner Jimmy Griffin stands at the entrance to what used to be a jail cell, now a popular spot to have one's photograph taken.

of their children, who stood inside, clutching the bars like the prisoners many of them had seen in *Pirates of the Caribbean*. Next to the cell, another barred window looked down at the brewhouse, where Berg and his assistant were mixing ingredients for a new brew.

The second floor was closed this afternoon, but Jimmy and I went upstairs where we could quietly talk about the story of the building and of his and Vince's building of a brewpub. The floors were of repurposed wood, and in what had probably once been a storeroom stood an old safe. Windows, which were opened on warmer days and evenings, looked out onto balconies and across the city, giving the space a bright, airy feeling. Although we were the only two there that spring early afternoon, the second floor was opened when there were too many people to be seated downstairs, and in the winter. "We certainly depend on tourists, particularly during vacation periods," Jimmy remarked. "But in the winter, it's primarily used by the local people. We make it available to the community for weddings, birthdays, anniversaries, and other special events. It's our way of giving back to the community. And, of course," he added with a smile, "they do buy our beer and food." The locals particularly enjoy two winter activities: beer and yoga nights and "History and Hops," a lecture series sponsored by the town's historical society. "It's a way of helping the people who live here reconnect with their history," Jimmy said.

Born in Utah, Jimmy Griffin had moved to Astoria and fallen in love with the place. When he found out that a management position had opened at Astoria's Rogue Ales Public House, which had opened in 2007, he went to Rogue headquarters in Portland for an interview with Jack Joyce, the brewery's legendary founder. "I was in the waiting area and was sipping from a bottle of beer, when I was called in to Jack's office. He frowned and asked if I thought it was suitable to show up for a job interview with a bottle of beer in my hand. I sheepishly said no. But the interview went well, and I was offered the manager's job."

In his time at the Public House, Jimmy learned that one of the most important aspects of craft beer is that "it's about community. Craft beer helps create a community. People don't bond over a Bud. I learned from Jack to feed the fishermen." That is a reference to what Joyce himself had been told by legendary Newport restaurateur Mo Neimi, who, when the Rogue founder was seeking a coastal location for the rapidly growing brewery, had emphasized the importance of giving back to the people of the community. How well he and partner Vince Berg learned that lesson is evidenced by Seaside Brewing's generous donation of the second floor space, the yoga and lecture nights, and the financial support of such Seaside area charitable organizations as "Seaside for Kids," and "Dimes for the High School."

Although he had enjoyed his work with Rogue, Griffin wanted to start a business of his own, one that would be located on the northern Oregon coast. "I was sitting in the waiting room of a Denver hospital, where my younger brother was being treated for a serious brain injury. To relieve the stress, I started writing down business plans for businesses I thought I might like to start up. I kept coming back to the idea of a brewery—one on the coast. I realized that Seaside, which was a really booming tourist town, didn't have a brewpub of its own." Later, he talked to his friend Vince Berg, the general manager for all the Rogue Meeting Houses, as they had been named, and the two became partners.

"When I saw this old building, which had been empty for years, I saw one big beautiful brewpub," Jimmy said enthusiastically. "It had a back story, it was right next to the highway, there was room for parking, and it was only a block away from the tourist shops." And the rest, to repeat the cliché, is history. But it's history with a struggle. "We were in the middle of the financial crisis, we were underfinanced, and so we basically lived on our cash flow for a while after we opened in 2012."

Getting the beer side of the business running also presented challenges. At first, the partners could not find a brewer with both the ability and suitable temperament to run the brewhouse. "So Vince learned to brew and he's getting pretty good at it. We both take care of the business side of things, he runs the beer making, and I get to talk to people like you," he laughed. Making enough beer was also a problem. "We started with a 10 gallon restaurant soup kettle as a mash tun; then moved to a one barrel system. But we were always running out and had to have other people's beer on tap." Now that a 15-barrel system has been installed, on site demands are always met and product is distributed to areas along the north coast and other parts of northern Oregon.

In describing Seaside's beers, Jimmy stated, "We have a basic quiver. We can't be too scattered; we offer the basic spectrum with something for everyone. A lot of tourists begin by asking us what's the lightest beer we have." The lightest of the beer offerings is Honey Badger Blonde Ale. Although it's 5.65 percent ABV, it's light and crisp. Vienna lager malts give it a more robust flavor than might be expected, but this is balanced by a hoppy finish. Lock Up IPA, the brewpub's best seller, is a standard American IPA, well balanced, with citrusy notes. At 8.58 percent ABV, it's not for the faint of heart or for anyone heading south on the long, curving highway right after lunch or dinner. Northcoast Seaside Red (7 percent) is malt forward, toasty and sweet. But the Chinook and Centennial hops provide a crisp finish.

Muther Hefer-Weizen does not have much of the yeasty flavors and textures usually associated with this style; but at 6 percent, 16 IBUs, it is surprisingly crisp and clean. Black Dynamite is an 11 percent Imperial stout that includes whole vanilla beans and cacao nibs. Nitro infusion gives it a rich, creamy texture, while the Chinook hops provide an understated bitterness. It was too late in the season to try the 5 Mil, a winter warmer that includes caramel and chocolate malts, along with molasses.

During our conversation, the noise from the dining room below increased. Jimmy looked out the window and remarked that the parking lot was nearly full. "Spring break week is like that; it's one of our busiest times. I'd better go down there and help out the servers. It's part of the job description for an owner." I turned out to be one of the first customers he served. I'd ordered a sampler tray of beer, which included a malty dunkelweizen and a pale ale that wasn't too hoppy.

I next visited Cannon Beach, a very curvy, 20-minute drive south of Seaside. Although both towns are tourist destinations, each has a unique personality. Seaside is not only bigger—by 4,500 people—it seems more commercial. Highway 101 runs past strip malls and many of the side streets leading to the beach seem to have large, high rise resort hotels at the end of them. Cannon Beach, by contrast, is not on the highway. Its main street has a village-like appearance, although many of the quaint buildings do house tourist stores. It was a popular place for the hippies and flower children of the 1960s and is now the home to a large number of artists' studios and galleries. Even so, long-time residents complain that it is too crowded on spring break and holiday weekends and all summer, and that the cost of housing is far too high.

By early summer 2016, Cannon Beach would be one of only three (the other two are Olympia and Astoria) three-brewery towns along Highway 101 in Washington and Oregon. (Had I made my trip three weeks earlier, Brookings, just north of the California border, would have been a fourth. However, when I phoned Tight-Lines Brewery to set up an interview, owner Nate Smith explained because of financial pressures and increased family responsibilities, he would be closing his small brewery and tap room.) Bill's Tavern and Brewhouse, which I would be visiting that morning, would be joined in a few months by Public Coast Brewing Company and Pelican Brewing. The former, named in honor of a 1967 state government declaration that made all Oregon Coast beaches free and open to everyone, is housed in a renovated restaurant at the north edge of town, while Pelican, near the south edge of town, will be in a new eleven-thousand-square-foot building that will house a restaurant, tap room, and brewery. In newspaper articles, officials for both of the new businesses spoke enthusiastically of the economic growth and prosperity of the area. When I asked the people at Bill's what they thought of the arrival of two competitors, they remarked that the two would be welcome and that their presence would take some of the pressure off of their own establishment. "In the summer, we

By the summer of 2016, Cannon Beach, a town of under two thousand, would be the home to three brewpubs. The nearly two-decades-old Bill's would be joined by Public Coast Brewing and Pelican Brewing.

can hardly seat all the people who show up and we have to brew constantly to keep enough beer on tap," Jim Oyala, one of the owners, explained.

Oyala was sitting at the bar tabulating the previous night's receipts when I arrived at the Tavern, which, although it was built in the 1990s, had the retro look of a large West Coast style 1920s home. Oyala told me that, while this building was new, there'd been either a restaurant or tavern on the site since 1917, when Bill Gallagher, after whom the tavern is named, opened a restaurant. At the end of Prohibition it became a tavern and passed through several owners before Ken Campbell purchased the restaurant in 1980. Four years later, Carpenter and Jim Oyala formed a partnership and purchased the property.

"It was a great old place, but it was in terrible condition," Jim remembered. "It was beyond renovation. By the mid–1990s, we realized that we needed to tear it down and start from the ground up, We wanted to make it bigger and to install a brewery. There was McMenamins brewpub in Lincoln City and Rogue in Newport, but nothing else. Tourism was growing—we knew it would work." But the city objected, not wanting to lose an historic edifice, no matter how run down it was. It wasn't until 1997 that they were permitted to demolish and rebuild. The new Bill's opened in November 1997, just after Pelican Brewing in Pacific City and Wet Dog in Astoria. Oregon's Northwest coast was on the verge of becoming a destination for beer tourists.

We were joined by Ken Campbell, Bill's other owner. The two jokingly filled in details of their longtime friendship. "Jim pulled me out of the Columbia River one time; he was coming along in a tow boat he skippered, and there I was," he laughed. Details of the rescue were sketchy and I came away unsure whether the two of them already knew each other. It is certain that they often played basketball with a mutual friend. Ken, a tall, lean, healthy looking sixty-something, who had played at the University of Portland, wouldn't comment on the skills of his friend and now business partner.

Jim excused himself and left to deal with other business concerns he had in Cannon Beach, while Ken showed me around the building and talked about how the tavern he'd taken over in 1980 had become a brewpub. The bar at which we'd been sitting divided the ground floor into two sections: on one side was the family area, where kids were welcome; on the other the adults only bar room. Wood repurposed from the old building gave the two spaces a homey and, at the same time, venerable look. Just inside the entrance, an old crank telephone was mounted on the wall. "It's not connected, of course," he laughed, "so we don't have wives calling up to tell their husbands to come home." Vintage photographs of the original Bill's and other old Cannon Beach buildings lined the walls. The image of a cigar-smoking, unshaven, bowler-hat-wearing older man, which was also on the outside sign and on the company logo, looked down from one of the walls. "We found it on an old steel engraving," Ken remarked.

"I'd been a homebrewer," he told me, as we walked to the beer garden at the back of the building, "and I'd wanted to own a brewery for a long time. Around the time that we bought the property in the mid–1980s, the modern brewpub movement was just beginning. I followed closely what McMenamins was doing in the Portland area and down the coast at Lincoln City and I thought that a brewpub would do very well in Cannon Beach. But the old building wasn't suitable for one; when we designed the new one it was as a brewpub. We'd visited several Portland brewpubs and talked to owners and brewers and used their input during the planning stages."

"One of the things everyone told us was that we had to make good beer," he continued. "Jim and I liked good beer, but we really didn't know that much about brewing it; we realized that if we were going to be successful, we had to hire a first-class brewer." They advertised and one of the applicants was Jack Harris, who had won many awards brewing in Colorado, but wanted to get back to Oregon, specifically to the coast. "I remember the morning he came for his

Rick Amacher, one of the brewers at Bill's Tavern in Cannon Beach, stands beneath the ceramic parrot perched above one of the brewing tanks. There is no report of the bird's location having created any problems while brewing is taking place.

interview," Ken recounted with a chuckle, "I'd come in a half an hour early and he was sitting on the steps waiting with his dog and with some of his own beer he wanted us to sample." Ken and Jim liked the beer and shortly after offered him the job. Within two years, Harris put Bill's on the craft beer map, winning two bronze medals at the 1999 Great American Beer Festival competition: one for Blackberry Beauty, a fruit beer; the other for Garden Party Elixir, a honey ale. Before he left Cannon Beach to start Fort George in Astoria, Harris brewed another GABF award winning beer, Duck Dive Pale Ale, the 2004 gold medalist in the American Pale Ale category.

Ken completed the tour by taking me up a steep set of stairs to the brewhouse, located on the second story. There was no lift apparatus for getting the grain up to the seven-barrel brewing system, so one of the essential requirements for becoming a brewer at Bill's was a strong back. There he introduced me to Rick Amacher, a burly fellow who looked like he had the requisite muscles, and who, along with Dave Parker, currently handled brewing duties. Ken returned downstairs and Rick and I talked beer as we stood beneath a ceramic parrot fastened to a perch that hung from the ceiling.

Rick had started his brewing career in Fort Collins, working as a bartender and helping when he could at the newly formed H.C. Berger Brewery. "I learned on the job," he noted. He later moved to breweries in Reno, Nevada, and Port Townsend, before coming to Cannon Beach, where, in addition to brewing, he creates stained glass pieces.

In discussing his philosophy, he referred to the *Reinheitsgebot*, the 1516 German Purity of Beer Law, which limited the ingredients used in making beer to malted grain, hops, yeast, and water. "I like to see what I can do with the basic ingredients; I think that less is more; making quality beer is more important than doing something that's far out." Some of the regular beers include Blackberry Beauty, a 4.1 percent fruit beer that uses 50 percent wheat; Duck Dive Pale Ale (4.8 percent), which is hoppier than usual for the style; Rudy's Red, an Irish ale, and Allie Mae's Irish Stout. There are also two lagers brewed each year—Billsner, a Czech style pilsner, and a kölsch. Bill's does, however, produce some less familiar beers—"something for the beer geeks," is how Rick puts it. One of these is a jalapeño beer available for Cinco de Mayo. Bill's has introduced a barrel aging program, purchasing containers from a recently opened nearby distillery.

While we talked, I sipped from a sample of Rick's alt beer, a German style infrequently brewed in the United States. It was based on a home brew recipe given to him by a friend. It was a very balanced beer with a malty mellowness. As I sipped, I glanced nervously above me, even though I knew the parrot wasn't real.

10. The Birds and the
Yeasts In Tillamook

de Garde Brewing (Tillamook),
Pelican Brewing (Tillamook and Pacific City)

The first part of the 40-mile drive from Cannon Beach to Tillamook is close to the sea, passing Haystack Rock, which rises 235 feet into the air, and, in places where the road is particularly close to the seashore, signs announcing "Tsunami Hazard Zone" and "Tsunami Evacuation Route." Just outside the northern city limits of Tillamook, a city with a population of 5,000, is one of the area's major tourist attractions, the Tillamook Cheese Factory, which offers free tours and, at the gift shop, a chance to purchase the factory's famous dairy product and a great variety of souvenirs. The city's other major attraction is located south of town, near the airport. Hangar B, built during World War II to house the enormous blimps used in submarine spotting operations, is the world's largest clear span wooden structure (so high that a small airplane can fly through it) and the home of the Air Naval Museum. Since 2013, Tillamook has also been the home of two well-respected breweries, Pelican and de Garde.

I was greeted just outside Pelican's production brewery, located at the north edge of downtown, by Brent McCune, the brewery's "Brand Ambassador" (that is, sales and marketing executive). He led me to a table in the small restaurant that overlooked the production facilities and, as we awaited the arrival of head brewer Darron Welch, McCune briefly outlined the two-decade history of Pelican Brewing. It had opened in May 1996 in the small coastal village of Pacific City, 24 miles to the south. The brewpub became very popular, Darren Welsh's creations won dozens of awards, and demand for the beer came from places far beyond Pacific City. The brewery was expanded, but couldn't keep up with the ever-increasing demand. So, in 2013, the present production facility was opened in Tillamook. "Some people have asked us why the brewery wasn't located to a more central location like Portland," McCune remarked and then went on to explain that the owners, Jeff Schons and Mary Jones, wanted to stay in Tillamook County, where they had other businesses, and that the city of Tillamook had provided funding toward the project. Production increased from 3,879 barrels in 2013 to 12,983 in 2015. A couple of months after my visit, a 14,000-foot expansion adjacent to the present facility would be complete. It would contain more conditioning tanks and cold storage space as well as a new bottling line that would enable Pelican to package six-packs of 12-ounce bottles, in addition to the 22-ounce ones presently in use. This repackaging was essential if the brewing company was to make inroads into the chain grocery store market, where six-packs were essential. The Pacific City brewhouse would be used as a test brewery and would produce special limited editions for the pub there. In addition, in the summer of 2016, the Cannon Beach brewpub would open and would produce nearly all the beer for that facility.

Just as Brett was finishing his brief account of the brewery's history, Darron Welch, who has been Pelican's only head brewer, arrived. He'd grown up in Eugene, Oregon, and after high school graduation had gone on a trip to Germany, where he had an experience similar to that of many people who had become craft brewers. "I realized that I loved beer—if it was great beer. And the German beer certainly was. It tasted good, and there were so many wonderful varieties. When I went to university, I decided I'd learn to homebrew. I didn't know how my beer would turn out, but at least it would have flavor." It turned out well and, in fact, one of his beers—which would later become the basis for Doryman's Dark Ale—won a homebrew contest. "I experimented with different combinations of malts until I got just what I wanted."

After graduating from university with a major in history, Welch headed to Appleton, Wisconsin, to work on a major history project. But the brewing bug had bitten him and one day he showed up at a local brewpub and asked what he would have to do to get into the business. "You can start by learning how to wash kegs," the owner told him. After this lowly start, Darron learned the various operations of commercial brewing and worked his way up to a position of assistant brewer. However, his heart was still in Oregon, and, in the mid–1990s, he asked his boss if he could go to a small brewer's conference in Portland. He said that it would expand his knowledge and, he admitted to me, he hoped that he might find a job opening that would bring him back home. At the conference he noticed a very small hand-written sign pinned on a notice board: "Brewer wanted—ocean side brewery."

As Darron reached this point of his story, Jeff, Schons and Mary Jones, Pelican's principal owners, stopped at the table. They'd heard Welch speaking of the note and offered their side of the Pelican story up to the Portland conference. During the earlier 1990s, the couple had been active in real estate and development in the area. "Pacific City was a beautiful area—the ocean, the beaches, Haystack Rock, Kiwanda Point—but it need something more to attract visitors and make it a vibrant tourist destination," Jeff remarked.

"We'd often driven past this old building on the beach at Pacific City," Mary continued. "It had been abandoned for a long time, and it was nearly covered by sand dunes. One day, the owner of the place, who'd been trying to interest us in it for a while, climbed up the dunes with us. We looked through a hole in the roof down into the dark interior." It was certainly a fixer-upper, but it definitely had location. "We didn't know what we were going to do with it, but we bought it."

Jeff remembered that they'd signed the agreement on a Saturday afternoon. "I spent a pretty sleepless Saturday night thinking about what we'd done and wondering what we would do. Then, on Sunday morning, I was reading the paper and came across an article about a beach front brewpub somewhere on the east coast. That's what we could do—we could build a brewpub! And so we got started. But we didn't know anything about making beer, so we went to this conference in Portland, hoping to find somebody who did. When we

Pelican Brewing co-owners Jeff Schons and Mary Jones stand with head brewer Darron Welch (right) in front of the 30-barrel production brewery located in Tillamook, Oregon.

passed that bulletin board, Mary told me to stop. She dug a pencil and paper out of her purse, wrote the note, and pinned it up."

After Jeff and Mary left for a meeting, I asked Darron what the first beer he brewed for Pelican was. His answer surprised me: it was a wheat beer. "At that time, Oregon was in the middle of a wheat beer war. The Widmer Brothers' Hefeweizen had been very popular for several years, and everyone else wanted to make something like it. We didn't introduce an IPA until 1997; at that time it was pretty much a niche beer; we offered it as a seasonal," he explained. In 1998, Pelican won its first Great American Beer Festival awards, bronzes for Doryman's Dark and Tsunami Stout. A year later, Doryman's Dark won the gold medal, the first of 12 golds Pelican has garnered. Pelican was twice named GABF small brewpub of the year and twice large brewpub of the year.

With so many styles (nine) winning so many GABF medals (a total of 32 including the 12 golds), it was difficult to decide which ones to talk about. Darron mentioned four of the beers—two light and two dark—that he felt best exemplified his approach to brewing. These were ales that "we worked very hard for a long time to get them where we wanted to be." Before discussing the four, he outlined the philosophy that underlay the creation of all Pelican beers. Conceptualization was very important. "We first ask ourselves, why is this beer here? How does it fit into our lineup and how does it relate to the other beers in terms of aroma, flavor, color, and alcoholic strength? We want each of our beers to have a distinct personality within the family. We start with the aroma; each one has a specific aromatic presence. For Kiwanda, it's a blossomy aromatic; for MacPelican Scottish Ale, it's a rounded maltiness, and for Doryman's, it's a mixture of cocoa, floral and caramel notes." Each Pelican beer must have a clean, snappy, balanced finish. "Aromatics and that clean snappy finish are like the anchors of a suspension bridge. They are what we build the flavors on."

Kiwanda Cream Ale (two golds, two silvers, and one bronze) was created, Welch laughingly explained, "as my solution to losing sales to Bud. We introduced it as a seasonal; but in the second year it was outselling our hefeweizen, so we made it a regular and soon dropped the wheat." Designed as Pelican's crossover beer, it's his interpretation of a pre–Prohibition cream ale. Golden in color and fairly light-bodied, its maltiness is balanced by the hop bitterness and floral aromatics. It's an easy drinking beer (5.4 percent ABV, 25 IBUs) which, when it was first introduced in the late 1990s, quickly converted legions of craft beer novices to the new, flavorful ale styles that were becoming increasingly well-known on the West Coast.

Surfer's Summer Ale (one gold, one silver and 2 bronze; 5.3 percent ABV, 25 IBUs), the other lighter beer we talked about, was also created because

Welch was confronted with a problem. In this case, the question was what kind of beer he could make with a sample of new hops an English salesman had given him at a craft beer conference. "I'd heard of an English beer called a summer ale, but I didn't know anything about it. I had a degree in history and so I used my university training to do some research. I gathered all data I could find, analyzed it, and came up with a flavor profile. From there I designed a recipe and those sample hops worked really well in it." It's like an English pale ale with a malty sweetness and toasted notes contributed by the Maris Otter malt. The new hops provided a floral aroma and crisp refreshing finish. After using the English hops for a while he found that they had a tendency to spoil, and replaced them with Glacier hops.

Doryman's Dark Ale (four golds, one silver and one bronze; 6.2 percent ABV, 42 IBUs), started as an experiment with a pale ale recipe into which Welsh wanted to introduce more malt complexity. At first, he added chocolate malts, but now there are four: pale, wheat, caramel and chocolate, which provide a malt sweetness with cocoa and caramel notes. The floral aromatics and citrusy flavors of the Cascade and Mount Hood hops provide balance. Although it is a malt-forward beer, it has that characteristically Pelican clean, snappy finish. Unfortunately, brown ales are now hard sells in a land that has gone overboard for big, hoppy beers, and so Doryman's is now available on draft only, at limited locations, and during limited times of the year.

Although Tsunami Foreign Style Stout (two golds, one silver, and two bronze, 7 percent ABV and 45 IBUs) will not tip you out of your dory and sweep you out to sea, it does provide a flavorful punch. To a pale malt base are added dark chocolate malts and roasted barley to give a complexity of tastes. A malt sweetness is complemented with a rich, somewhat bitter espresso-like finish, which is slightly different from the clean, snappy finish the hops provide in other Pelican beers.

The drive along 101 as it passed through downtown Tillamook was slow, as spring break visitors seemed to be cruising, inspecting the signs on the tourist shops on either side of the street. Outside of town, I turned left on Long Prairie Road, passing by green grazing lands, the pastures of the cows from whose milk came the area's famous cheeses, and then onto Blimp Boulevard. As I pulled into the back of the long, one-story warehouse building that housed de Garde Brewing, Hangar B, that World War II home of giant airborne vessels, loomed up a few hundred yards away. I parked and entered this ordinary looking building, in which some extraordinary beer making was taking place.

To the right, just inside the large rollback door, stood de Garde's 15-barrel brewing system. The mash tun and kettle didn't look much different from most of the ones I've seen. But, to the left of the door was something very different:

a rectangular, flat-bottomed stainless steel trough, roughly eight feet wide and twelve feet long and just under two feet deep. As I walked toward the office and taproom where I was to meet owners Linsey and Trevor Rogers, I glanced through a large door that opened onto the rest of the brewery. There were no stainless steel fermenting tanks, just hundreds of wooden barrels, most of them quite small, but a few of them enormous. In my discussion with Rogers, I would learn that the trough and the wooden barrels were part of what makes de Garde completely different from any of the other breweries I'd ever visited.

Linsey and Trevor met in Ashland, Oregon, the original home of Rogue Brewing. She was a graduate in history from Los Angeles's Occidental College; he, in art, sculpture, and painting from Southern Oregon University. They'd both been wine drinkers until they discovered what are called "wild" or "spontaneously fermented" beers, in which fermentation is induced not by pitching commercially produced yeast into an enclosed tank, but by letting the wild yeasts floating in the air interact with the wort to turn it into alcohol. They fell in love with these beers, which, Trevor explained, were brewed the same way that most beers were before the industrial age. "There wasn't much wild beer around here a few years ago and what there was was pretty expensive, so we started making our own," Linsey remembered. "We read a lot of books and did a lot of experimenting."

Both Linsey and Trevor, who was working in the restaurant at Pelican's Pacific City brewery, decided that they should turn their hobby into a profession. But to do so, they needed more than just funding; they needed the right location for their business. This wasn't a matter of a place with relatively easy access to large markets or the right demographics. (Besides, Tillamook was known as a town of with a large number of consumers of mass-produced lagers and so was unlikely to provide their main clientele.) It was a matter of finding somewhere with the wild yeast that was right for the kinds of beer they wanted to make. "We did a lot of tramping around, looking for a location with the yeast we wanted. We'd make a batch of wort [prefermented beer] and each evening take a bucket of it to a specific place, leave it out overnight, and then ferment it, to see if the area had the yeast we wanted. The sea breezes and the agricultural land around Tillamook helped to create just the right yeast we wanted."

In 2013, they opened their brewery, which they named "de Garde" in honor of a traditional French farmhouse ale, "Biere de Garde," in a small outbuilding next to the rural house in which they lived. The outbuilding quickly became too small and late that year they moved operations to the present location, using first part of the warehouse, then more and more of it, until now de Garde occupies the whole building. In 2014, the taproom was moved from downtown to the brewery. Like so many of the breweries I visited, this one is expanding

Trevor and Linsey Rogers of de Garde Brewing stand in front of one of the giant wooden foeders used to ferment and condition their wild-fermentation beers.

to meet increased demand. Production has grown from 92 barrels in 2013 to 1,127 in 2015. Later in 2016, the taproom and brewery will be moved into town.

Trevor invited me on a tour of the brewery. We stopped first at the mash tun and kettle. "What we do here is pretty standard. We make and boil wort in the same way that other brewers do. Our grain bill is developed to create the style and alcoholic strength we're looking for. We use hops—both the older and newer varieties—for flavor and aroma." He did not mention bittering hops, which would counteract the subtle flavors they wanted in the finished product.

"It's when we get over here that things get different," he said as we walked toward the shallow rectangular vessel near the door. It was, I learned, a coolship, derived from the Dutch/Flemish word "koelschip," and was used to cool the wort and to begin the process of wild fermentation. "There's a lot of flat surface," Trevor explained. "That speeds up the cooling and provides more area for the wild yeasts to settle on." Its being near the door enhanced the cooling process and made it easier for yeasts and bacteria carried by the night breezes to get inside. "We put the wort in the coolship later in the afternoon and then, after 18 hours, we put it in barrels to begin the fermentation." Essentially, after they've made the wort, the brewers don't have much more to do with creating the finished product; the yeast does the work. Their main job is to move the liquid from kettle to coolship to barrels and finally to bottles and kegs.

The barrels into which the yeast infused wort is placed can be roughly categorized as either foeders (the enormous ones I'd seen) and simply barrels. de Garde has seven foeders, three with a 92-barrel capacity, two with 60, one with 50 and one with 25. There are, as well, 80 oak tanks, each with an 8.5 to 15-barrel capacity. After a fermentation period ranging from three or four months to three years, the end product is bottled. "We can't make these beers anywhere but here," he emphasized, using the word terroir, a term used to describe the influence of a specific place of growing on wines, to explain that, unlike regular brewing, which can use the basic ingredients anywhere, de Garde can't get the airborne yeasts that give the beers their specific flavor anywhere but in the Tillamook area. "We are a deviation from the norm in current brewing," he announced, a note of pride in his voice, "Many breweries use computers for every step of the brewing process and so, a brewery with multiple production facilities can make a specific style taste the same no matter where it comes from. They have complete control over every step of the process; we don't."

One batch of Bu Weisse (Berliner Weisse), one of the brewery's most popular styles, may taste quite different from another. And sometimes, the results will be terrible—undrinkable beer. "We have to pour out between five and fifteen percent of what we brew," Trevor explained. "That's just one of the things that happen when you're using spontaneous fermentation."

In late July 2016, Ratebeer.com, the consumer beer evaluation site, listed descriptions of 201 de Garde beers. While that is certainly a large number for a brewery that was barely three years old, many of the listings were for variations on five basic styles, each based on a traditional European style associated with a specific location. Ten of the beers evaluated were lambics, the funky, often fruit-flavored beers from the Brussels, Belgium, area. Thirteen were listed as goses, the salty, tart, crisp finishing wheat beer originally brewed in the Leipzig, Germany, area. Many of the de Garde versions were given the name Hose, indicating that they were brewed with aroma and flavor hops. Nineteen were saisons, the usually robust, often peppery brews from the western Belgium–eastern France region. Sixty-five were Berliner Weisses (identified with the nickname Bu on de Garde labels). These tart, sour, fruity, effervescent beers have been dubbed "the people's Champagne." By far the largest category is "sour beers/wild beers," spontaneously fermented beverages that are local to wherever they are brewed, as they are influenced by the "airoir" (as opposed to "terroir"), the yeasts floating about around and inside of the brewery.

There are several variables which make each brewing of one of these styles unique. The quantity of the grain bill influences the final alcoholic percentage of the end product and with it the flavor. Most of de Garde's beers are fairly low in alcoholic content, with 20 percent being measured below five percent. There are some stronger ones, with ten of them over ten percent. The highest is Morning Star, a sour beer that tops the list at 15.9 percent ABV. Interestingly the term "Imperial," which in other breweries is often applied to their big beers, ones that weigh in at over eight percent, is applied by de Garde to those Berliner Weisses that are between five and 5.6 percent. Not just the amount of fermentable sugars in the wort, but the nature of the yeast to which it exposed, will result in variations. Different strains of yeast will result in different flavors from batch to batch.

Almost a third of the beers have fruit additives, nearly all of which are sourced in Oregon. "If it's grown around here, we've probably used it," Trevor laughed. "Local is very important to us." Further flavor nuances are often added when some of the brews are aged in barrels that had previously contained hard liquor or wines. A glance at the details for the Bu beer, which comes as close as anything to what could be called a flagship beer, reveals the tremendous variety of flavors. There are many types of berries: raspberries, blackberries, blueberries, boysenberries, cranberries, gooseberries, and marionberries. Also used are local fruits like apricots, cherries, nectarines, peaches, and plums. Some of the fermented brews will be aged in whiskey, rum, gin, Chenin Blanc, or Merlot barrels and acquire subtle tastes from these containers. Different grain bills, yeasts, fruits, and barrels—that's a lot of permutations and combinations.

As we walked the length of the building, passing rows and rows of barrels, Trevor Rogers remarked, "We thought we'd be selling our beer out of the back of our truck for years and years. But look at this space, we started at one end, and in just over two years we've expanded from one end to the other." He went on to say that the success, which culminated just a few weeks ago in early February 2016 with de Garde being voted the fifth best brewery in the world by participants in the Ratebeer website poll, was not the result of an advertising campaign. "We didn't spend a dollar on advertising; it was all word of mouth." The success certainly wasn't based in Tillamook, with its lovers of megabrewed lagers. Beer lovers from Portland soon heard of de Garde and made the two-hour drive to the brewery. A Midwesterner regularly flies his private plane in to replenish his stock. Word even spread overseas. "When we were vacationing in Spain, we were talking with an Irishman. When he heard we were from Oregon, he asked if we knew about de Garde."

"We price our beer reasonably because we can. We make beer for beer lovers. We're not out to get rich and we don't want to get too big. About 2,000 barrels annually would be about as far as we'd want to go. You don't need a wealthy lifestyle to be wealthy. We want to share our passion for good beer." By these terms, Trevor and Linsey Rogers are very wealthy people indeed.

Highway 101 turned inland as I drove out of Tillamook and it wasn't until I'd left the main road to drive into Pacific City that I again saw the ocean. I drove through the streets of what advertises itself as "Your Little Beach Town" and turned into the parking lot of the Pelican Pub and Brewery. The view was spectacular. To the north, Cape Kiwanda, in the lee of which dorymen used to shelter their small fishing boats during rough weather, jutted into the sea. Straight ahead, well beyond the shoreline, rose Haystack Rock, at 327 feet the tallest sea stack along the Oregon coast. Near the shore, surfers rode the waves; children, under the watchful eyes of their parents, stepped gingerly into the cold water; and a dog, escaped from its leash, chased a gull. Behind the low dunes stood Pelican Pub and Brewery, which Jeff Schons and Mary Jones had created inside the building that had once been nearly covered by sand dunes.

Ken Hanson, general manager of the pub, gave me a brief tour, from the lobby where people waited for tables, through the brewery which, although the space had been expanded, looked very cramped, and down a hall the walls of which were covered with medals and plaques, not just from GABF competitions, but from other regional, national, and international competitions. "Here, we cater mainly to tourists," he told me, leading me into a room generally reserved for such special events as the Pub's three-times-a-year beer and food pairings dinners. It was open today to handle the overflow crowd of spring vacationers. "We have over half a million visitors a year. We want them to have the best beer in the world. But it's more than just good beer and good food.

When Jeff Schons and Mary Jones bought the property that is now Pelican Pub and Brewery in Pacific City, the vacant building was nearly completely buried in sand dunes. The brewpub is now one of the most popular beer destinations along the Oregon and Washington coasts.

We're here to provide an experience that we want them to remember whenever they see a bottle of Pelican beer."

I looked around the room, noticing the surfboards, wet suits and an oar decorating the walls and then out the window. Beyond the dunes loomed Haystack Rock. I'd been at several places that used the slogan "Brews with a View." Pelican didn't use that slogan, but as I sipped a MacPelican Scottish Ale I knew I was enjoying the best brew with a view I'd experienced in all my beer travels.

Courtesy Misty Mountain Brewing Company.

Courtesy Pelican Brewing Company.

Courtesy Fish Brewing Company.

Courtesy Buoy Beer Company.

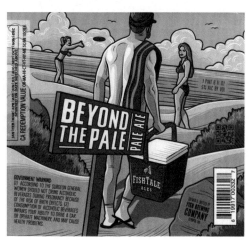

Courtesy Rogue Ales.

Courtesy Fish Brewing Company.

A

B **Courtesy Fish Brewing Company.**

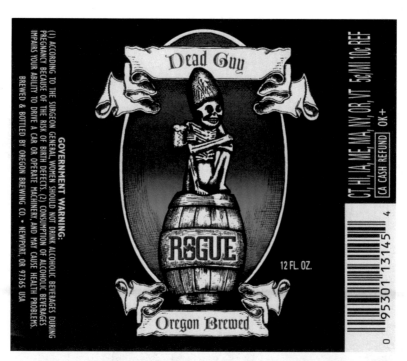

Courtesy Rogue Ales.

C

Courtesy Arch Rock Brewing Company.

Courtesy Chetco
Brewing Company.

Courtesy Top Rung
Brewing Company.

D   Courtesy Top Rung Brewing Company.

Courtesy Astoria Brewing Company.

Courtesy Port Townsend Brewing Company.

Courtesy Astoria Brewing Company.

Courtesy Astoria Brewing Company.

E

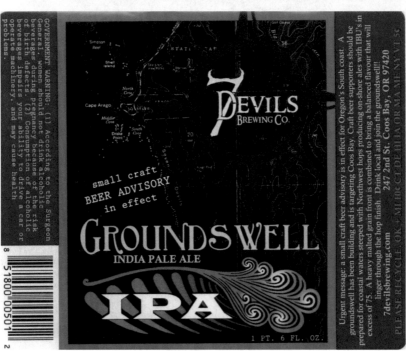

F

Courtesy 7 Devils Brewing Company.

Courtesy Propolis Brewing.

Courtesy North Jetty Brewing.

G

Courtesy Wolf Tree Brewing
Company.

Courtesy Port Townsend Brewing Company.

Courtesy Rusty Truck Brewing Company.

Courtesy North Jetty Brewing.

Courtesy Fort George Brewery and
H   Public House.

Courtesy Seaside Brewing Company.

Part IV

After the Beer Drought: The Central and Southern Oregon Coast

When I was doing preliminary research on Oregon breweries, I came across a 2004 comment that described Highway 101 from south of Newport to the California border as a "beer desert." Although the central Oregon coast was the home of two of the state's earliest craft breweries, McMenamins Lighthouse Brewpub in Lincoln City (1986) and Rogue Ales in Newport (1989), the observations was a fairly accurate one. Before 1915, when Prohibition was legislated in the state, there had been breweries along the central and south Oregon coast in Bandon, Mansfield (Coos Bay), Newport, and North Bend. After that, over seven decades passed before a brewery opened there. Of the three craft breweries that opened in the 1980s, only McMenamins and Rogue survived. A place called "Roger's Zoo" in North Bend was open from 1989 to 1993. During the last decade of the twentieth century and the first of the twenty-first, breweries opened and then closed in Newport (SKW Brewing), Florence (Wakonda Brewing) and Coos Bay (Bank Brewing).

It wasn't until the beginning of the second decade of this century that the coast below Newport ceased to become a beer desert. Between 2011 and 2015, nine breweries opened in Lincoln City, Newport, Seal Rock, Yachats, Coos Bay, Gold River, Brookings, and Harbor. Only one, Tight Lines in Brookings, failed to survive. In the summer of 2016, Defeat River Brewing would open in Reedsport, and, later in the year, The Horn Public House and Brewery in Depoe Bay. With the exception of Rogue Ales, which produced over 100,000 barrels in 2015, they were small operations. Of these, only Arch Rock, with 1,154 barrels, had production numbers above three figures.

11. A Landlocked Lighthouse
and a Very Old Truck:
Lincoln City

Mcmenamins Lighthouse Brewpub
and Rusty Truck Brewing (Lincoln City)

McMenamins Lighthouse Brewpub, located in a Lighthouse Square shopping center, near the northern edge of Lincoln City, a long, narrow town of 8,500 people, is four blocks away from the sea. The only lighthouses to be seen from the parking lot are one next to the sign for the strip mall and another on the side of the building housing the brewpub. In the mid–1980s, the developers of the mall approached Mike and Brian McMenamin, who had just opened a brewpub in Hillsdale, a suburb of Portland, to see if they would like to establish one in the coastal town. The far-seeing brothers, recognizing the area's potential as a tourist destination and noting that there were no breweries along the Oregon coast, liked the idea and, in July 1986, opened the first Oregon coast brewery since pre–Prohibition days.

Although the brewpub isn't housed in a restored historic building such as a church, dance hall, or school, as many of the McMenamins properties are, its interior shares the same fun and funky decorative style as the others do. The restaurant/brewpub occupies two floors, the second being a balcony that wraps around the four walls and looks down at the first. The walls are decorated with old tin signs advertising long-forgotten soda pops, tobaccos and other products. In between several of the signs are paintings done in the humorous, almost grotesque style the company has become known for. In one of them, a man clings to a buoy rocking in a choppy sea. An octopus waves his tentacles at the man, who reaches out, offering the cephalopod a pint of beer. A lighthouse stands long the rocky shore in the background. The west wall is completely windowed and, looking out across several low buildings, I thought I could see a thin, sparkling line that might have been the ocean.

Opposite the ground floor bar, behind glass walls, stands the cramped six-barrel brewing system, surrounded by empty kegs that have been cleaned and are awaiting refilling. Around the tops of the fermentation tanks, which are painted purple, are ornately decorated bands; little faces are painted on the pipes coming out of them. The equipment looks old. The bottoms of the fermentation tanks are flat rather than conical. But the system has been doing yeoman duty for thirty years, and, in 2015, turned out 663 barrels, which is about average for most of the McMenamins breweries. Since December 2015, this cramped area has been the workspace for Gary Stallings, the latest of the 25 brewers who have worked at Lighthouse. These have included Rob Vallance, who is now the General Manager overseeing operations for all the company's 25 breweries, and Jack Harris, co-owner of Astoria's Fort George Public House and a young legend in the craft beer industry.

There was nowhere for Gary and me to sit among the kegs and tanks, so

Gary Stallings, recently installed brewer at McMenamins Lighthouse Brewpub in Lincoln City, stands before the playfully decorated and rather old brewhouse equipment. McMenamins brewers follow established recipes for beers that are available throughout the brewpub system, but are free to use their creativity in making beers for their own brewpub.

we moved to a booth to discuss his brief brewing career and the McMenamins brewing philosophy. A native of Idaho, he'd been a drinker of what he called "clear beer" until the day he tasted a Deschutes Mirror Pond Pale Ale. "Wow, I thought! This has flavor!" he remembered. He'd been at McMenamins Lighthouse for 14 years, first as a cook, then a bartender, and then an assistant manager of the restaurant. When Doug Ashley, who'd been the brewer since 2008, decided to move on, Gary decided that taking over brewing duties would be a very interesting change. "They brought one of the more experienced brewers over to teach me. He showed me the basics, and walked me through a couple of batches. And here I am."

He explained that each McMenamins brewer was expected to follow exactly the style guidelines and recipes for what are called "the corporate beers," the year-round offerings and seasonal releases that are available at all locations. "Then we're encouraged to become creative, to design our own recipes." Gary showed me the placemat used for sampler trays and pointed out a quotation. "It is the unique qualities of each brewhouse, combined with the brewer's whimsy, creativity and spark that ensures a special pint every time"

Ruby, the most popular and the oldest of the three "corporate beers," had been created just a few months before Lighthouse opened, and this year there had been celebrations for the brew's thirtieth anniversary in all the pubs in the McMenamins chain. In the first ale in the United States to legally use fruit in it (according to the website), pale malts provide the base for the understated fruit flavor, imparted by raspberry puree. Chinook hops give a delicate contrast to the sweetness of the fruit. At 4 percent ABV and with very little bitterness (5 IBUs), this light-bodied, golden colored ale has long been McMenamins' entry level beer and go-to session ale.

The website defines Terminator Stout (6 percent, 30 IBUs), another regular, as "Black as the darkest night and as rich as the most decadent dessert." Coffee and roasted notes, which seem a little harsh at first, become more rounded as this full-bodied beer warms up. The third regular, "Hammerhead Ale," is an American pale ale. At 5.9 percent ABV and 44 IBUs, it is certainly not a weak beer, but it isn't overwhelming. The crystal malts introduce a caramel flavor, while the Cascade hops provide a slightly bitter finish. Among the "corporate" seasonals is an Irish stout (4.9 percent, 38 IBUs), which is released in time for St. Patrick's Day, and Kris Kringle Winter Ale (6.8 percent, 76 IBUs). Some beers have been created at Lighthouse and are only occasionally offered at other locations. These include Spring Fever Wheat (4.6 percent, 47 IBUs), Cascade Head Golden Ale (4.12 percent, 12 IBUs), and I Can Play Porter. And there are others newly created by Stallings. "I love hops," he said. He's used them in abundance in an IPA he created for the 100th anniversary of Hotel Oregon (another

McMenamins property) and the Alienator IPA (7.5 percent, 68 IBUs) for the UFO Fest held at that hotel.

Gary was looking forward with enthusiasm and excitement to one of the biggest events to take place in his new career—the midsummer Lighthouse Brewfest. "Each of the head brewers at one of McMenamins brewing locations picks a number out of a hat. That number corresponds to a specific style and the brewer has to make an original recipe for the style and present it at the brewfest. This year, I'll be a contestant, not just an employee working in the restaurant and watching. And, I'll be one of the hosts. I'm getting excited already and there's over four months to go!"

Stallings is certainly enjoying his late career change.

A few miles south on Highway 101, at the edge of a large parking lot, sits a somewhat rusted 1958 Chevrolet flatbed truck. It gives its name to the large roadhouse restaurant that the parking lot serves and the brewery building behind it. The restaurant was originally called "Roadhouse 101" when Brian Whitehead acquired it in 2005. "It was operational," he explained, "but barely. It needed a lot of work and I thought it would be a good project for my son and I to work on. Then, when we added a brewery in 2011, we called it Rusty Truck. As of the spring of 2016, the "Roadhouse 101" name was dropped; Rusty Truck now included both brewery and restaurant.

Giving a brewery or brewpub an unusual name is not that unusual. Already on this trip I'd visited places called Three Magnets and Wet Dog and in the next couple of days I'd be stopping by Wolf Tree and 7 Devils. But none of these unusually named places had as interesting a back story as Rusty Truck. I heard this story after I'd parked my car, walked through the batwing doors into the bar area, and past the small bandstand where area musicians performed. The manager of the roadhouse, Branden Fowler, had been delayed by an unexpected doctor's appointment. "But," said the young man tending bar, "the owner is here. You could talk to him while you're waiting." Brian Whitehead, whose day job was being a trial lawyer in Salem, had come to the coast for the weekend and was enjoying brewer Jon Anderson's latest creations.

When I asked him about the rusty truck, he told me that there was quite a story behind it and how it came to give its name to the brewery. He'd bought it several years ago because he wanted to use it in the July 4th parade held in Glen Eden Beach, a seaside community just south of Lincoln City. "We put the local band on the back and the name Roadhouse 101 on the doors. Most of the time, we parked it at the Roadhouse."

That's where the problems began. City officials didn't like seeing the truck there and made several attempts to remove it. First, they claimed it was an abandoned vehicle that had to be towed. "I told them it worked and sent them

This aging rusty Chevrolet flatbed truck gives its name to the brewpub in front of which it's parked. Brewpub owner Brian Whitehead, a trial lawyer, had to go to court several times to establish his right to park the vehicle there.

a copy of the license and insurance, and a picture of it in the parade." Then officials complained that, sitting on the lot as it was, its door signs were visible to passersby. It was illegal, they told him, to use a parked truck as a sign. Brian responded by covering the signs with cardboard. But the city wasn't finished: parking on dirt or gravel was also illegal. So Brian and his son shoveled away the gravel to reveal the concrete underneath it.

There was more to come: the truck was declared a public nuisance, and if Whitehead wanted to dispute that, he'd have to appear before the City Council. "I'm a trial lawyer. So I carefully planned my defense of the truck. I took pictures of 50 other local trucks that were also in violation and I made a Power-Point presentation that included photographs of the Chevy in parades. I won my case. I've been in bigger cases—but this was by far my most famous." The city fired one last salvo: the code enforcer said that the parking spot had to be clearly delineated. A little paint fixed that. "I'd fought so hard for that truck," Brian concluded, "that I felt it deserved recognition. That's how the brewery got its name."

"Rusty," as the Chevy is affectionately called, is not the brewery's only truck. There are three others which, although they haven't enjoyed the fame of Rusty, are visible at many outdoor events in the area. They've been converted into beer trucks, complete with refrigeration units, and with beer taps along the side. And they have names as well "Rocky," "Bullwinkle," and "Rescue" (a converted first responders' vehicle).

As we chatted, Brian invited me to try a couple of samples of brewer Jon Anderson's beer. "I've never brewed," he remarked. "But I really like good beers. So I've hired the best brewers I can find, and sometimes I make suggestions to them." The first beer, Strawberry Wheat Tonic (4.6 percent ABV), did what a good fruit beer should: it offered subtle hints of the fruit without letting it overpower the beer. The other I tried, Cherry Chocaholic Baltic Porter (7.2 percent), did the same thing. The cherry notes came through the chocolate malts. Although stronger and fuller-bodied than the Tonic, it was lighter than I expected, no doubt because lager yeast had been used.

Our conversation turned to Rusty Truck's involvement with the Lincoln City Community. "We support the local civic organizations," Brian told me. "But one of the best things we do is support local people who need help. When somebody needed a new set of false teeth and couldn't afford them, we paid for them. One time we paid for a bum's funeral and cremation. Another time we helped a person with chemotherapy expenses." When I asked where the money came from, thinking perhaps that Rusty Truck had nights when a portion of the price of each pint sold was donated to a charity, he pointed upward. He wasn't pointing to heaven, but to the ceiling of the roadhouse, where hundreds of dollar bills (and, I learned, larger denominations) were stuck to the ceiling. Customers are invited to give a bill one of the servers who sticks a pin through it, folds it around a quarter and flings it upward. The coin gives weight to the bill and when it hits the ceiling drives the tack into the wood. The quarter falls to the ground. "We take the money down when it's needed," Whitehead explained. "Usually, there's ten thousand dollars thrown up there each year."

Brewer Jon Anderson was away that afternoon, so I made arrangements to return the next day when he could show me the expansions that were taking place in the brewhouse and discuss his beers. I gave one of the servers a dollar bill and he nailed it to the ceiling. As I went out of the swinging saloon doors, I wondered if I had perhaps made a very small contribution toward buying someone else a new set of false teeth.

When I arrived the next morning, Rusty was the only vehicle in the parking lot. I walked around the roadhouse, past "Rocky," "Bullwinkle" and "Rescue," and into the brewery, which was being expanded from a 10-barrel system to a 20. The building also housed 15 fermenters. Beer was being brewed not just for the restaurant, but also for markets in Portland, Salem, and Eugene. It was expected that the distribution area would increase as Rusty Truck beers became more widely known. The installation of a bottling line was being considered.

Head Brewer Jon Anderson, who had been a homebrewer for a dozen years, had come to Rusty Truck to learn the trade at a professional level, studying under one-time Pelican brewer Paul Thomas, who Jon said "has the highest beer IQ of anyone I've ever known." After two years as Thomas's assistant, Anderson took a month's leave of absence to take an intense course at Chicago's prestigious Siebel Institute of Brewing. "It was nine and a half hours a day. We learned the whole process: selecting ingredients, building recipes, brewing, quality control, packaging. We did some practical work at the downtown Chicago Goose Island Brewery." The course over, he returned to Lincoln Beach and, when Thomas moved on, assumed the role of head brewer.

Before discussing some of Rusty Truck's flagship beers, he described the brewery's house style. "We produce beer made by beer drinkers—craft beer drinkers. We tweak styles a little bit, but we want to create sessionable ales; someone can enjoy two or three and not worry about getting home safely." Some of the seasonal ales are more experimental and he used as an example his Saison de Noel (9.0 percent ABV, 25 IBUs). A new take on the traditional summer beer, it included cranberries and winter spices and was aged for several months. He spoke of the saison yeasts he used in the recipe. "People are discovering that you can do very interesting things with saison yeasts that you can't do with the usual ale and lager yeasts. Using them is as close as you can get to spontaneous fermentation."

Not surprisingly, Road Wrecker IPA (7 percent ABV and 70 IBUs) is Rusty Truck's top selling beer. Columbus, Zytos, Centennial and Nugget hops provide not only bitterness, but also citrus and floral notes. Munich malts give balance to what might be an overwhelming hoppy drink. Surprisingly, the second-best seller is Moonlight Ride Blackberry Ale (5.3 percent ABV and 20 IBUs). The tartness of the berries—126 pounds of puree for each ten barrel batch are added post-fermentation—is lessened by the maltiness. It's a kind of blackberry sandwich. Other popular beers include Low Rider Lager (5.5 percent ABV and 15 IBUs), a Mexican-style beer which uses 50 pounds of flaked maize in the mash; Beach Blonde Ale (5.2 percent), a light-bodied crossover beer; and Pacific Grind Espresso Stout (5 percent ABV, 33 IBUs), which uses two and a half pounds of ground coffee in the mash and then adds four gallons of brewed espresso just before kegging.

12. The Small and the Very Large in Newport

Bier One Brewing and Rogue Ales (Newport)

Newport, home of Rogue Ales, the largest brewery I'd visit, and Bier One, one of the smallest, was first settled by non-native peoples in the 1860s. The newcomers soon discovered beds of oysters, established commercial oyster farms, and sent their harvests to high-end restaurants in San Francisco and New York. Commercial fishing developed during the latter part of the nineteenth century, and the area soon became a popular tourist destination, as beaches were developed and luxury hotels built. But it wasn't until the spring of 1882, a few months before the area around Yaquina Bay became officially incorporated as Newport, that the first brewery was built. Two men identified only as Blattner and Brandt began Newport Brewery in 1882. It was renamed Yaquina Bay Brewery in 1886, when it was taken over by Robert Schaibold, who operated it until 1897.

Although the commercial fishing, fish processing, and tourist industries grew, and Newport became an important port, for the nine decades after that, residents and visitors had to be satisfied with beer shipped in from elsewhere (usually Portland). Brewing returned to Newport in 1989, when Rogue Ales, which a year earlier had opened business in Ashland, Oregon, established its second brewery in the coastal town. Since then Rogue has grown to become one of the larger regional breweries in the country, and its beverages are available in all fifty states and several foreign countries. A second brewery, SKW, opened in 2008, but closed after two years. Then, in 2013, Luke and Christina Simonsen started Newport Brewing Company, a garage operation which dispensed its brews at Bier One, a bottle shop and homebrew supply store they operated. In 2015, it produced 72 barrels, less than one tenth of a percent of what Rogue, their very large neighbor, brewed that year. In 2016, Newport Brewing changed its name to Bier One Brewing Company.

What would be one of the busiest days during my beer odyssey would begin with a visit to Bier One, followed by lunch at the original Newport home of Rogue Ales, and finally, a tour of the Rogue production plant and an interview with John Maier, the company's storied, some would say legendary brewer. The words "David and Goliath" came into my mind. David, of course, would be Bier One, and Goliath, Rogue. It would be a story of the little guy working out of his garage taking on a West Coast giant.

Bier One's taphouse was certainly not in a touristy part of the city. Located in the center of town on Highway 101, a half-mile away from the Yaquina Bridge that later in the day would lead me to Rogue's production facility, it's in what would be called an aging, rather than historic, area. It wasn't open when I arrived, but as I got out of the car I noticed that a nearby tavern, with a Bud sign in the window, was open and that someone was going in for a morning libation.

Luke and Christina Simonsen arrived, invited me into Bier One and began discussing their brewery and the role they saw it playing in Newport. I quickly realized that the David and Goliath analogy was incorrect. The two weren't some unknowns trying to bring the neighboring giant to its knees. "We see ourselves as a local business," Luke explained. "We want to be Newport's 'local' just like the places in German towns. We don't have to be in fifty states, and we're not here for just for the tourists. People here like us for this."

Luke and Christina proudly showed me around Bier One, telling me about the paths that led them to the Oregon coast. Local art decorated the walls, a foosball table and old-fashioned looking shuffleboard (sold to them by a long-time customer) stood between tables, and the stools at the bar were made from driftwood and repurposed wood, including the "remains" of broken barstools. "One of our bartenders does this as a hobby," Luke, who used to make custom designed furniture in his garage, explained. The chairs were unique and certainly very local.

Luke had developed a taste for good beer, he admitted, while he was an army brat in Germany. "I began homebrewing when I was 20 and, even though I studied oil painting and sculpture at university, I always thought it would be great to be a brewer." He met Christina, who began university as a Russian history major, before studying to become a pastry chef, at a beer festival in Utah.

"I was working as a volunteer," she remembers. "He came up to my booth and tried to sell me a raffle ticket. I told him. 'No!'" But Luke persisted and, he noted with a smile, "I got her telephone number." She'd grown up with a brother who was a homebrewer. "I was the bottle scrubber," she laughed. She and Luke discovered they had a common interest, and soon after married. When they read in 2009 an advertisement about a bottle-shop, homebrew supply, and taproom for sale in Newport, they made an offer, which was accepted, and moved from the Utah desert to the Oregon coast.

Luke and Christina Simonsen see Bier One, a small homebrew supply store, bottle shop, and taproom, as being "Newport's Local," a neighborhood pub which the area's residents can feel is their own. The Simonsens do not see themselves as being in competition with Rogue, the craft beer giant located across Yaquina Bay.

"We were doing well, but I kept wanting to add a brewery," Luke explained. "I joined the local homebrew club and kept working at my skills. One of the members was John Maier [the head brewer at Rogue], and he helped me a great deal. We turned pro in 2013; we still have guest taps, and people can buy bottles and drink them here for a one dollar corkage fee. But, in the long run, it's more profitable if you make your own beer." Bier One operates out of the Simonsens' garage. "The first year, we produced 69 barrels on a 20-gallon system," Luke remembered. The first brews, a kolsch and a Berliner Weisse, reflected his early love of German brews. These were followed by Smooth Hoperator IPA and a stout.

Asked to discuss the beers he regularly brews, Luke began by remarking: "Variety is the spice of life. It's boring to drink the same beer over and over. I'm small, so I can try new and different things and never be bored." This sense of variety was seen in his description of his Smooth Hoperator IPA (6.5 percent ABV, 60 IBUs), where necessity became the mother of invention. He began by noting that because he didn't have a hop contract, which would insure that he regularly received certain varietals, he had to be flexible. In different batches, he has used, among hop varieties, Columbus, Centennial, Simcoe, Crystal, Amarillo, Citra, and Polaris, while still achieving the floral and citrusy notes he desired. He added that occasionally Rogue Ales, the giant with whom he isn't competing, helped out by loaning him hops.

Conte Blonde, named after Conte McCullough, the architect who designed the Yaquina Bay Bridge, is intended to be a gateway beer. Luke said that the 5 percent ABV, 18 IBUs ale represented his view of what a "super light IPA might be like." The use of wheat and light crystal malts created an easy-drinking, relatively light-bodied beer. His Heffe Me! (5 percent, 14 IBUs), which he emphasized is a true German interpretation of the hefeweissen style, was developed for a German patron of Bier One. "I wanted to make a beer he would like— and he did." A chewy, yeasty beer, it has clove and banana flavors. Alsea Amber (6.6 percent) was the end result of experimentation with a pale ale recipe. "I wanted to brew something like a 1990s pale ale, but then decided to make it different, so I added some chocolate malt."

Luke saved the discussion of his most interesting beer, Berlinerweiss (3.9 percent ABV), until last. This relatively unknown German style—although it has recently been drawing the attention of craft beer aficionados—has, he says, "the taste of a dehydrated apricot." It uses pale malts for a base and adds 30 percent wheat. The result is a tart, slightly sour, light-bodied beer that finishes crisp and clean. In Germany, patrons frequently alter the basic flavor and mouth feel of the beer by adding some type of simple syrup. Among syrups available to fans of the Bier One version of the style are lavender, marionberry, grapefruit, pineapple, and ginger. "Alone, or with the syrup, it's a wonderful introductory beer for people interested in discovering sour beers."

Recently, Bier One upgraded from a 20-gallon to a three-barrel brewing system. "I enjoy having the guest taps at Bier One," Simonsen remarked. "That means there'll always be a lot of variety. But we're gradually easing out of being a bottle store and homebrew supply shop. I want to make sure that we always have plenty of our own brews available." Asked about the future of craft brewing in Newport, he noted that, while Rogue Ales would dominate the area, there was plenty of room for growth. "I hope someday to move brewing operations from my garage to the pub/taproom and to increase the system to seven or ten barrels. And I'd certainly not object to seeing another small brewery open here. Competition makes us all better." He might have added that variety really is the spice of life.

After leaving Bier One, I drove a few blocks south along Highway 101, took the exit just before the bridge and then proceeded along Naterlin Drive and south down a steep hill to South West Bay Street. The street passed through a working waterfront district which was also a tourist destination, where such fish plants as Bornstein's (owned by one of the copartners in Astoria's Buoy Beer Company) stood side-by-side with art galleries, gift stores, and restaurants. My destination was Rogue Ales Public House, where, in 1989, the brewery's Newport operations had been established.

This was the second of three visits to a Rogue establishment I'd make during my travels. Before I'd stood on the bridge in Olympia, I'd stopped at Rogue's Portland, Oregon, headquarters to chat with Brett Joyce, son of cofounder Jack and now president of the company. He'd worked for Rogue, as a dish washer, cleaner, driver, and later assistant pub manager, while he was a high school and university student. "People used to say that I got special treatment because I was the boss's kid. I did," he said with a laugh, and then added, "I got all the dirty jobs."

Our conversation focused mainly on the creation and marketing of the Rogue brand, one of the most interesting elements of which were the accounts of the founding of the brewery's Newport operations and the hiring of brewmaster John Maier. The events seem almost like incidents in a legendary history. As the story goes, in early February 1989, Jack Joyce, a former criminal lawyer and then Nike executive, had been dispatched to the coast by his partners Bob Woodell, Rob Strasser, and Jeff Schultz, to find a second location for the rapidly expanding Rogue Ales brewpub they had started the previous year in Ashland. Joyce was caught in a rare snowstorm that descended upon the coastal town of Newport. As he was looking for a place to shelter he met Mo Niemi, the owner of a very popular chain of seafood restaurants. When she learned of his quest, she told him that she had the ideal location for a brewery, a large garage in a building she owned near her restaurant. The rent would be reasonable, she said, but there would be two conditions. When they opened their brewpub, Jack and his friends would have to display above the bar a large picture of Niemi hunched over in an old four-legged bathtub and, if they didn't go broke, they would be required to "feed the fishermen." In other words, they would give back to the community that was supporting them. The photograph is still found above the bar in all the Rogue public houses (which extend from San Francisco, through Oregon, and up to Issaquah, Washington) and the Rogue Foundation gives generously to area charities.

The choice of the brewer for the Newport plant also involved a chance meeting during a snowstorm. Not too long before his February adventure, Jack Joyce was sitting at a bar in the Denver airport, awaiting the announcement of the departure of his flight to Portland—which had been delayed by a snowstorm. He struck up a conversation with a bearded young man also sitting at the bar.

The young man was John Maier, a brewer for Alaskan Brewery who had grown up in Oregon and wanted to return there, particularly now that the craft beer industry was booming. The two exchanged cards and, after the snow stopped, went their separate ways. When Jack and his partners were firming up their plans for opening a brewery in Newport, he remembered the young man he'd met at the airport. John Maier became the head brewer for the new brewery.

The Newport facility opened in May 1989, and since then there have been two constants. Production and distribution have grown steadily, and the beers John Maier brewed soon began (and continue) to win awards. By 1992, the brewery had been unable to keep up with demand and moved across Yaquina Bay to its present location on the south shore, where expansion has occurred regularly since. In 1996, when a flood severely damaged the original Ashland location, all brewing operations were moved to the coast. Annual number of barrels produced quickly moved into five figures and, then, in 2012, production reached and soon exceeded the 100,000 barrels mark. By 2015, Rogue Ales were available in every state and in 49 other countries.

It didn't take long for John Maier to start winning awards for his beers. Before he'd arrived in Newport, his Alaskan Amber had won two gold medals at the Great American Beer Festival. Then from 1990 to 1992 Rogue Smoke, a rauch beer, won a gold and two silvers, and in 1992, Old Crustacean Barleywine, based on his own award-winning homebrew recipe, earned a silver medal. Over the years, 11 Rogue ales have won 32 Great American Beer Festival medals, including 10 golds. "We were very lucky to get him," Brett Joyce said. "We gave him free rein and then we figured out how to sell the beers."

Maierbock Ale

One of the rooms in Rogue Ale's restaurant on the north side of Yaquina Bay is called "Rogue Gallery." Lining the walls are large blowups of beer labels featuring real people the brewery wishes to honor. The label for Maierbock Ale, named after John Maier, Rogue's first and still head brewer at their Newport operations, features his bearded likeness.

"You can make the best beer in the world, but if people don't buy it you are in trouble." That's a statement frequently made in the craft brewing industry. People having been buying Rogue's very good beers, not just because they're very good, but also because the company has developed very good marketing strategies. That isn't surprising given that the founders were all involved in the sales and marketing for Nike and that Brett, who took over the running of the company in 2006, had worked in similar roles for Nike's chief competitor, Adidas.

The name Rogue had originally signified the area of southern Oregon where the original brewery was situated. But when all the brewery operations moved to Newport, 175 miles north of where the Rogue River reaches the Pacific Ocean, the geographical implications of the name became obsolete. So brewery officials developed a brand around the denotative and connotative meanings of the word Rogue. "Rogue isn't just a beer. It's a brand," Brett Joyce emphasized. "All that we do is to honor the spirit of the Rogue brand." He listed four elements of that brand: world class products, world class packaging, "unique thunder," and community integration. The website states: "The spirit of the Rogue brand, even the name suggests doing things differently, a desire and a willingness to change the status quo." He went on to emphasize the importance of the terms "dare," "risk," and "dream." "When we make decisions, we ask what are we daring, risking, and dreaming? Is what we want to do a good idea for Rogue?"

The company not only declared that the spirit of roguishness animated it, it invited drinkers of its beer to share in that by becoming members of the "Rogue Nation." The card-carrying citizens (who became so by filling out an application on the website and including a picture with the application) were urged to "Rise up" and celebrate the rogue within themselves. "Have a Rogue and see what happens" they were challenged. In early 2016, the website announced that the population of this "Global alliance without borders" had more than three times as many citizens as Greenland. One of the citizens was from Antarctica! "The whole idea was to create a fun framework to make people feel they're part of the company."

This spirit of mischief and unconventionality was extended to brewing several unconventional—one might say "roguish"—beers, "novelty" beers as they are termed by some beer critics. They are what Brett Joyce and his marketing people have referred to as members of the "Collision series," an unusual joining with brands that are themselves somewhat unusual. "There's been a lot of publicity in the last few years about collaboration beers, when two breweries work together to make a special beer. We decided to give the idea a bit of a twist and look for a collaboration with a company that wasn't a brewery," he said. The first of these collisions was with Voodoo Donuts, a very popular company in Portland and Eugene which had created some unusually flavored donuts. As the Voodoo website explained it: "Many breweries had come to Voodoo before in hopes that their beer would wind up in a doughnut. Rogue flipped this notion and proposed an ale inspired by our doughnuts." The first of what the advertising called "The Collision of Crazies" was a beer that included maple and bacon flavors, two of the ingredients found in one of Voodoo's unusual donuts. Another was based on their "Lemon Chiffon Cruller." Rogue Ales also teamed up with the producers of Huy Fong hot chile sauce to create Sriracha HOT Stout—certainly one of the most unusual additive-flavored stouts. Of course, the releases of all these collision beers were well publicized online and in print media. "We do crazy things like that to keep lively and to keep the brand alive," Joyce remarked.

But perhaps the most widely-publicized and roguish of Rogue's very different brews has been "Beard Beer," available on draft and in bottles. "We had been using grain and hops grown on our own farms, and we thought it would be great to make beer with our own yeast. We looked around our farms and the brewery, but didn't discover anything that would work." Then someone jokingly suggested that they look for yeast in head brewer John Maier's beard—which, according to rumor, hadn't been trimmed since the late 1970s. "He'd been professionally brewing for over a quarter of a century, and so some wild yeast must have gotten in there," Brett explained. Nine hairs were clipped from the hirsute masterbrewer's beard and sent to a lab. Traces of yeast were discovered, and from these was cultured the yeast strain used in the beer that was released on April 1, 2013. The release generated tremendous publicity all over the country, including a front page story in the *Wall Street Journal*, a framed copy of which hangs on the wall of Brett's office. A Belgian-style golden ale, it is still available, and labels on bottles containing it bear a picture of Maier with his signature facial hair. The Rogue website includes a blog entitled "John's Beard."

Two extremely important components of the Rogue brand are farms located in the Willamette and Tygh Valleys. In 2007 a severe hop shortage had North American brewers scrambling to acquire enough hops to fill their beer-making needs. Rogue decided that, in order to avoid being caught by future shortages, the company should grow and process its own hops, and, in 2008 purchased land in the Willamette Valley, prime hop growing territory. In later years, they grew pumpkins, marionberries, and jalapeños, harvested hazelnuts from trees they'd planted, and established a large colony of bees. In the Tygh Valley, in eastern Oregon, they raised barley and rye. All of these crops provided ingredients for their beers. The names of the hop varieties developed echoed the idea of the Rogue revolution: Liberty, Revolution, Independence, Freedom, and Rebel. The prime ingredient for one of a very popular fall seasonal beers is "Dream" Pumpkin; the varieties of malt used in some of the beers are Risk and Dare.

The relationship between the finished products and the farms is often described in terms that satirize writings about wine. One website article is titled "No More Pinot Envy." In my visit to Propolis Brewing, Piper Corbett had used the term "terroir" in referring to the unique taste of the beers that used local wild ingredients, and in my visit to de Garde Brewing, Trevor Rogers and I had tossed around the word "airoir" to describe the airborne wild yeasts of the Tillamook area. At Rogue, the word "terroir" is replaced by "dirtoir." "One of our most valuable resources at Rogue farms is our dirt," the website explains. "It all begins in the dirt. We grow beer. When you grow it, you know it."

As our conversation drew to a close, Joyce remarked: "This is the best time in the world to be a beer drinker." When I asked him if selling beer was more fun than selling shoes, he enthusiastically replied: "Way more fun—you can't drink shoes!"

I didn't have to look at street numbers to find the Rogue Ales Public House in Newport, the place where a much younger Brett Joyce had worked as a dishwasher and assistant manager. The plain, white-sided two story building at 748 Southwest Bay Boulevard was decorated with several signs proclaiming its identity. Rogue Museum and Card Room was painted above one set of windows, Rogue Gallery above another. Hanging above one of the doors was a sign reading Rogue Wolf Eel Café. At the entrance to the bar, a placard stated: "No minors beyond this point. Loggers and fishermen welcome." The first part of the statement fulfilled a legal requirement; the second made implicit reference to Mo Niemi's instructions to Jack Joyce on that snowy February 1989 evening.

I found a table near the bar, ordered Kimchi Crab Sliders for lunch and, while I was waiting for my order to arrive, poked into the three other rooms of the Public House. A back room that had once been the home of the 15-barrel brewing system named Howard now housed a pool table. The walls of one of the front rooms became the Rogue Gallery, with large reproductions of faces that had appeared on the bottles of several of the ales. Among them I recognized the legendary Mo Niemi and the equally legendary John Maier, whom I was to meet later that day. When I returned to my table, I was offered a sample of a recently released stout and, as I sipped, looked for but couldn't find the bathtub picture of Niemi that was supposed to be above every Rogue bar. When I asked my server, "Where's Mo?" he pointed to a corner next to the bar. And there she was, crouched in the four legged tub, looking up and smiling. Unfortunately, the print was behind glass and I wasn't able to get a good picture of the brewery's famous benefactress.

Located on the south shore of Newport's Yaquina Bay, the humorously named "Rogue Nation World Headquarters" is a popular destination for beer tourists from across the country and beyond. Visitors walk through the brewery to the restaurant and gift shop, which look out on a marina.

After lunch, I retraced my route to the Yaquina Bay Bridge and crossed it to the south shore. As I pulled into the parking lot of a long industrial building that proclaimed it was "Rogue Nation World Headquarters," I noticed two significant things: first, the large number of out-of-state cars, no doubt many driven by members of the Rogue Nation who had made a pilgrimage to the "capital," second, the construction going on at the far end of the building. Later, I learned that in what was just the latest in a series of renovations and expansions, new warehouse space was being added. Rogue had certainly grown since that day in 1992 when Howard the brewing system had been loaded on a barge and towed to the south shore. In fact, in the last eight years, Rogue's beer production has increased by 50 percent, and Howard has been replaced by a 100-barrel brewhouse. There are now 37 fermentation tanks, including two with 400-barrel capacity.

To reach the restaurant, where I was to meet John Maier, I had, along with people coming for a meal, to pass through an opening at the bottom of a large red cylinder on which was a sign announcing that within, in addition to a restaurant and gift shop, would be found the "Roguesonian Cultural Heritage Interpretive Center & Beerquarium." A winding path led through a forest of fermenting tanks into the restaurant, which looked out on yachts and sailing boats docked at the edge of Yaquina Bay.

The restaurant was nearly empty, but even if it hadn't been, it would have been easy to spot John Maier. He didn't look like any of the members of the Rogue Nation who had made a trip to this brewing Mecca. Instead, he looked exactly like what he was, a working brewer. He wore calf-length rubber boots, tan overalls, and a dark work shirt—standard brewing issue. And even if he had dressed like the tourists, I'd have recognized him by the bushy beard he sported.

Maier recalled that he'd first become interested in beer when he was a teenager and his father had bought home a mixed six pack of beer. "I really liked Anchor Steam Beer," he said. "I wondered what it was that made it taste so different from the mainstream beers." When he went to Los Angeles to work for Hughes Aerospace, he joined the famous Maltose Falcons homebrew club. His beers won many awards and attracted national attention, and wanting to learn more, he decided he'd like to attend the Siebel Institute in Chicago. The higher-ups at Hughes turned down his request for a leave of absence, so he resigned, attended the Institute, and in 1986 began a career as a professional brewer with Alaskan Brewing of Juneau. Alaskan Amber, which he played a large role in developing, won GABF gold medals in 1987, 1988, and 1990. He also used one of his homebrew recipes to develop a smoked porter, which won a GABF silver medal in 1988.

Then came the airport meeting with Jack Joyce, and in the spring of 1989, Maier began brewing for Rogue in Newport. His first beer was based on a maibock recipe and was called Maier Bock. It's still available under the name Dead Guy Ale (6.5 percent ABV, 40 IBUs). The website makes reference to its "malty aroma, rich hearty flavor, and well-balanced finish." While he was developing this and other early beers, John acquired a nickname that has remained attached to him for over a quarter of a century: "More Hops Maier." "You've got to remember that this was before everyone was making very hoppy IPAs. I was accused of wanting to over hop my beers. When we opened, we were really on the cutting edge. We pushed style to the max. Now some people think we're almost tame," he remarked, before stating, "I've retired from the hop wars."

Since then John and his fellow brewers have created dozens and dozens of different beers (close to 250 are on a recent list published by Rate Beer). With so many possible beers to discuss, we agreed to talk about only four, two standbys and two recent releases. Mocha Porter, a regular winner on the international competition circuit, began its life as Newporter, until government regulators insisted that a hyphen be placed after the syllable "new." "It's a recipe I'd been playing around with for years," Maier said of the 5.6 percent, 54 IBU ale. "One time the supplier sent a different malt—a pale chocolate one—which I accidentally used. But it gave the beer a wonderful coffee flavor, so we kept using it." Hazelnut Brown Nectar (5.6 percent ABV, 33 IBUs), the winner of two GABF gold medals, is based on a recipe that Chris Studach, one of Maier's homebrewing friends, had made for an American Homebrewers Association conference in Portland. "I helped him and then brought it to Rogue, where we adjusted the recipe. We use specialty malts to tone down the hazelnut extract." The website referred to it as an English brown with a Northwest twist.

The two newer beers we discussed, Good Chit Pilsner, and Cold Brew IPA, could be called products of Rogue's "dirtoir," using most, if not all, locally sourced ingredients, including hops and malts from Rogue Farms. Good Chit Pilsner, which takes its name from the term applied to barley at the point when germination is about to begin, uses floor malted barley and Liberty hops from the farms, along with a Czech pilsner yeast to produce a golden colored, smooth 5.3 percent ABV, 38 IBU lager that starts with a malt presence and has a crisp hop finish. Cold Brew IPA (7.5 percent, 82 IBUs) blends coffee from Portland's Stumptown Coffee Roasters, with Liberty, Rebel, and Freedom hops and Dare and Risk malts from the farms. Packman, the brewery's proprietary yeast, used in most of Rogue's ales, is also part of the recipe. It is a clean, surprisingly refreshing drink in which neither hops nor coffee dominates. Each of the four beers we discussed, as well as all Rogue ales, use another local ingredient, which is listed on labels as "free range water."

Had anyone overheard our conversation, they would never have guessed that the soft-spoken man with the bushy beard was one of the most decorated craft brewers in the country, and certainly of the hundreds of bearded brewers, the only one whose facial hair had garnered national, even international, attention. He spoke simply of his brewing career as something that gave him satisfaction and a sense of fulfillment. He was certainly pleased that many people had started their careers under his direction and mentioned that they could be found at Fish, Deschutes, Full Sail, Golden Valley, Great Divide, and Amnesia, "to mention a few breweries." There was a sense of pride in his voice when he mentioned that he'd been awarded a lifetime membership in the American Homebrewers Association. "I'm still a homebrewer," he said, noting that he attends meetings of the area club. "It's fun to experiment, to try new things with people who love making beer as much as I do."

13. Forest Brews
and Farmstore Ales:
Seal Rock and Yachats

Wolf Tree Brewery (Seal Rock),
Yachats Brewing (Yachats)

Seal Rock and Yachats, 10 and 23 miles respectively south of Newport, were two of the smallest brewery towns I visited. The former is an unincorporated community marked by a reduced speed zone and a few commercial buildings; the latter is a village with a population of just over seven hundred people. My first stop wasn't even in Seal Rock, but just over five miles east on North Beaver Creek Road, past several small ranches surrounded by hillsides of spruce trees. The second was in a village so small that it extended for only two or three blocks on either side of Highway 101. Small though it was, it was becoming a tourist Mecca and was often referred to as the Oregon coast's "hidden gem."

After I'd been driving up North Beaver Creek Road for twenty minutes or so, it turned into little more than a two track surrounded by forest and I realized that I'd messed up on the directions Joe Hitselberger, brewer/owner of Wolf Tree Brewing, had given me. I back-tracked, asked directions at the first house I saw, and then found my destination. Cattle grazed in nearby fields, and, on the hillside, a man was using a bulldozer to clear away the debris from felled trees. When he saw me standing beside the car, he waved and came down to greet me. It was Joe. He explained that this was a working ranch and that brewing was basically a side activity. In fact, in 2015, he produced only 23 barrels, an amount that ranked Wolf Tree 2,163rd among the country's craft breweries. "Getting a license to establish a commercial brewery on agricultural land was very difficult," he said. "I wasn't allowed to have a taproom; state law won't allow beer tasting on agricultural land. If I was a running a winery it would be okay. But at least that means I'm not distracted by visitors."

The ranch/brewery was on land Hitselberger had grown up on during the 1980s. After studying agriculture at Oregon State University, he travelled to Alaska, where he worked for the state's fish and game department and discovered spruce tip beer. "I really liked it, and when I came back to Oregon to work for the Department of Forestry, I began to make my own spruce beer. I gathered spruce tips from the all trees on the property. Then I realized that there weren't any breweries making spruce beer on a year-around basis, so, in 2013, I opened a brewery, doing 20-gallon batches." He named his brewery Wolf Tree, after the logging term for the tallest tree in the forest. In the case of the forest around Hitselberger ranch, that would be a spruce tree. When he told me the meaning, I was reminded of the term "peckerpole," a reference to the scrawniest tree in a forest and the name of one of the beers from Highway 101 Brewery in Quilcene, Washington.

Hitselberger estimates that 75 percent of Wolf Tree beers include spruce. The flagship beer, Spruce Tip Ale (6.5 percent ABV, 15 IBUs), adds 120 pounds of the tips for each seven-barrel batch. The pale malt base, with added Crystal

On the hill behind Joe Hitselberger, the owner and brewer of Wolf Tree Brewery, is a stand of spruce trees, the tips of which he uses in many of his beers. Because the brewery is located on agricultural land he is unable to have a taproom in the brewery, which is in one of the ranch outbuildings.

and Black malts, creates a sweet brown ale that is complemented by the spruce. No hops are included in the recipe. There is also a version of the spruce ale that has been aged in red wine barrels. Other beers using spruce tips are Tail Hold IPA (6 percent, 60 IBUs), which mixes the tips with hops; Irish Chocolate Stout (5.5 percent), in which the bitterness of the hops is balanced by the sweetness of the spruce; and Donker Boom (6 percent), a Belgian ale that uses spruce and tart cherries and is aged in red wine barrels.

In addition to the ranch's spruce tips, Joe also uses the Cascade, Chinook and Nuggett hops grown on the ranch. They are included in IPAs named after his dogs: Camille's Golden IPA and Camille's Golden Fresh Hop IPA (both 7.5 percent ABV, 80 IBUs), and Cali's Black IPA (6.5 percent, 104 IBUs). Hitselberger has also created Pom el Hefe, a German style wheat beer with pomegranate puree. He plans, as his market expands, to brew saisons and a gose.

It's hard work being the owner, brewer, salesman, and distributor of a small brewery, as well as the owner of a working cattle ranch. Although he admits that the current craft beer bubble may soon burst, he is optimistic that Wolf Tree will be one of the survivors. "We produce some of our own ingredients, including hops and spruce tips, and, of course, the water is free and I don't have to pay rent for brewery space. But the most important thing is that we are a niche brewery. We do have IPAs, but we're a year-around supplier for spruce beer. And the people who own the places that sell our beer really like being able to have something that's local and different."

A couple of hours later, when I parked in front of Yachats Brewery, the sign on the building read "Yachats Brewery, Market, and Farmstore." Although it would soon be shortened to just Yachats Brewery and Farmstore, the three designations signified the unique nature of the place and the stages of its short history. In 2012, Nathan Bernard, a home designer and builder, and his wife, Cecily, decided to start a business that would contribute to the local agricultural scene and that would enable him to spend more time in Yachats with his family. With the economic downturn at the end of this century's first decade, he'd had to travel further and further from Yachats for his business. And so, the couple purchased a vacant building that had been erected in 1965 as a bank but was now vacant, and completely remodeled it, often using recycled and repurposed lumber, along with planks made from trees Nathan had cut down on his own property. The Yachats Farmstore opened that year, selling growing supplies, garden implements, small farm tools, seeds, books on fermentation, gardening, permaculture, and sustainable agriculture, as well as in-house vine-maple smoked tuna and salmon.

A few years before opening the business, Nathan and Charles Porter, a professional brewer and Nathan's fishing buddy, had started a homebrewing

Nathan and Cicely Bernard originally established Yachats Brewing as a farm store to serve the farmers in the area near the small coastal town of Yachats. The brewery has been expanded and the menu items increased, making the brewpub the most important part of the business.

club in Yachats. Then, as the farmstore became successful and a popular community gathering place, Nathan realized that establishing a small brewery and taproom would make it even more popular. By June 2015, they had installed a 20-gallon brewing system and made their first beer, Perpetua Xtra Pale (5.4 percent ABV), an ale named after a local landmark and inspired by Sierra Nevada Pale Ale.

When he added the small brewery, Bernard had plans for enlarging the building and increasing the size of the brewhouse to seven barrels. By the early winter of that year, work began on an addition, which would be in a space literally chiseled out of the hillside behind the building. With expansion would come the need to hire a fulltime brewer and brewery operations director. Nathan still ran other businesses and Charles Porter was the cofounder and owner of Logsdon Farmhouse Ales, located in the Hood River area of north-central Oregon. It was at Logsdon that Bernard located the person he needed. Charlie Van Meter, who had majored in philosophy at university and homebrewed when he wasn't studying, had worked at homebrew supply stores, at Sasquatch Brewing in Portland and at Logsdon. "I had lots of on-the-job training and some wonderful mentors," he told me. One of these mentors was Dave Logsdon, who in addition to having cofounded Full Sail Brewing and Logsdon Farmhouse Ales had founded Wyeast, a laboratory that produced many yeasts used by Oregon brewers. Charlie got a thorough grounding on the use of yeasts and the brewing of saisons. "I fell in love with farmhouse beers and tried different ones whenever I could. I liked the wonderful diversity of flavors in this style."

His wife Jenna Steward, who had majored in nutrition and restaurant management and had homebrewed with him after their marriage, came to head up the business side of the brewery. She had worked managing the beer and wine section of a Whole Foods store and for a beer distributor and a mobile canning and bottling company. At Yachats, she handles graphic design, manages the web site, orders, keeps inventory, and does the paperwork. "I also help Charlie with the brewing and recipe development," she said.

About himself as a brewer, Van Meter remarked, a grin on his face, "I'm a recovering hopaholic. I'm learning with age that balance is important and that you have to make beer people would enjoy having more than two of." That is not to say that Charlie has foresworn brewing big hoppy IPAs. Among those that regularly appear at the taproom are Cone Picker Imperial IPA (9.5 percent ABV), Imperial Black IPA (10.2 percent), along with Thor's Well (7.2 percent) and Pacific Wind (6 percent). However, it is when he names the saisons he has brewed and will soon be brewing at Yachats that a sparkle comes into his eyes. Plum Loyal (5.2 percent) includes plums and lavender; Saismon (6.2 percent), stone fruit; Garden Beer (4.4 percent) sage; Salal Sour Saison (6.6 percent); and Catacea (6.5 percent), Szechwan peppercorns. He's also created Marbled Murrelet Dry Stout (4.8 percent), named after an endangered species of bird that lives high in area forest trees, and Tears of the Innocent Sour Wit (4.5 percent).

As I sat talking with Nathan, Charlie, and Jenna in the fairly cramped taproom/restaurant/store, I could hear construction noises from behind the bar. The new brewery and an expanded kitchen were taking shape. Had I been able to come back in the late spring, when the renovations had been completed, I'd have noticed not only an increase in the size of Yachats (now called Yachats Brewing and Farmstore), but also in the number of beverages available and the number of items on the menu. The website listed thirty taps offering probiotic beverages, meads, ciders, wines, and beers (12 of which had been brewed in-house). Descriptions of menu items frequently used the words organic, gluten-free, in-house, and local.

Less than three years after it opened as a farm store and market, Yachats Brewing and Farmstore has become a very large presence in this small village.

14. A Desert No More: Coos Bay, Gold River, Brookings, Harbor

7 Devils Brewing (Coos Bay), Arch Rock Brewing (Gold River), Chetco Brewing (Brookings), Misty Mountain Brewing (Harbor)

As I came off the Coos Bay Bridge, the thirteenth of the fourteen Conde McCulloch bridges I'd cross, I quickly saw that Coos Bay (called Marshfield until 1944) was very unlike the tourist towns I'd been visiting for the past several days. With a population of 16,182, it was the largest city along the Oregon coast, and the largest I'd stopped in since leaving Port Angeles, Washington. It was a working city, with shipyards, lumber companies, commercial fishing outfits, and the world's largest wood products port. The buildings of the downtown area had not been renovated, retro-style, to lure in tourists; they were fairly plain and functional.

I parked, got disoriented, and asked a passerby where 7 Devils Brewing Company was. She pointed me my way and remarked, "They're good people." The entrance to the brewpub was reached by a short walkway that passed between the outdoor patio and a plot of miniature evergreen trees, what the web site referred to as an "Ocean-Friendly Rain Garden." The website had also said, "Walking through our doors should create the same restorative feelings of walking toward the shore."

The building, which had at various times been a storage warehouse and appliance repair store, had been transformed not just into a taproom, but into a gorgeous art gallery with stained glass windows, a glass-blown chandelier, a copper-topped bar, ceramics and paintings. I would later learn from co-owner Carmen Matthews that the art and furniture had been created by local artists and craftsmen, including his wife and co-owner Annie Pollard, and that to pay the contributors, the brewpub had instituted an "Investor Pint Program." The three hundred people who invested one hundred dollars received a pint glass, free beer twice a week, and the satisfaction of knowing that they had helped make the taproom/restaurant one of the most elegant places to drink in the Coos Bay area. "It made it their pub," Carmen explained.

Carmen and Annie had met at a ceramics class at the local college. "Our friends kept saying that we should get together," he laughed. "One night we were both at a party and they shoved us into an empty room and locked the door. We became friends very quickly!" He didn't say whether the two, who were both homebrewers, exchanged recipes when they were left alone. However, within a couple of months they were homebrewing together. One thing they discovered is that they both felt Coos Bay needed its own brewery and that each had dreamed of starting one. He'd been working as a regional manager for Dutch Brothers, an Oregon-based drive-through coffee franchise company. She was a marine biologist, whose work had taken her as far afield as Antarctica. Both liked surfing, music, and art. "She's a real crafty person," Carmen laughed. "She likes to make things—beer, art work, organic gardens."

"We wanted a pub to celebrate our community and why we lived here. We're not touristy; this is a real town. People are crafty here—we showcase local beer, food, art, and music. The tourists who come in get a taste of the area. Every town needs a brewery—like its own bakery. People want things from closer to home. We love craft products for their authenticity and character. People are getting tired of cookie-cutter places." The emphasis on local was seen in the name they gave to the brewery—7 Devils, a reference to a spectacular recreation area near Coos Bay—and in the names of many the beers, which referred to local landmarks.

The two saved for five years before they leased space in a very rundown building and began renovating. They repurposed and recycled many of the materials they used: an old home entertainment center became part of the bar, the copper from an old water heater the bar counter, old pallets made of South American hardwood became table tops, and the chairs had been salvaged from a long-gone restaurant.

"We set up a pilot brewing system in the summer of 2012 and Annie and I began developing recipes and tweaking them," related Carmen. "When we opened in 2013 with a seven-barrel system, we both brewed; now Annie focuses mainly on recipe development. It was a challenge for a couple of years; neither of us had brewed professionally or run a restaurant. And this wasn't a craft beer drinking community. At first people wondered why our beer was so much warmer than what they were used to drinking. Now, they are learning about the nuances of various styles and about brewery things like cask-conditioned beers and beer engines."

When Carmen Matthews and his now wife Annie Pollard first met, the two homebrewers discovered that each of them had wanted to open a brewpub in Coos Bay. The result is 7 Devils Brewing, which, in addition to serving good beer and food, displays works by local artists and craftspeople.

As he showed me through the brewhouse, which had just been expanded from a seven- to a fifteen-barrel system, Carmen described the beers he and Annie had developed. "Our first beer was Lighthouse Session (4.2 percent ABV, 21 IBUs). It's much lighter on the hops than a session IPA and it has a malty sweetness." The 7 Devils crossover beer is Endless Summer Blonde (5.9 percent, 20 IBUs), the name a tribute to ardent surfer Carmen's favorite movie. "We wanted something that was easy to drink, but had more flavor than the lagers from the macrobrewers." The top seller is Groundswell IPA (6.2 percent, 70 IBUs). The name is a reference to the groundswell of popularity for IPAs that began in the Northwest but had now reached the southern Oregon coast. When he told me that the recipe included Nugget, Apollo, Simcoe, Amarillo, Cascade, Mt. Hood and Citra hops, I remarked that they must create a tsunami of hoppy flavor. He agreed, but went on to add that the ale was quite malty as well. Other 7 Devils beers that were "quite malty as well" included Blacklock Oat Porter (5.4 percent, 34 IBUs), Coal Bank Stout (7.9 percent), and Arago Amber (5.4 percent, 28 IBUs).

There was one beer, not named after either surfing or local landmarks, of which Carmen was very proud: Advocate Ale, a Northwest-style pale ale (5.4 percent, 35 IBUs). Not part of the brewpub's year-round offerings, its release coincides with announcement of the 7 Devils Advocate Award. Both Carmen and Annie have been deeply involved in local service organizations and charity activities, and wanted to recognize other locals who shared their commitment. "It celebrates our fellow citizens who advocate for a better life for all around them. It's for people who fight apathy with action."

As the tour was finishing, Carmen looked around him at the community gathering place he, Annie, and their fellow citizens had created in the rundown shell of a building they'd leased four years earlier. "It's mind blowing," he said enthusiastically. "I'm here in my own brewery—it's a dream come true!"

As I entered Gold Beach, my next destination, I crossed the Isaac Lee Patterson Bridge, the last of the Conde McCullough bridges I'd encounter. Below the bridge flowed the Rogue River, where, in the middle of the nineteenth century, the precious metal that gave the town its name was discovered. Within a decade, most of the gold had been washed away by a flood and the town became a center for logging and commercial fishing operations. As the twentieth century wore on, these two industries gradually faded away, and now Gold Beach was primarily a tourist destination attracting river fishing enthusiasts, hikers, beach combers, and, very recently, beer tourists. In 2013, Arch Rock Brewing began business and quickly started a new gold boom, both with the color of their beer and with the gold medals their brews almost immediately began to win.

Located south of town near Hunter Creek, Arch Rock Brewery is sandwiched between Kerr's Truck and Auto Repair and Hunter Creek Bar and Grill. It's a small building, with a large sliding garage door dominating the front wall, and with a fork lift parked just in front of it. Just as I arrived, so did Larry and Marjie Brennan, the owners of the building and the brewery inside. The couple had moved from the hot, dry desert climate of Phoenix to the evergreen forests and the rivers by the shores of the Pacific Ocean in order to start a cabinet building business. In fact, where the brewery's mash tun and kettle three fermentation tanks stood, lumber and tools were once stored. "Several years ago, the construction business slowed drastically," Larry explained. "There was no house building going on at all around here. I had this building and Marjie and I started thinking about what to do with it. That's when I realized that there weren't any breweries between Newport and Eureka, California. I figured that Gold Beach would be a good location and that this building was just the right size for a small brewery."

Larry knew nothing about setting up a brewery or making beer and real-

When the economic slowdown hit Gold Beach late in the first decade of the new century, Larry and Marjie Brennan decided to transform the building that housed his cabinet-making business into a small brewery. Standing in front of the converted building are (from left) owners Larry and Marjie Brennan, brewery operations director Kristen Smith, and her husband, award-winning brewer James Smith.

ized that if his new business were to be successful, he'd have to hire a brewer—a good one. There might not be any breweries on the south coast, but to sell sufficient beer to be financially viable, they'd have to distribute beyond the immediate area to places where there was a lot of competition. Only well-brewed beers had a chance of making inroads into the market. And that's where James and Kristen Smith came in.

James, who grew up in Salt Lake City, became interested in making beer after he and his "quite liberal" Mormon father watched the movie *Strange Brew*, in which the brewmaster was named Smith. He'd been a homebrewer and had worked at a homebrew supply shop before accepting a job as a keg washer at Salt Lake City's award-winning Uinta Brewing. Within five years he'd become head brewer, with GABF medals to his credit. In 2009 the direction of his professional and personal life changed. As Kristen, who, at the time had been working in quality control at Grand Teton Brewing, another award winning brewery, remembered: "I'd seen James around at the GABF conference and, one evening when I was at a restaurant, he came over and asked if I'd like to join him for a beer later. He's not the kind of person who does things like that, and I'm not a person who usually says yes, but I did." Not too long after, James left Uintas and moved to Victor, Idaho, to take a lesser position at Grand Teton.

"When we saw the ad that Larry and Marjie had placed in probrewer.com, it was over two months old," Kristen said. "But James and I had been talking about working together in a small brewery, so we decided to send an email, and we got invited for an interview." During the meeting, Larry and James each made a statement that, in a sense, meant that the Brennans' planned brewery and the young brewing couple were right for each other. When James asked what beers Larry wanted brewed, the owner replied that the brewer would have complete control and freedom over the making of beer. James said that if he brewed a batch that didn't meet his standards, he'd pour it out. (Kristen noted with pride that that hadn't happened yet.) This seemed to be the ideal owner-brewer relationship and the Smiths were invited to create and run the new brewery.

"They said that they'd get back to us," Marjie recalled. "And then they headed back to Idaho. We were sad and worried; we were afraid that they wouldn't want to come to this isolated little place. But they called us as soon as they got home." She paused, and then added enthusiastically, "This was meant to be."

"It would be a challenge, we knew," Kristen remarked. "Uinta and Grand Teton were very large breweries with a lot of employees. James and I would be the only employees here [there's now a four-days- a-week driver] and the brewery would be a much smaller system than we were used to, only 15 barrels. But we could make the brewery exactly what we wanted and make the beer we wanted the way we wanted it." One of the big difficulties during the startup was transporting equipment along very winding two-lane roads to a relatively remote area. However, the job was finished in 2013 and then, gold (in the form of brewing prizes) was again discovered in Gold Beach.

"We didn't want to drown in a sea of IPAs," Kristen stated when I asked her about Arch Rock's beers. "There were enough of those around in Oregon and a lot of them were very, very good. We thought that there was market for a good lager. So we decided to limit ourselves to a lager and two other core beers: a pale ale and a porter. James wanted clean, dryer, lighter-bodied beer—basic, simple, good beer. He didn't try to reinvent the wheel; he stayed pretty close to style."

Early in 2013, Arch Rock sold its first beer, State of Jefferson Porter (6 percent ABV), named after the area of southern Oregon and northern California that had often been mentioned as a possible new state. It was a brown, light-bodied, smooth ale with chocolate and mocha notes. Lightly hopped, it didn't have the bitterness of many porters. It earned the brewery its first gold medal beer, taking first place at the 2013 North American Beer Awards. Gold Beach Lager (5 percent ABV), Arch Rock's best seller, is, Kristen explained, a cross between a Helles and a Dortmunder, both classic German styles. It is a simple beer, using Hallertau hops, German yeast, and German Wyermann pilsner malt. "But," she said, "it's harder to brew. If you make any mistakes, it's very difficult to hide them." Evidently James didn't make any mistakes with this light gold, crisp, slightly malty lager; it won a gold medal at the Great American Beer Festival in 2014, along with a gold at the North American Beer Awards. "Winning at the Great American Beer Festival got us into Portland," Kristen remembered. "There where are so many IPAs around and everyone was happy to find a good lager."

The last created of the three regulars, Pistol River Pale Ale, named after a river that flows into the ocean a few miles south of the brewery, quickly established itself. At 6 percent ABV, the strongest of the core list, it's a Northwest-style pale ale. "We keep the bitterness down, and we double dry hop it [during fermentation] to add flavor and aroma." The CTZ, Bravo, Nugget, and Centennial hops add citrusy notes to the finish. Pistol River won a gold medal at the 2016 World Beer Cup and helped the brewery win the Very Small Brewery of the Year award there. "By keeping our core list down to three," Kristen remarked, "we can achieve consistency. When places order our beer, they know what to expect." But she went on to add that when there is time and tank space, James does create one-offs, called Brewers Select. These have included IPAs, which are different every time, an Imperial Stout, and an Imperial Red Ale.

While we were talking, several people dropped into the tasting room. Two were locals, one wanting a growler refill, another asking if Arch Rock could supply some beer for an upcoming charity event. Another was a vacationer who had joined the Uintas brew crew sometime after James had left. He was taken to the back where James was in the early stages of brewing a new batch of beer. "We've had visitors from all over the world," Kristen said enthusiastically. "Germany, New Zealand, South Africa."

When James had reached a stage in the process that allowed him to take a few minutes off, he rested his trident shaped brewers' paddle against the mash tun and came outside to pose with Larry, Marjie, and Kristen in front of the big garage doors. He only had a couple of minutes and so I could only ask him a few brief questions. One of these was about the water—was it good form making beer. "Yes, it's really good," he replied. Then he paused before adding: "At least for now." After he'd returned to his duties, climbing the steps to the mash tun, trident gripped firmly in one hand, Kristen elaborated on his remark. The Wild Rivers, which included Hunter Creek, which ran behind the brewery, Chetco River, and Winchuck River, the sources for the brewing water for Arch Rock, Chetco, and Misty Mountain breweries, faced a serious threat. Strip mining companies had made applications to take nickel from the mountains in which the Wild Rivers originated. "Nickel strip mining is probably the most devastating to the environment. When chemicals seep into the surface and ground water, it harms not just brewing water, but everyone's drinking water. It will have a terrible result on the fish in the rivers and all the habitat around them," she explained. Kristen and James have been active in Wild Rivers, Wild Brews, an advocacy group that includes Arch Rock, 7 Devils, Chetco and Misty Mountain breweries. They are spearheading a campaign to have people protest the proposed mining developments to national, state, and local governments. "It's our livelihood, but more important, the health and well-being of the human and natural environment depend on the health of the rivers."

On the way out of Gold River, I crossed the Pistol River, one of the threatened Wild Rivers and the namesake of Arch Rock's pale ale, and then stopped at a viewpoint to look at Arch Rock, one of the last major off-shore landmarks along the way to the California border. The frothy surf surged through the arch in the center of the towering basalt rock. Then, I drove through Brookings, a town of just over 6,300 people, which had once been a company town controlled by the Brookings Lumber and Box Company and had become, since the 1980s, a very popular destination for retirees seeking to relocate from the major metropolitan areas of Oregon and California. At the south end of town, I turned onto the North Branch Chetco River Road, made a left on Yellowbrick Road (which looked very un–Ozian) and stopped at 16883, the home of Chetco Brewing Company and its owners, Mike Frederick and Alex Carr-Frederick. My arrival was announced by the barking of Florence, a vigorously tail-wagging rescue dog. (Both Mike and Alex are ardent supporters of the work of the South Coast Humane Society and donate 10 percent of the profits of their annual Beat the Brewers Relay Run and Block Party to the organization.)

Mike, who had been working on an enlargement project for the brewery, which was located in the garage and in a large adjacent cold storage locker, was the next to greet me. He led me through the brewery and out on to a veranda on which, in addition to outdoor furniture, were a couple of the brewing tanks that had just been replaced and would soon be carted away. His brewing systems had a history that linked Chetco Brewing to two other South Coast breweries. When he was first starting out, he realized his 20-gallon brewing system was not going to be large enough. "James and Kristen of Arch Rock rescued me; they loaned me the 1.5-barrel system that had been James's when he homebrewed.

We couldn't have survived without him." The new 7-barrel system that was being installed had come from 7 Devils in Coos Bay. The brew kettles from both the old and the new systems had the name "Grace," in honor of a benefactress who had left money in her will to support the brewery.

The balcony looked down on the Chetco River, the source of the brewery's and the town's water and a very popular place for river fishermen. It was a warm afternoon and a green sheen on the trees on the opposite bank proclaimed the arrival of spring. When I remarked how idyllic the area was, Mike agreed and said that it was exactly what they had been looking for when, as he put it, he and Alex escaped from Los Angeles. The couple had come to southern California from Minnesota's Twin Cities, and he worked as a message therapist, she as a yoga instructor and real estate agent. In fact, even now, as they owned and managed both the brewery and its downtown taproom, they continued working at these jobs.

Michael Frederick and Alex Carr-Frederick stand on the balcony of their home, which is also the site of their seven-barrel brewhouse. Immediately behind them is a small brewing tank that was removed during expansion and temporarily stored on the deck. The Chetco River, which is the source of their brewing water, flows through the valley below.

Alex, who had been showing a home, joined us on the deck. Mike poured us each a glass of Block and Tackle Stout. "We'd opened in 2013 and early the next year, I decided to enter it in the American-Style Imperial Stout category at the World Beer Cup competition just to see what would happen." The category attracted 60 entries, and Block and Tackle earned a silver medal. "I'd always enjoyed Rogue's Imperial Russian Stout, and I wanted to create something big, heavy, rich, and thick. I fiddled with the recipe until I found just what I wanted. We age it for six months." The web site described the 8.4 percent, 52 IBU beverage as "rich and robust enough to warm you on a fog shrouded boat or windy bluff."

When the couple lived in Minnesota, Alex had enjoyed Moosehead Ale from Canada and the now-defunct Pete's Wicked Ale. Mike confessed to starting his beer drinking life with Old Milwaukee; but he soon graduated to Minnesota's Summit Pale Ale. In California, they developed a fondness for the state's microbrewed ales, and particularly enjoyed Anchor Steam Beer. "I can take the credit for getting him started in homebrewing," Alex said with a laugh. "I gave him a homebrew kit for a present. But he quickly moved beyond that into all-grain brewing. And when we had space, he began to grow hops in the garden." He still does, and many of the hops they use in their ales are home grown, as are the blackberries that form one of the main ingredients for Unite Pink Ale. The brewing hobby sparked in Mike a desire to own a brewery and, when the couple moved to Chetco and noted that there were no breweries operating on the southern coast, they decided to take action. Others had similar ideas and, by the end of 2013, Chetco Brewing was one of three breweries operating along the south coast, turning the oft-called beer desert into a beer garden.

As he showed me his hop garden, Mike remarked, "I really do like hops," and told me about his fondness for Pliny the Elder, a renowned Imperial India pale ale, brewed by Russian River of northern California. "I found clone recipes for it and tinkered with these till I found something I liked." The result was Thunder Rock Imperial IPA, the brewery's top seller. At 8.0 percent ABV and 100 IBUs, it is a big beer, with notes of citrus, pine, and tropical fruit. The names of various hop varieties he grows and uses flow off his tongue—Fuggles, Chinook, Cascade, Glacier, Galena, Centennial, Sterling, Zeus, Magnum, Horizon, and Nugget. (In the fall, he would use eight of these in his fresh hop ale.) "Two hops provide the humorous nickname for one of his IPAs: Willa Nelson, which uses Nelson Sauvin and Willamette hops." In addition to using various combinations of hops, he also enjoys making single hopped IPAs, such as Lilly Brew (6.2 percent, 68 IBUs), which uses Centennial hops, and Summer Salmon (6.2 percent, 71 IBUs), which uses Chinook hops.

Another regular Chetco beer is Unite Pink Pale Ale, a 4.1 percent ABV, 18 IBU beverage that contains a hint of the home grown blackberries included in it. It's a beer created for International Woman's Day. "The Pink Boots Society, an organization of women in the brewing business, sends its members general guidelines each year and encourages them to create something uniquely their own within the framework supplied," Alex explained. "The blackberries don't overwhelm the pale ale; Mike's the king of subtlety." Other regulars include The Chetco Effect, a 5.0 percent, 32 IBU summer ale that is light bodied, clean and crisp; Anastacia's Amber (5.6 percent, 49 IBUs), which has roasted caramel and toasted notes and a dry citrus finish; and Save for Ted, a robust porter (6.1 percent, 28 IBUs). I asked about the names given to some of these beers and found out that they referred to relatives or friends. Anastacia was the nickname of a high school friend, Lilly is a niece and Mike Row (MikeRoe Brew IPA) her dad. Raymond's Fathead Red honored the owner of Vista Pub of Brookings, one of the first local supporters of Chetco Brewing. Ted was a regular customer with a fondness for Porter.

While happily admitting his fondness for creating hoppy beers, Mike does enjoy malty ones as well—there is a brown ale and two porters and stouts on the Chetco beer list. However, whatever the style, one aspect underlies them all, they are all vegan beers. Of course, that means you won't find any oyster stouts or bacon and maple syrup ales. But it's more fundamental and subtle than that. "I'm definitely not going to make a milk stout, because the lactose in that recipe is derived from milk," Mike explained, "And I don't use isinglass or gelatin as a clarifying agent because it's made from animal byproducts; instead I use Spanish moss." Alex added that they'd both been vegetarian and vegan most of their lives and that it seemed important to continue that way as brewers. She remarked that it was part of a philosophy of doing the least harm to the environment and the most good possible. She added that all the snacks served at the taproom are vegan, although most people didn't realize it.

After Chetco Brewing was on firm ground, Mike and Alex decided to open a taproom at the north edge of downtown Brookings. "We didn't want a place that was just somewhere where people could drink our beer, along with our friends' beer, and Oregon wines. We wanted it to be a community gathering place. People could play board games, chat, listen to music, have some of our peanuts, or bring food in with them, and, on nice days, sit on the patio with their dogs." To fund the new venture, the owners created a series of memberships in what they called a "Mugless Mug Club." At the thirty dollar Half Pint level, donors received a t-shirt; at the $125 Full Pint Level, one pint a week for a year; and at the $1,250 Design a Brew level (memberships limited), a person could design a beer recipe, assist Mike in brewing it, and have it named after him or her.

Later that evening, I dropped by the taproom. The long narrow space was fairly crowded, but not noisy. Although there was nobody there called "Norm," it seemed as if most people knew each other's name, and, if they didn't, they were just as friendly to each other. Alex and her assistants greeted customers cheerfully, often asking if they wanted the regular or would like to try something new, from Chetco or another brewery. In one corner, Mike was chatting with Rick White, who was starting a new brewery in Crescent City, 26 miles south across the California border. "Mike has really helped me and made me feel like family," Rick said. "That's the way a craft brewery should be—everyone here, owners, beer makers, servers, patrons, feel they're part of a big extended family. When I open Port O'Pints, that's the way I want my place to be."

Early the next afternoon, I made the short drive south, across the Chetco River through the unincorporated district of Harbor to the Tap Haus of Misty Mountain Brewing. In early 2015, Hanna and Mark Camarillo had fulfilled a dream by establishing a brewery in the large garage in their home in the hills east of Highway 101, and a few months later had opened the Tap Haus next to the highway and a few hundred yards from the ocean. The couple greeted me as I entered and led me to a table that looked out across the highway to the sea, where at periodic intervals we spotted spouts made by migrating whales. The only other occupants of the simple but elegant taproom were a couple who had retired here and had become semi-regular patrons.

Until they'd opened Misty Mountain, Mark and Hanna had also been retirees. "I'd been with the Orange City [California] police department for 25 years," Mark told me. "I knew that I wanted to escape the loud noise and the fast pace of southern California. We'd liked southern Oregon and wanted a place where we weren't far from the ocean and where there were forests and rivers around us—somewhere that was quiet, peaceful, and natural."

As a young man, Mark had developed a fondness for imported beers, particularly German lagers, but gave them up—very briefly—when "lite" beers came on the market. "I was worrying a little about the calories," he laughed. "But then I discovered Firestone Walker and Stone [two award-winning southern California breweries] and forgot about the calories." He became a home-brewer and continued the hobby after the move to Oregon. He, Hanna and their two sons, Mark and Matt, had often discussed the possibility of starting a family microbrewery, but it had remained talk until just a few years ago when a family emergency arose.

Matt had developed problems with the aortic valve of his heart and when the condition worsened, he'd left a brewing job in California, to join his family in Harbor; surgery soon followed. It was while he was recovering at home that the idea of opening a family brewery resurfaced. "We had the space for a small brewing system in our garage and Matt had the experience, so we started the procedures for opening a brewery. There were two other breweries in Brookings, Tight Lines and Chetco, and Wild Rivers Pizza had a taproom here. But we weren't worried about being the new and smallest guys on the block. We'd just do our best, be true to style, and not try to outdo the others."

Although they soon placed their beer in a local sports bar, it turned out to be more of a challenge to get noticed than they expected. Getting to Oregon's many, but often far away, beer festivals was proving difficult. They realized that they needed to open a taproom in a location where they'd be easily accessible the locals and visible to motorists coming from or heading to California, just three miles away. "We needed a place to showcase our beer," Hanna said. "One morning, Mark noticed there was a vacancy in this building and that it was very close to and visible from Highway 101. It used to be a sleep disorder treatment center." The Camarillos didn't sleep on it; that afternoon Hanna wrote a deposit check and gave it to the building's owners.

On October 31, 2015, just over eight months after they'd begun to legally sell beer, they opened the Tap Haus. The use of the word *haus* was both a nod to Mark's early fondness for German beer and an indication that this wasn't just some roadside bar, but a place where people could feel at home, comfortable among friends. Patrons could watch—but not listen to—television. "We don't want it to be noisy; we want people to be able to talk with each other or just sit quietly and look out the window," Hanna explained. "Children are welcome; we even have a special corner for them, with coloring books and games. People can sit on the patio with their dogs."

At this point in our conversation, Hanna excused herself. More patrons had arrived and wanted to order food from a relatively simple menu that included such items as bratwurst and sauerkraut, grilled sandwiches, tacos and nachos. Mark invited me to sample a few of the Misty Mountain brews. The first beer son Matt had created was Grey Pilgrim Pale Ale (5.5 percent ABV, 35 IBUs). "He kept it true to style; it's not over hopped and somewhat malt forward." It was a smooth, rounded beer with a clean finish. The top seller was Weatherhop IPA (6.5 percent, 70 IBUs), made with Citra, Cascade, Perle, and Mt. Hood hops and possessing citrus notes. An imperial version (9.7 percent, 85 IBUs), is not only stronger and hoppier, it has a big grain bill—"To balance out the hops," Mark explained—and has a smokiness and a slight sweetness.

It was when Mark told me the names given to their saison and kölsch, "Rivendale" and "Goldberry," that I understood what the underlying theme for the brewery was, what some of its decorations were, and what the individual names signified. These were places and people from some of the most popular fantasy works of the twentieth century. "Are you J.R.R. Tolkien fans?" I asked, referring to the author of *The Hobbit* and *The Lord of the Rings.* "Hanna loved the books when she was young," he replied. "And the kids too. Matt designed our logo to be to look like a Tolkien design, and we even have one of Tolkien's sayings on the wall." It read: "Not all those who wander are lost." As he told me this, I thought back to one of the first brewery visits I'd made on this trip— to Fish Brewing in Olympia. The Hobbit beers that Fish had brewed were part of a large merchandising plan for a major Hollywood motion picture. Here at Misty Mountain, the Tolkien theme was a celebration of a family's favorite author.

At this point Matt dropped by and talked briefly about his brewing background. "I've been brewing since I was 20," he said, "often with my Dad and my cousin." He sheepishly admitted that he'd once been a drinker of Mickey's Malt Liquor and Miller High Life, but hastened to add that Stone's Double Bastard Ale had made him realize that there was much more than Mickey's or Miller. He'd begun his professional brewing career working on the bottling line at Bayview Brewing, a contract brewery in Orange County, and then moved

Matt Camarillo, brewer for the family-owned Misty Mountain Brewing, stands in front of a map he drew of Tolkien's Middle Earth. The family's love of J.R.R. Tolkien's fantasies inspired the name of the brewery and several of the beers.

on to work in packaging at Hangar 24 in Redlands. "I tried to help the cellarmen as much as I could. I asked a lot of questions, because I wanted to learn as much about the process as I could. I wanted to understand the does and don'ts of brewing on a large scale. It was when I was recovering at home from my surgery that we all made a vow that we'd open our own family brewery."

He talked about Rivendale Saison (7.2 percent ABV, 30 IBUs) which uses blackberries grown in the Camarillos' garden to give a tartness to counteract the Belgian yeast's pepper notes. Goldberry Kolsch (5 percent, 30 IBUs) uses German pilsner malts and is gently hopped to create a clean effervescent drink. Longbottom Lager (5 percent) uses smoked cherry malts to create what Mark referred to as "our version of a smoked Munich Dunkel." Sea of Ruin Imperial Red, even though it is strong (9.0 percent) and hoppy (75 IBUs), is not overwhelming, Matt emphasized. Organic ginger gives it a slight nip, and it has a very velvety finish.

Hanna rejoined us for a few minutes, her kitchen orders filled. The three Camarillos and I sat quietly looking out the windows toward the ocean, sparkling in the late afternoon sunlight. "Look!" Hanna exclaimed. "there's a whale spouting. All this is a wonderful new adventure," she continued. "We do it ourselves. It's about the beer, but it's one hundred percent about family. We share the love we have for each other, one pint at a time."

Conclusion

My beer odyssey, which began on a bridge arching over the Deschutes River, in Tumwater, Washington, near the northern terminus of Highway 101, concluded on a bridge spanning the Winchuck River, three miles as the crow flies from where Highway 101 leaves Oregon and enters northern California. This final destination hadn't been planned. But, while I'd been talking with Mark, Matt, and Hanna Camarillo at the Misty Mountain Tap Haus in Harbor, I mentioned my starting point on the bridge still depicted on Olympia Beer cans. "We have a bridge near our house," Hanna said. "You could come up to our place, see the new brewhouse Matt and Mark are installing, and then we'd take you down to the bridge and you could take photographs."

And so I did. There were many striking contrasts between the bridges and the breweries near them. As I'd stood on that first bridge on a damp, grey, misty morning, I looked at the graffiti covered building that had been the initial home of Olympia Brewery. Started as a family business, it had grown into one of the largest regional breweries in the United States, producing well over a million barrels of beer annually, most of it pale American lager (aka that fizzy, yellow stuff). Then it had been bought by a bigger brewery, the brewery was later closed, and brewing operations contracted out to a Miller plant in Irwindale, California. Local residents still mourned its demise. It many ways, its rise and fall represented that of many twentieth-century American breweries that had prospered and then been overrun in the advance of the megaliths, Anheuser-Busch, Miller, and Coors.

As I stood on the bridge over the Winchuck, sunlight sparkled off the slowly moving waters; the mists that frequently shrouded the mountains and gave the Camarillos' brewery its name had burned off; the sheen of new growth on the riverbank trees gave evidence of the spring to come. The spring growth symbolized to me the bright future of the small brewery up the hill and the futures of so many of the breweries I'd visited. As Olympia had been long ago, they were part of their communities. They brewed a wide variety of beers, most of them unknown to most people a couple of decades ago, and shared them with customers, many of whom felt like family. They weren't out to take over

Not far from the California border, the author stands on a bridge spanning the Winchuck River, the source of brewing water for Misty Mountain Brewing (courtesy of Hanna Camarillo).

the American beer market; they wanted to make a living practicing a craft in which they took great pride.

The Camarillos and I spent a few minutes taking photographs of each other standing on the bridge and then shook hands and said goodbyes.

During my journey of nearly 800 miles, I had visited 36 breweries (one of which, Grove Street Brewhouse in Shelton, Washington, would fold in the summer of 2016). They varied tremendously in size, annual production, and distribution range. Rogue Ales, on the south shore of Yaquinna Bay, produced over 100,000 barrels annually on its 100-barrel system and distributed product to all fifty states, as well as internationally. Several, like Fathom and League Hop Yard Brewery, in Sequim, Washington, a league or so from the shores of the Strait of Juan de Fuca, produced well under 100 barrels a year on systems that were often one barrel or less, and distributed their brews to two or three nearby bars and restaurants.

What was most interesting to me was that 25 of these 36 breweries had begun operations in 2010 or later and that nearly all of them had just completed or were in the midst of expansion projects designed to increase both brewing capacity and the ability to can or bottle beer, thus enabling them not just to meet growing local demand, but also to increase distribution areas.

The town and cities, and in one case, ranch, along Highway 101 in Washington and Oregon were clearly participants in the craft beer boom which had seen the number of breweries in the United States increase by 135 percent between 2010 and 2015. I asked myself why there were so many breweries along Highway 101, often in villages and quite small towns and why most were doing so well that they were in the process of expanding.

The first answer is that the breweries I visited were providing alternatives to the bland pale American lagers that have dominated the beer scene for nearly three-quarters of a century. They have offered what has become the standard range of craft beer ranging from blonde ales, through pales, ambers, reds, and browns, to porters and stouts. Within the recognized styles, the breweries have created a variety of interpretations. A good example is India pale ale, a style which nearly every brewery has at least one or two versions of, ranging from what a friend laughingly called IHBs (Imperial Hop Bombs), high in bitterness and alcoholic content, to session IPAs, which decrease the alcohol levels to five percent ABV or less without sacrificing the nuanced flavors.

In addition to the now well-recognized styles, brewers have rediscovered long-forgotten styles and brewing techniques. German and Belgian wheat beers became very popular early in this century, then such-lesser known styles as saisons and kolschs. European pilsners, relatively ignored in the early days of the craft brewing movement, have made a comeback. And recently such traditional German styles as gose and Berliner Weisse, virtually unknown in America, have begun to appear on the beer lists of many craft breweries and brewpubs. Several breweries have begun barrel aging programs, in which fermented beer is conditioned in containers that have formerly contained wines and alcohol. One of the breweries I visited has resurrected the practice of open fermentation, in which the wort is placed in open vats and exposed to wild, airborne yeasts to begin fermentation; these wild yeasts import distinct flavors to the finished product.

Not only have the craft brewers made available a wonderful range of beers to locals and to visitors to these areas, as well as those lucky enough to live in other areas where they are distributed, they are making superior products. With the obvious exception of the very bland can of California-made Olympia I had on the first evening of my trip, I didn't have a bad beer, and usually I enjoyed very flavorful, very well-made beers. My decidedly amateur judgment was more than confirmed when I surveyed the lists of winners of major beer competitions.

In addition to such large, older and regular medal winning breweries as Fish, Rogue, and Pelican, such smaller and recently established breweries as Arch Rock, Chetco, Buoy, Three Magnets, and Propolis have won medals. Since the conclusion of my trip Fish, Pelican, Arch Rock, Fort George, and Propolis have received recognition at major festivals.

In addition to the quality of the beers I sampled, I was impressed with the taprooms and brewpubs in which they were served. Many, most notably Wet Dog Café and Buoy Beer in Astoria, Pelican in Pacific City, and Misty Mountain in Harbor, offered spectacular views of the rivers or seashores next to which they were located. Others were just a few minutes' walk away from the ocean. The walls of the interiors of many of the taprooms and brewpubs were hung with works by local artists, themed decorations such as ships bells and whistles, portraits of brewers, and mock-ups of labels. Pool and foosball tables, board games, and well-read books provided entertainment. Nearly all of the taprooms/brewpubs featured regular live music afternoons or evenings. And, on days, when the lands along the shores of the Pacific weren't living up to the nickname "Wet Coast," patrons could sit outside on decks and patios or in beer gardens. Clearly, in the taproom and brewpubs along Highway 101, pounding back several cans of mass-produced lager and then driving home to sleep them off wasn't the focus. Drinking a couple of well-made and interesting beers was just part of the enjoyable experience of an afternoon or evening's night out. And if the outing has been an enjoyable one, a patron can order a growler of his or her favorite to take home or buy a souvenir t-shirt, ball cap, or beer glass as a reminder of the experience.

Perhaps the best word to describe the success of many of the craft breweries and brewpubs I visited is "local." The craft beer industry has often been considered a part of the locavore movement, the trend toward the purchase and consumption of locally grown and produced foods. During my journey, I heard the words "airoir," "dirtoir," and "terroir," terms used to explain the significance of the local environment in which products are grown or nurtured. From the "free range water," jokingly listed as one of the ingredients in Rogue Ales to the airborne yeast used to ferment beers, a large numbers of the brewers I visited used local ingredients. The water from Olympia's artesian wells; the hops grown in backyards in Sequim, Washington, or Brookings, Oregon; the wild cherries harvested outside of Port Townsend, Washington; the Sitka spruce tips picked in the hills above Seal Rock, Oregon—each imparted a local quality to beer in which it was one ingredient.

As the locals in the different towns and villages I visited become more and more familiar with and educated about craft beer and its vast difference from the products that come from giant breweries located in places like Milwaukee,

St. Louis, and Golden, they became more appreciative of their local brewers and their "local"—in the traditional English sense of neighborhood brewpub. Here they could sit with friends enjoying a beer that was made only a few dozen yards, or in a couple of cases, a couple of miles away, by people who were part of their community and who used area ingredients as often as possible. And if touring beer geeks or other tourists dropped in for a pint, they were welcomed and made to feel at home.

The owners and brewers worked to make their taprooms or brewpubs part of the community. "We like tourists, and we probably couldn't do without them," one brewer confessed to me. "But we also couldn't survive without a strong local base." They want to establish community gathering places. As Chris Simonsen told me, "We want Bier One to be Newport's local," something different from Rogue Ales, which she respected, but which had become a kind of international beer tourist Mecca. As the theme song from *Cheers* emphasized, "everyone knows your name" in a local taproom. The paintings of local artists that hang on the walls enhance the sense of localness. And the fact that several of the small breweries are family-owned increased the idea of community.

The owners of the places I visited not only created community gathering places, they worked very hard to give back to the community. During my conversations, I asked them to list their community outreach and charitable activities. The number of such activities is too great to list here, but they range from donating beer for organizations to sell at non-profit events to sponsoring activities, to in one case donating money tacked to the brewpub ceiling to worthy local causes.

One of the things I wondered about both before and during my trip was how long the craft brewing boom could continue. Would the bubble burst as it had in the late 1990s, when after a decade of growth, there was a drop in the number of breweries operating followed by a leveling off period? When I asked these questions of the brewers and owners, most were very optimistic. The two main things that could doom a brewery, several brewers told me, were underfunding and, more important, bad beer. Craft beer drinkers had become very knowledgeable and discriminating, particularly in Oregon and Washington. With such good beer available, they didn't have to settle for something inferior. "This is a great time to be a craft brewer and craft beer drinker in America," one of them told me. "Every town should have its brewery."

Certainly in the months after my trip, the boom continued unabated. In the late spring of 2016, three new breweries opened: Public Coast and Pelican Pub in Cannon Beach, Oregon, and Defeat River in Reedsport, Oregon. Four others were well into the startup process—Matchless Brewing (Tumwater, Washington), Keelhaul Brewing (Shelton, Washington), Reach Break (Astoria,

Oregon), and The Horn Public House (Depoe Bay, Oregon). In addition, breweries in planning were listed for Olympia and Hoquiam in Washington State.

As one brewer remarked when I asked about the future of brewing along Highway 101: "The best is yet to come!"

I'll drink to that!

Appendix A:
Directory of Breweries

The following directory includes factual information for 35 of the 36 breweries I visited, along Highway 101 in Oregon and Washington, in the early spring of 2016. (Grove Street Brewhouse in Shelton, Washington, went out of business in the summer of 2016.) Also included are details for Defeat River Brewing (Reedsport, Oregon) and Public Coast Brewing (Cannon Beach, Oregon) which I did not visit and which opened in the summer of 2016. The names and addresses of breweries well into the developmental stage and expected to open later in 2016 or early in 2017 are also listed. First comes a listing of cities hosting breweries, followed by an alphabetical list of the breweries, with details about each.

The information in this directory, which is up to date as of late 2016, is based on facts taken from brewery websites and responses to a questionnaire sent to each brewery. Production figures are those published in the May/June 2016 issue of *The New Brewer*. Each brewery has been sent a completed copy of its directory entry to be checked for any errors and admissions.

The word "menu" following "Food" signifies that the taproom or brewhouse has a food menu and that patrons are not permitted to bring food into the establishment. "BYOF" means "Bring Your Own Food." Patrons are welcome to bring food into or to order take-out to be delivered to the taproom or brewpub.

Cities with Breweries or Brewpubs

Washington

LACEY
O-Town Brewing, Top Rung Brewing

OLYMPIA
Cascadia Homebrew and Brewing, Fish Brewing, McMenamins Spar Café, Three Magnets
    Brewing

PORT ANGELES
Barhop Brewing, Dungeness Brewing

PORT TOWNSEND
Port Townsend Brewing, Propolis Brewing

QUILCENE
101 Brewery and Twana Roadhouse

SEAVIEW
North Jetty Brewing

SEQUIM
Fathom and League Hop Yard Brewery

SHELTON
Keelhaul Brewing (in development)

TUMWATER
Hoh River Brewery, Matchless Brewing (in development), Triceratops Brewing

WESTPORT
Blackbeard's Brewing

Oregon

ASTORIA
Astoria Brewing Company/Wet Dog Café, Buoy Beer Company, Fort George Brewery
    and Public House, Hondo's Brew and Cork, Reach Break Brewing (in development)

BROOKINGS
Chetco Brewing Company, Misty Mountain Brewing and Tap Haus

CANNON BEACH
Bill's Tavern and Brewhouse, Pelican Brewing Company, Public Coast Brewing Company

COOS BAY
7 Devils Brewing Company

DEPOE BAY
The Horn Public House and Brewery

GOLD BEACH
Arch Rock Brewing Company

LINCOLN CITY
McMenamins Lighthouse Brewpub, Rusty Truck Brewing Company

NEWPORT
Bier One Brewing, Rogue Ales/Brewers on the Bay

PACIFIC CITY
Pelican Pub

REEDSPORT
Defeat River Brewery

SEAL ROCK
Wolf Tree Brewery

SEASIDE
Seaside Brewing Company

TILLAMOOK
de Garde Brewing, Pelican Brewing Company

YACHATS
Yachats Brewing

Individual Breweries

7 Devils Brewing Company

247 South Second St., Coos Bay, OR, 97420
541-808-3738; www.7devilsbrewery.com
Founded: 2013
Owners/brewers: Annie Pollard and Carmen Matthews
Brewery size: 15-barrel
2015 Production: 700 barrels
Core beer list: Ground Swell IPA, Endless Summer Blonde, Lighthouse Session Ale, Advocate Pale Ale, Arago Amber, Blacklock Oat Porter, Coalbank Stout
Available in draft, growlers, bottles (seasonal releases)
Distribution area: area taps within 60 miles
Food: menu
Kid friendly: yes *Dog friendly:* yes, on patio
Handicapped accessible: yes
Special events, music nights, etc.: Pub trivia nights, live music, Science Pub (lecture series)
Community involvement: support for local artists and craftspeople

101 Brewery & Twana Roadhouse

294793 U.S. 101, Quilcene, WA, 98376
360-765-6485; www.101brewery.com
Founded 2012
Owner: Melody Bacchus
Brewer: Mark McCrehin
Brewery size: 15-gallon
2015 production: 47 barrels
Core beer list: Hook Tender Honey Brown Ale, Look Out Stout, Peckerpole Pale, Sidewinder White Wheat
Available in draft, growlers
Distribution area: in house and local beer festivals
Food: menu

Kid friendly: yes *Dog Friendly:* no
Handicapped accessible: yes
Special nights, live music, etc.: N/A
Community involvement: sponsor four concerts at Quilcene Historical Museum

Arch Rock Brewing Company

28779 Hunter Creek Loop, Gold Beach, OR, 97444
541-247-0555; www.archrockbeer.com
Founded: 2013
Owners: Larry and Marjie Brennan
Brewer: James Smith
Brewery size: 15-barrel
2015 Production: 1,154 barrels
Core beer list: Gold Beach Lager, Pistol River Pale, State of Jefferson Porter, Brewer's
   Select Series (different style each release)
GABF Medal: Gold Beach Lager (gold, 2014)
Available in draft, growlers
Distribution area: Oregon
Community involvement: member of Wild River, Wild Brews environmental advocacy
   organization; donate product to local charities

Astoria Brewing Company/Wet Dog Café

144 11th St., Astoria, OR, 97103
503-325-6975; www.wetdogcafe.com
Founded: 1997
Owners: Steve and Karen Allen
Brewers: John Dalgren and Chris Olsen
Brewery size: 15-barrel (Astoria production brewery), 4-barrel (Wet Dog Cafe)
2015 Production: 242 barrels
Core beer list: Astoria Old Red-Beard Amber, Astoria Poopdeck Porter, Trolley Stop Stout,
   Astoria Bitter Bitch Imperial IPA, Wet Dog Da Bomb Blonde, Astoria Strawberry
   Blonde, Wet Dog Solar Dog IPA, Wet Dog Volksweissen, Astoria Lincoln Lager,
   Astoria Bad Ass Imperial Oatmeal Stout, Astoria Stone Cold Strong Ale
Available in draft, growlers, cans (Wet Dog only)
Distribution area: Astoria area in Washington and Oregon
Food: menu (Wet Dog Cafe)
Kid Friendly: yes *Dog friendly:* yes, on patio
Handicapped accessible: yes
Special events, live music, etc.: live music Wednesday to Sunday
Community involvement: sponsor Fisher Poets Gathering (February), sponsor Astoria-
   Warrenton Crab and Seafood Festival (April)

Barhop Brewery and Tap Room

124 W. Railroad, Port Angeles, WA, 98362
360-797-1818; www.barhopbrewing.com
Founded: 2010
Owner: Tom Curry
Brewer: Josh Blue

Brewery size: 3-barrel
2015 production: 66 barrels
Core beer list: Citrasonic IPA, FnA IPA, PA 7 Pale Ale, Patio Pale Ale, Redneck Logger
  Pale Ale, Screaming Seagull Pale Ale, Predecessor ESB, Judge Porter, Big Nothin'
  Wheat IPA, Hophead Willie IPA, Winter Hop Imperial Stout, Last Tangelo IPA
Available in draft, growlers
Distribution area: Port Angeles
Food: menu
Kid friendly: yes *Dog friendly:* yes, on patio
Handicapped accessible: yes
Special nights, live music, etc.: Friday night live music

Bier One Brewing
424 SW Coast Highway, Newport, OR, 97365
541-265-4630; www.bier-one.com
Founded: 2013
Owners: Luke and Christina Simonsen
Brewer: Luke Simonsen
Brewery size: 3-barrel
2015 production: 74 barrels
Core beer list: Smooth Hoperator IPA, Three Goats Stout, Berlinerweisse, Luke-cifer
  Imperial Barrel Aged Double Stout, Conde Blonde IPA, Alsea Amber
Available in draft, growlers
Distribution area: at the brewpub only
Food: Menu
Kid friendly: no *Dog friendly:* no
Handicapped accessible: yes
Special events: live music nights, special nights (local art show, costume party, etc.), Super
  Bowl Pot Luck
Community involvement: Coast to Hill Bike Classic (proceeds to local rec center), Brewers
  Memorial Fest (proceeds to Humane Society)

Bill's Tavern and Brewhouse
188 North Hemlock St., Cannon Beach, OR, 97110
503-436-2202; www.billstavernandbrewhouse.com
Founded: 1997
Owners: Ken Campbell and Jim Oyala
Brewers: David Parker and Rich Amacher
Brewery size: 7-barrel
2015 Production: 676 barrels
Core beer list: American Bilsner, ASA's Premium Blonde, Blackberry Beauty, Duck Dive
  Pale Ale, Foggy Notion Weissbier, Ragsdale Porter, Rudy's Red Irish Red
GABF awards: Blackberry Beauty (bronze, 1999), Garden Party Elixir (bronze, 1999),
  Duck Dive Pale Ale (gold, 2004)
Available in draft, growlers
Distribution area: locally
Food: menu
Kid friendly: yes *Dog friendly*: yes, on patio

Handicapped accessible: yes
Special nights, live music, etc. House Band Thursday nights
Community involvement: many local sponsorships and support to Public Radio

Blackbeard's Brewing Company
700 West Ocean Ave., Westport, WA, 98595
360-268-7662; www.blackbeardsbrewing.com
Founded: 2015
Owners: Ryan and Katy Montes de Oca
Brewer: Ryan Montes de Oca
Brewery size: 10-barrel
2015 production: 71 barrels
Core beer list: Ahoy! Amber, Hop Fever IPA, Puffin Porter; Strawberry Blonde, Yo! Ho
    Golden
Distribution areas: at the brewpub
Available in draft, growlers, kegs
Food: menu
Kid friendly: yes *Dog friendly:* yes, on patio
Handicapped accessible: yes
Community involvement: Art Festival, Pirate Daze, Washington Tuna Classic

Buoy Beer Company
1 Eighth St., Astoria, OR, 97103; 503-325-4540 (brewery and restaurant)
42-7th St, #100; 503-468-0800 (office); www.buoybeer.com
Founded: 2014
Owners: Luke Colvin, David Kroening, Andrew Bornstein, Dan Hamilton, Jerry Kasinger
Brewers: Kevin Shaw (head brewer), Dan Hamilton (founding brewer)
Brewery size: 20-barrel; 3-barrel pilot system
2015 Production: 3,125 barrels
Core beer list: Helles, Czech Pilsner, Pale Ale, NE Red Ale, Dunkel, Cream Ale, IPA, Oat-
    meal Stout, Meridian Single Hop IPA, Roggenbier, Cascadia Dark Lager, Golden
    Wheat Hefeweizen, Breakfast Porter, Milk Stout, ESB
GABF award: Dunkel (silver, 2014)
Available in draft, growlers, bottles, cans
Distribution area: Oregon, southern Washington
Food: menu
Kid friendly; yes *Pet friendly:* yes, on patio
Handicapped accessible: yes
Special nights: Trivia night each Wednesday
Community involvement: Pilot Pints for a Purpose: proceeds from beers brewed on pilot
    system to local charities and foundations. Donate swag and kegs to various charities.
    Title sponsor for Run on the River which benefits the Astoria Parks Foundation

Cascadia Homebrew and Brewing Company
211 4th Ave E, Olympia, WA, 98501
360-943-2337; www.cascadiahomebrew.com
Founded: 2015
Owner/Brewer: Chris Emerson

Brewery size: 1-barrel

2015 Production: 60 barrels

Core beer list: Speakeasy SMASH Pale, Respect Your ELDERberry, Butternut Squash Beer, Brambleberry Vanilla Stout on NITRO, Ginger Saison, Gluten-free IPA, Double Rye IPA, Root Gruit

Available in draft, growlers

Distribution area: at the brewery and a few local taps

Food: BYOF

Kid Friendly: yes *Dog friendly:* yes

Handicapped accessible: yes

Special nights, live music, etc.; "Brewgrass" first Thursday of month, "Free Music Friday" second Friday of month, homebrewing classes

Chetco Brewing Company

16883 Yellowbrick Road: Brookings, OR, 97415 (brewery—open by appointment only)

541-661-5347; chetcobrew.com

Tap room: 927 Chetco Ave., Brookings, OR, 97415

Founded: 2013

Owners: Michael Frederick and Alexandra Carr-Frederick

Brewer: Michael Frederick

Brewery size: 7-barrel

2015 production: 204 barrels

Core beer List: Unite Pink Pale, Block and Tackle Stout, Chetco Effect Summer Ale, Chetco Logger Pale Ale, Anastacia's Amber, Lilly Brew Single Hop IPA, Raymond's Fathead Red, Summer Salmon Single Hop IPA, MikeRoe Brew IPA, Willa Nelson IPA, Thunder Rock IPA, Save for Ted Robust Porter, Black Thunder Coffee Stout

Distribution area: Brookings area, Southern Oregon, Portland

Available in growlers and draft

Food: snacks, BYOF

Kid friendly: no *Dog friendly:* yes, on patio

Handicapped accessible: yes

Special nights: live music, new beer release parties

Community involvement: Official brewery of the Siskiyou Mountain Club; active fundraiser for South Coast Humane Society and the Brookings Harbor Food Bank; organizer: Beat the Brewery Relay Team; co-sponsor: Brookings Oktoberfest; Run the Wild Rogue relay; Brookings-Harbor Crabfest; member Wild Rivers, Wild Brews coalition

Defeat River Brewery

473 Fir Ave., Reedsport, OR, 97467

541-808-8862; www.defeatriverbrewery.com

Founded: Summer 2016

Owners: Levi Allen, Trevor Frazier, Herb Hedges

Brewers: Levi Allen, Trevor Frazier

Brewery size: 10-barrel

2015 production: N/A

Core beer list: 1.21 Jigahop! IPA, Beachhead ISA (session ale), Bravest Pale Ale, Communion IRA (red ale), Thor Cascadian Dark Ale, Early October SMASH Ale.

Distribution area: taproom, area taps
Available in: draft, growlers
Food: BYOF
Kid friendly: yes *dog friendly:* no
Handicapped accessible: yes
Special nights, live music, etc., live music, Public Service workers Pint discount (Thursday),
    music nights
Community involvement: sponsor Defeat River History Nights (lectures) at the tap room

de Garde Brewing
114 Ivy Ave., Tillamook, OR, 97141
503-815-1635; www.degardebrewing.com
Founded: 2013
Owner: Linsey Rogers
Brewer: Trevor Rogers
Brewery size: 15-barrel
2015 Production: 1,127 barrels
Core beer list: 200 rotating beers—all wild fermentation; styles include gose, saison,
    Berliner Weisse
Distribution: Limited areas in Oregon, Washington, and California
Available in draft, bottles
Food: n/a
Kid friendly: no *Dog friendly:* no
Handicapped accessible: yes
Community involvement: support New Avenues to Youth (Portland), by cash donations,
    products, and proceeds from a beer dinner, sponsorship of numerous local charitable
    and social organizations

Dungeness Brewing Company
Production brewery only—no taproom or tours
4017 S. Mt. Angeles Rd; Port Angeles, WA, 98362
360-775-1877; www.dungenessbrewing.com
Founded: 2012
Owner: Mic Sager, Kelly Sager
Brewer: Mic Sager
Brewery size: 1-barrel
2015 production: 35 barrels
Core beer list: Agnew Amber, Jalapeño IPA, Kelly's Stout, Railroad Pale Ale, Trail 90 IPA,
    Crab Stout
Available in draft
Distribution area: Port Angeles

Fathom and League Hop Yard Brewery
Production brewery only—no taproom or tours
360 Grandview Drive, Sequim, WA, 98382
360-286-0278; www.fathomandleaguebrewery.com
Founded: 2009
Owner/Brewer: Tom Martin

Brewery Size: 1-barrel

2015 production: 13 barrels

Core beer list: Alderwood Smoked Stout, Dark Edge American Strong Ale, Dungeness Dunkle Weizen, Four Leaf Irish Style Stout, Krabben Kolsch, Mastodon Scotch Ale, Raingold Pilsner

Available in draft

Distribution: Port Angeles and Sequim

Fish Brewing Company/Fish Tale Brew Pub/Leavenworth Biers

515 Jefferson St. SE, Olympia, WA, 98501

1-360-943-6480; www.fishbrewing.com; www.fishtaleales.com, www.leavenworthbiers. com

Founded: 1993

Owner: Sal Leone, major shareholder, President and CEO

Head brewer: Paul Pearson

Brewery Size: 40-barrel

2015 Production: 13,200 barrels

Core beer List: Fish Tale Organic Amber Ale, Fish Tale Organic India Pale Ale, Fish Tale Organic Wild Salmon Pale Ale, Fish Tale Mud Shark Porter, Fish Tale Vicious Circle Amber, Fish Tale Beyond the Pale Ale, Leavenworth Boulder Bend Dunkelweizen, Leavenworth Premium Lager, Leavenworth Whistling Pig Hefeweizen

GABF Medals: Boulder Bend Dunkelweizen (gold, 2011; bronze, 2015, 2016); Whistling Pig Hefeweizen (bronze, 2011), Old Woody (gold, 2007—strong ale)

Available in draft, growlers, cans, bottles

Distribution area: 13 states (mainly Western)

Food: menu

Kid friendly: yes *Dog friendly:* no

Handicapped accessible: yes

Special nights/events: Hosts for annual SLURP (Shellfish Lovers Ultimate Rejuvenation Party) in May with Pacific Coast Shellfish Growers Association; host annual Oktoberfest with live music and special foods; host quarterly Brewers Dinners (with food-beer pairings).

Fort George Brewery and Public House

1483 Duane St., Astoria, OR, 97103

503-325-7468; www.fortgeorgebrewery.com

Founded: 2007

Owners: Jack Harris and Chris Nemlowill

Brewer: Jack Harris

Brewery size: production brewery 30 barrel; pilot brewery 8.5 barrel

2015 Production: 13,783 barrels

Core beer list: Big Guns Session IPA, The Optimist IPA, 1811 Lager, Vortex IPA, Cavatica Stout, 3-Way IPA, Fresh IPA, Java the Hop, Magnanimous IPS, Overdub IPA, Plaid Scotch Ale, Spruce Budd Ale, Suicide Squeeze IPA, Quick Wit, Working Girl Porter, Sunrise Oatmeal Pale ale

Available in draft, growlers, bottles, cans

Distribution area: Washington, Oregon, Idaho

Food: menu

Kid friendly: yes *Dog friendly*: yes, on patio
Handicapped accessible: yes
Special events: Sunday live music, Festival of the Dark Arts (Stout Festival) February, Thursday lecture series, brewer's dinners
Community involvement: Magnanimus Mugs award to deserving community member who raises most money for a charitable cause; Mug Club raises money for charities; Giving Tuesdays (last Tuesday of month), dedicate proceeds and provide a forum for community organizations to raise money and promote themselves.

Hoh River Brewery
2442 Mottman Road SW, Tumwater, WA 98512
360-705-4000; www.hohriverbrewery.com
Founded: 2015
Owner/brewer: John Christopherson
Brewery size: 2-barrel
2015 Production: N/A
Core beer list: Frostbite IPA, qweets IPA, Hoppy Hoh Double IPA, Hawk Hefeweizen, Pacific Beach Pilsner, High Divide Pale Ale, Hoh River Porter, Ruby Beach Red
Available in draft, growlers
Distribution area: Thurston County
Food: snacks
Kid friendly: yes *Dog friendly:* no
Handicapped accessible: yes

Hondo's Brew & Cork
2703 Marine Dr., Astoria, OR, 97102
503-325-2234; www.hondosbrew.net
Founded: 2013
Owner/brewer: R.J. Kiepke
Brewery size: 1-barrel
2015 Production: 19 barrels
Core Beer List: Double Dog IPA, Dry Hopped Belgian Pale, Hellhound Mocha Imperial Stout, Old Yeller Wiezen, Red Dog India Red Ale, Triple Dog Dare Imperial IPA, Dexter Joe's Mocha Porter, Dog Day IPA, CitaWit Belgian Style Witbier, Czesky Dog Pale Lager, Pug Tail Pale, Ho Ho Hondo's Winter Ale, Schnauzer Sour
Available in draft, growlers, bottles
Distribution area: at the taproom
Food: light snacks
Kid Friendly: no *Dog friendly:* yes, on patio
Handicapped accessible: yes
Special events, live music, etc. Open mic Saturday, board games; home brewers' competition (December)

The Horn Public House and Brewery
110 Highway 101, Depoe Bay, OR, 97341
Planned opening late 2016 or early 2017

Keelhaul Brewing
233 1st St., Shelton, WA, 98584

1-360-259-8233; www.keelhaulbrewing.com
Founded: planned opening late 2016, early 2017
Owners: William Handley, Eric McLemore
Brewer: William Handley

Matchless Brewing Company
8108 River Dr. SE, Suite 104, Tumwater, WA, 98501
503-317-3284; www.matchlessbrewing.com
Founded: planned opening late 2016–early 2017
Owners/Brewers: Pat Jansen and Grant Bolt

McMenamins Lighthouse Brewpub
4157 North Highway 101; Lincoln City, OR, 97367
541-994-7238; www.mcmenamins.com/279-lighthouse-brewpub-home
Founded: 1986
Owners: McMenamins, Inc.
Brewer: Gary Stallings
Brewery size: 6-barrel
2015 Production: 662 barrels
Core beer list: Hammerhead IPA, Ruby Raspberry Ale, Terminator Stout, I Can Play
    Porter, Cascade Head Golden Ale, Spring Fever Wheat, Kris Kringle Holiday Ale,
    Irish Stout, Sleepy Hollow Nut Brown, Jam Session India Session Ale
Available in draft, growlers, bottles
Distribution area: at the brewpub and other selected McMenamins locations
Food: menu
Kid friendly: yes *Dog Friendly:* yes, on patio
Handicapped accessible: yes
Special events: Lighthouse Brewfest (August) with all McMenamins breweries represented
Community involvement: sponsors of ArtoberFest at Lincoln Beach Cultural Center

McMenamins Spar Café
114 4th Ave E; Olympia, WA, 98501
360-357-6444; www.mcmenamins.com/spar
Owner: McMenamins, Inc.
Brewer: Brian Lawrence
Founded: 2007
Brewery size: 3-barrels
2015 Production: 6 barrels
Core beer list: Hammerhead Pale Ale, Ruby Ale, Terminator Stout, Cascade Golden Ale,
    Spar-tesian IPA, Sleepy Hollow Brown, Sunbreak IPA, Wilhelm's Nitro Cream Ale,
Available in draft, kegs, growlers, mason jars, bottles
Distribution area: at the brewery
Food: menu
Kid friendly: yes *Dog friendly:* yes, on patio
Handicapped accessible: yes

Misty Mountain Brewing and Tap Haus
15440 Museum Rd. # B, Harbor, OR, 97415
541-813-2599; www.mistymountainbrewing.com

Owners: Mark Camarillo, Hanna Camarillo
Brewer: Matt Camarillo
Founded: 2015
Brewery size: 6-barrel
2015 production: 16 barrels
Core beer List: Goldberry Kolsch, Grey Pilgrim Pale Ale, Rivendale Saison, Longbottom Lager, Buckland Brown Ale, Weatherhop IPA, Black Gate India Black Ale, Sea of Ruin Imperial Red Ale, King Under the Mountain Pumpkin Russian Imperial Stout, Sting Imperial IPA
Available in draft, growlers
Distribution area: south Oregon Coast and inland
Food: menu
Kid friendly: yes *Dog friendly*: yes, on patio
Handicapped Accessible: yes
Special events, live music, etc.: occasional live music, cosponsor of car show with Currie County Cruise Car Club, motorcycle ride ending at Tap Room
Community involvement: Wild Rivers, Wild Brews Coalition (environmental advocacy)

North Jetty Brewing
4200 Pacific Highway, Seaview, WA, 98644
360-642-4234; www.northjettybrewing.com
Founded: 2013
Owners: Erik and Michelle Svendsen
Brewers: Erik and Michelle Svendsen, Kirk Hurd
Brewing size: 10-barrel
2015 Volume: 431 barrels
Core beer list: Cape D IPA, Discovery Coast Coffee Milk Stout, First Crack Pale Ale, Leadbetter Red Scottish Ale, Lights Out Imperial IPA, North Head IPA, Simquinox Hopped Up Dark Ale, Starvation Alley Weissbier, Yellow Boots Kolsch,
Available in draft, growlers, bottles
Distribution areas: Western Washington, Northwest Oregon
Food: BYOF
Kid Friendly: yes *Dog friendly*: no
Handicapped accessible: yes
Special Nights, live music, etc.: Firkin' Friday, Trivia Nights, Live Music, Holidays at the Jetty: Santa and vendors, two weeks before Christmas
Community Involvement: Brewed Straight Amber Ale with local teachers and staff. Fifty cents of every pint goes to Ocean Beach Education Foundation. Fifty cents from the sale each pint of a specially brewed beer, Red Cedar, donated of Friends of Willapa Bay

O-Town Brewing
Production brewery only—no taproom or tours
4414 Montclair Dr. SE, Lacey, WA, 985039
360-701-4706; www.o-townbrewing.com
Founded: 2015
Owners: Neil Meyer, Matt Smith, Bryan Trunnell, Jason Stenzel
Brewers: Neil Meyer, Matt Smith, Bryan Trunnell, Jason Stenzel

Brewery size: 2-barrel
2015 Production: 26 barrels
Core beer list: Brewtarsky -0.0 (German Pale Ale), Going Back to Oly (Helles Bock), Budd Bay IPA, The Hoppy Reverend IPA, Kapitol Kokomo Coconut Porter, Kolsch Kobain, O-Face Imperial IPA, Oly IPA, Oridian's Hammer Baltic Porter, O-Town Marzenbier, O-Town Oktoberfest, Priest Point Porter, Sails 'n' Gunpowder English/Caribbean Strong Ale, South Sound Saison (Heather Farmhouse Ale)
Available in draft
Distribution area: Thurston and Pierce County
Community involvement: participate in four annual festivals where funds go to support various community causes

Pelican Brewing Company

33180 Cape Kiwanda Dr., Pacific City, OR, 97135 (Pub and brewery); 503-965-7007
1708 1st St, Tillamook, OR, 97141 (Production brewery and tap room); 503-842-7007
1371 S. Hemlock St, Cannon Beach, 97110 (pub and brewery); 503-908-3377
www.pelicanbrewing.com
Founded: 1996
Owners: Mary Jones, Darron Welch, Ken Henson, Jeff Schons
Brewers: Darron Welch (brewmaster), Mike McGrath (Pacific City Pub, head brewer), Don McCandless (Cannon Beach)
Brewery size: 30-barrel Tillamook production brewery, 15-barrel Pelican Beach Pub, 10-barrel Cannon Beach
2015 production: 12,988 barrels
Core beer list: Tsunami Stout, Imperial Pelican Ale, Umbrella IPA, McPelican's Ale, Kiwanda Cream Ale, Bad Santa, Flock Wave Pale Ale
GABF Awards: Surfer's Summer Ale (2014, bronze; 2009, silver; 2008, gold; 2004, bronze); Silverspot IPA (2013, silver; 2012, silver); Tsunami Stout (2013, bronze; 2006, gold; 2004, silver; 2000, gold; 1998 bronze); Doryman's Ale (2013, bronze; 2007, gold; 2006, gold; 2005, gold; 1999, gold; 1998, silver): Kiwanda Cream Ale (2013, bronze; 2009, silver; 2007, silver; 2006, gold; 2005, gold; 2003, bronze; 2001, bronze); MacPelican's Ale (2013, bronze; 2006, silver; 2005, silver), MacPelican's Wee Heavy (2015, gold; 2007, gold; 2009, bronze); Mac:Pelican's Brun (2008, bronze); Imperial Pelican Ale (2004, gold; 2001, bronze); Pelicano Extra! (2016, silver)
Available in draft, growlers, bottles
Distribution area: California, Idaho, Hawaii, Nevada, Oregon, Washington, Utah, Vermont; Japan, New Zealand
Food: menu
Kid friendly: all locations; *dog friendly:* just off the patio in Pacific Beach (warm weather)
Handicapped accessible: yes
Special nights, live music, etc.: Three brewer's dinners each year
Community Involvement: "Flock of Pelicans" relay team raises money for American Cancer Association; host community events at the brewery

Port Townsend Brewing Company

330 10th St, Port Townsend, WA, 98368
360-385-9967; www.porttownsendbrewing.com
Founded: 1997

Owners: Kim and Guy Sands
Brewer: Carter Camp
Brewery size: 15-barrel
2015 *Production:* 2,500
Core beer list: Barley Wine, Beast Mode Imperial IPA, Bitter End IPS, Porter, Chet's
    Golden Ale, Hop Diggity IPA, Imperial Porter, Peeping Peater Scotch Ale, Porter,
    Red Barchetta IPA, Reel Amber, Single Hop IPA—Simcoe, Strait Stout, Winter Ale,
    Yoda's Green Tea Golden Ale
Available in draft, growlers, bottles
Distribution area: Puget Sound Region from Whatcom and Skagit Counties down to
    Olympia and back to Port Townsend.
Food: peanuts, BOYF
Kid friendly: no *Dog friendly:* yes, outside in the garden area
Handicapped accessible: yes
Special nights, live music, etc.: live music Sunday afternoons
Community involvement: sponsor many area events including Centrum's Music Series,
    Fiddle Tunes, Jazz and Blues Festivals, Wooden Boat Festival, Shipwrights Regatta,
    Kinetic Skulpture Race, Key City Public Theatre, The Film Festival

Propolis Brewing
2457 Jefferson St., Port Townsend, WA, 98368
360-344-2129; www.propolisbrewing.com
Founded: 2012
Owners: Robert Horner, Piper Corbett
Brewer: Robert Horner
Brewery size: 15-barrel
2015 *Production:* 138 barrels
Core beer list: new beers each month include: Wyrt Farmhouse Stout, Granum Herbal
    Saison Brett, Spruce Golden Saison, Beltane Golden Elderflowers Saison Brett,
    Erthe golden Herbal Saison, Zephyros Golden Elderflower Dryhopped Saison Brett,
    Achillea Farmhouse Dubbel with Yarrow, Hyssop, and Thyme
GABF Awards: Beltane Golden Elderflower Saison Brett (2014, gold), Pi (2016, bronze)
Available in draft, growlers, bottles
Distribution area: Washington, Oregon, California, Idaho, Chicago, British Columbia
Food: BYOF
Kid friendly: Yes *Dog friendly:* yes, on patio
Handicapped accessible: yes
Special events, live music, etc.: occasional music evenings, beer themed dinners
Community involvement: sponsors of area Herb Conference, participate in Taste of Port
    Townsend

Public Coast Brewing
264 Third St., Cannon Beach, OR, 97110
503-436-0285; www.publiccoastbrewing.com
Founded: 2016
Owner: Ryan Snyder
Brewer: Will Leroux

Brewery size: 10-barrel
2016 Production: N/A
Core beer list: The People's Pale Ale, Irish Red, NW Red, OIPA Oswald IPA, '67 Blonde Ale, Black Stack Stout, Uncle Fred's German Wheat, American Brown "Nut Ale."
Available in: draft, growlers, crowlers, cans, bottles
Distribution area: Washington, Oregon
Kid friendly yes *Dog friendly* yes, on patio
Handicapped accessible yes
Food: menu
Special nights, live music, etc.: Friday keg weekly FRESH TAP, live music monthly, or event specific
Community involvement: One dollar from sale of each Save Our Beaches Burger donated to Haystack Rock Awareness program. $40,000 annually donated locally and regionally through Martin Hospitality's Charitable Giving Program

Reach Break Brewing

1343 Duane Street, Astoria, OR, 97103
503-468-0743
Planned opening late 2016 or early 2017
Owners/brewers: Josh Allison, Jared Allison, Finn Parker

Rogue Ales

2320 OSU Drive, Newport, OR, 97365
541-867-3664; www.rogue.com
Founded 1988 (Ashland), 1989 (Newport)
Owner: Brett Joyce
Head Brewer: John Maier
Brewery Size: 100-barrel
2015 Production: 105,961 barrels
Core beer list: over 30 year-round beers including American Amber, Beard Beer, Brutal Bitter Ale, Captain Sig's Northwestern Ale, Chipotle Ale, Chocolate Stout, Dead Guy Ale, Hazelnut Brown Nectar, Irish Style Lager, Honey Kolsch, Mocha Porter, Moramoto Soba Ale, Shakespeare Oatmeal Stout, XS Old Crustacean Barleywine
GABF Awards: Rauch (gold, 1989), Welkommen (silver, 1991, silver, 1992, silver, 1993) Old Crustacean (silver, 1992; gold, 1993; bronze, 2004), Mogul Madness (bronze, 1994), Smoke (gold, 1997; gold, 1997; silver, 1998; silver, 2000; gold, 2011), Chocolate Stout (silver, 2000; silver, 2001), Mocha Porter (bronze, 2001; silver, 2009), Morimoto Soba Ale (silver, 2004), Shakespeare Stout (gold, 2005; bronze, 2010), Russian Imperial Stout (bronze, 2007), Hazelnut Brown Nectar (bronze, 2010; gold, 2011; gold, 2012; gold, 2014; silver, 2015).
Available in draft, growlers, bottles, cans
Distribution area: 50 states and 49 countries
Food: menu
Kid friendly: yes *Dog friendly:* no
Handicapped accessible: yes
Community involvement: Rogue Foundation—supports local charities through money raised at Rogue sponsored events

Rusty Truck Brewing Company
4649 SW Highway 101, Lincoln City, OR, 97367
541-994-7729; www.rustytruckbrewing.com
Owner: Brian Whitehead
Brewer: Jon Anderson
Founded: 2011
Brewery size: 20-barrel
2015 production: 723 barrels
Core beer list: 3 Hop IPA, Beach Blonde Ale, Cruiser Session IPA, Espresso Stout, Fender Bender Amber Ale, Hempeweizen, Low Rider Lager, Moonlight Ride Blackberry Ale, Road Wrecker IPA, Taft Draft Toffee Porter
Distribution area: Oregon
Available in draft, growlers, bottles
Food: menu
Kid friendly: yes *Dog friendly:* yes, on patio
Handicapped accessible: yes
Special events, live music etc.: Live Music Saturday, Bingo Thursday; three antique trucks with refrigeration serve beer at various community events.
Community involvement: Dollars in the ceiling—servers stick pins through bills donated by patrons and throw them onto the ceiling. Each year the money "collected" on the ceiling is donated to charities and needy people. Sponsor of Artober Fest—a beer and art festival

Seaside Brewing Company
851 Broadway St., Seaside, OR, 87138
503-717-5451; www.seasidebrewery.com
Founded: 2012
Owners: Jimmy Griffin and Vince Berg
Brewers: Vince Berg
Brewery size: 15-barrel
2015 Production: 631 barrels
Core beer List: Black Dynamite Stout, Seaside Blonde, Honey Badger Blonde, Lockup IPA, North Coast Seaside Red, Muther Hefer-Weizen, Stormcrow Stout
Available in draft, growlers
Distribution area: Oregon
Food: menu
Kid Friendly: yes *Dog friendly:* yes, on patio
Handicapped Accessible: yes
Special nights, live music, etc.: cosponsor of History and Hops lecture series; Pub Quiz nights, Fish bingo (win fish)
Community involvement: supporter of Seaside Kids, non-profit organization sponsoring children's activities

Three Magnets Brewing Company
600 Franklin St SE, Suite 105; Olympia, WA, 98501
360-972-2481; www.threemagnetsbrewing.com
Founded: 2014

Owners: Nathan and Sara Reilly
Head brewer: Jeff Stokes
Brewery size: 15-barrel
2015 Production: 1,010 barrels
Core beer list: Scherler Gold, Little Juice IPA, 3 Mag Rain IPA, 3 Mag Sun IPA, Brotherhood Brown, 3 Mag Supporters Lager, 1st Anniversary Ale, Old Shook Barleywine, Little Juice IPA, Big Juice IPA
GABF Award: Old Shook Barleywine (bronze, 2015)
Available in draft, growlers, bottles
Distribution area: from Bellingham, WA, to Portland, OR, along the I-5 corridor
Food: menu
Kid friendly: yes *dog friendly:* yes, on patio
Handicapped accessible: yes
Special nights: Seattle Seahawks and Seattle Sounders game nights (raffles and specials), special beer release nights
Community involvement: donations to causes chosen in consultation with beer namesake organizations, free kegs to charity events

Top Rung Brewing Company

8343 Hogum Bay Lane, NE Suite E, Lacey, WA, 98516
360-915-8766; www.toprungbrewing.com
Founded: 2014
Owners: Casey Sobol, Jason Stoltz
Brewer: Jason Stoltz
Brewery size: 10-barrel
2015 Production: 467 barrels
Core beer List: Three-Sixty Red, Lacey Lager, Lacey Dark Lager, Prying Irons IPA, Shift Trade IPA, My Dog Scout Stout, Heavy Irons Double IPA, Raspberry Wheat, Rotating Pale Ale series, Pyrolysis Imperial Stout, Bourbon Barrel Pyrolysis Imperial Stout, Good Jake CDA, Trashed Pumpkin Ale
Available in draft, bottles, growlers
Distribution area: Thurston County and from Seattle to Vancouver, WA.
Food: snacks, BYOF
Kid Friendly: yes *Dog friendly:* yes, on patio
Handicapped accessible: yes
Special nights, live music, etc.: Thirsty Thursday Randall Nights—run a different beer through a Randall containing a special flavoring ingredient
Community involvement: active in local Chamber of Commerce, work with Nisqually Land Trust, part of South Sound Craft Crawl

Triceratops Brewing Company

8036 River Drive SE, Suite 203, Tumwater, WA, 98501
360-480-5626; www.triceratopsbrewing.com
Founded: 2014
Owners: Rob Horn, Kelly Horn
Brewer: Rob Horn
Brewery size: 10-barrel
2015 Production: 7 barrels

Core beer list: Hawthorne Coffee Mill Stout, Rhythm and Rye IPA, Sammy IPA, Straw-
berry Sour, Craftsman Copper Ale, Ben SMASH, Citrasaurus Down Double IPA,
Molly IPA
Available in draft, growlers:
Distribution: Along the I-5 Corridor from Seattle to Portland
Food: BYOF
Kid Friendly: yes *Dog friendly:* yes
Handicapped accessible: Yes

Wolf Tree Brewery
Production brewery only—no taproom or tours
199 N. Wolkau Rd., Seal Rock, O,R 97376
541-563-6181; www.wolftreebrewery.com
Founded: 2013
Owner/Brewer: Joe Hitselberger
Brewery size: 7-barrel
2015 Production: 23 barrels
Core beer list: Spruce Tip Ale, Bull of the Woods Barley Wine, Tail Hold IPA, India Brown
Ale, Pom el Hefe, Camille's Golden IPA, Cali's Black IPA
Available in draft, bottles
Distribution area: western Oregon
Community involvement: donate Tumornator Triple IPA for charity functions

Yachats Brewing
348 Highway 101 North, Yachats, OR, 97498
541-547-3884; www.yachatsbrewing.com
Founded: 2015
Owners: Nathan and Cicely Bernard
Brewer: Charlie Van Meter
Brewery size: 10-barrel
2015 Production: 50 barrels
Core beer list: Perpetua Xtra Pale Ale, Coastal Dark Ale, a seasonal Saison, an IPA, Cetacea
Saison (with Szechuan Peppercorns), Ten Mile Oak Fermented Saison, Cone Picker
Imperial IPA, Jennaration IPA, Marbled Murrelet Dry Stout
Available in draft, bottles
Distribution area: Yachats and southern Oregon coast, Newport, Corvallis, Eugene, Port-
land, Bend
Food: menu
Kid friendly: yes *Dog friendly:* yes, on patio
Handicapped accessible: yes
Special events, live music, etc.: Brewers brunch, brewers' dinners, live music, beerfests, col-
laborations
Community involvement: Donate to Yachats Youth and Family Activity Program and donate
product to other local non-profit organizations

Appendix B:
A Guide to Beer Styles

The following guide to beer styles is divided into three sections: lagers, ales, and specialty beers. Following the description of each style are examples that breweries along Highway 101 have brewed over the last two or three years. Because breweries stop producing some beers and add others, some of the examples may no longer be available, while newer brews will not be included in this guide. In putting together the style descriptions, I have drawn on Randy Mosher's *Tasting Beer: An Insider's Guide to the World's Greatest Drink* (North Adams, MA: Storey Publishing, 2009), Garrett Oliver's *The Brewmaster's Table* (New York: HarperCollins, 2003) and the second edition of Dan Rabin and Carl Forget's *The Dictionary of Beer and Brewing* (Boulder, CO: Brewers Publications, 2008).

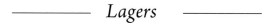

Lagers

Lagers use bottom fermenting yeast, are generally more highly carbonated and are lighter-bodied than most ales. With the development of refrigeration in the later part of the nineteenth century, lagers, which must be brewed and stored at lower temperatures, have become very popular in the United States, where brewers from Germany, the birthplace of most lagers, created versions of the beers of their homeland and established very large breweries and extensive distribution networks. Varieties of North American pale lagers are the most widely-consumed beers in the world.

Bock: a German style beer with much fuller and more robust flavors than most other lagers. Lightly-hopped, it is dark in color—from copper to a deep brown—and medium to full-bodied. Doppelbock is stronger in alcoholic content and more full-bodied and darker than bock. It often has chocolate and coffee notes.

   Bill's Billy Goat Bock, Buoy Doppelbock, Hoh River Spring Bock, Leavenworth Navigator Doppelbock

California Common Beer: (also called Steam Beer because of the hissing sound made when a keg is tapped): developed in California in the nineteenth Century, this beer is amber colored and medium-bodied and is fairly highly hopped. Amber Steam Brewing Company of California has copyrighted the term "steam beer."
Cascadia Steam

Dortmunder Export: pale gold in color, with a medium hop bitterness and a crisp finish. The malts contribute biscuit flavors to this medium-bodied beer.

Dunkel: light to dark brown in color, this is full-bodied lager with rich malty flavors.
Buoy Dunkel, Top Rung Lacey Dark Lager, Yachats Coastal Dark

Helles: from the German word meaning "bright," this medium-bodied beer balances malt and hop flavors. Light straw to golden in color, it often features toasty malt flavors.
Arch Rock Gold Beach Lager, Arch Rock Hunter Creek Jam Helles, Buoy Helles

Kellerbier: an unfiltered, fairly hoppy German style lager that is low in carbonation.
O-Town Grendel Keller, Three Magnets Supporters Kellerbier

Maibock: a golden-colored bock beer available in the later spring (May). It is distinguished by its sweet, malty notes and relatively light body.
Rogue Dead Guy Ale

Marzen/Oktoberfest: brewed in late spring and served in the fall, this is a medium to full-bodied, very malty, copper-colored beer with a crisp hop bitterness.
Fort George Chartzen Charge Marzen, Leavenworth Oktoberfest Ale, O-Town Marzenbier, Rusty Truck Oktoberfest, Yachats Kraut Hammer German Harvest Ale

Mexican Lager *see* **Vienna Lager**

North American Lager: pale in color, very light in body, and highly carbonated, with minimal hop and malt flavors.
Astoria Lincoln Lager, Fort George 1811 Lager, Fort George Booty's Back Lager, Hondo's Czesky Dog Pale Lager, Leavenworth Premium Lager, Misty Mountain Longbottom Lager, Top Rung Lacey Lager

Oktoberfest see **Marzen**

Pilsner: Bohemian (Czech) Pilsner is a light-bodied and clear, light straw to golden colored beer, with a crispness imparted by the hops. It was originally brewed in Pilsen, where the soft water enhanced the crisp cleanness of the beer. German Pilsner is a light to medium-bodied, straw to gold lager that has spicy hop notes and a slight malt sweetness. It is fuller in body and maltier than Czech pilsner.
Bill's American Bilsner, Buoy Czech Pilsner, Buoy IPL (imperial pilsner), Fathom and League Raingold Pilsner, Hoh River Pacific Beach Pilsner, Leavenworth Premium Lager, Rogue Good Chit Pilsner, Rogue Moromito Imperial Pilsner, Rusty Truck 50th Anniversary Pilsner, Three Magnets 13 Czech Style Pilsner, Three Magnets Proto Pilsner,

Rauchbier: from the German "rauch" for smoke, a dark-colored lager using malt roasted over open fires to impart a smoky flavor.
Rogue Smoke Ale

Schwarzbier: from the German word for "black," a very dark-colored, light-to-medium-bodied beer. The roasted barley malts impart chocolaty flavors that are balanced with a low to medium hop bitterness.

    Buoy Schwarzbier, Leavenworth Bakke Hill Black Lager, Rogue Black Brutal, Rogue Farms Dirtoir Black Lager, Three Magnets 14 Black Lager

Steam Beer *see* **California Common**

Vienna Lager: medium-bodied and reddish-brown to copper, this lager has a malt sweetness balanced with a clean, crisp, but not too strong, hop bitterness. Mexican lagers are often a variation of the Vienna lager style.

    Rusty Truck Low Rider Lager

Weissenbock: a dark, malty wheat beer with a fairly high alcoholic content.

    Leavenworth Blackbird Island Hopenweizen

Ales

Using top fermenting yeast, ales do not require the cooler temperatures for fermenting and conditioning that lagers do, and the brewing cycles are much shorter. Generally speaking, ales are fuller-bodied, darker in color, and richer and more robust in flavor. When the craft brewing movement began in the late 1970s and early 1980s, most craft brewers produced ales, offering beers that were different in taste from lagers made by the megabrewers.

Alt Bier: from the German word meaning "old" (traditional), this copper to brown ale has toasted malty flavors balanced by hop notes that help to create a clean, crisp finish.

    Leavenworth Eight Mile Alt

Amber Ale: this copper to light brown beer has been called a "darker fuller-bodied pale ale." It maintains a balance between caramel malt notes and citrusy hop flavors.

    7 Devils Arago Amber, Astoria Old Red Beard Amber, Bier One Alsea Amber, Blackbeard's Ahoy! Amber, Dungeness Agnew Amber, Fish Tale Organic Amber Ale, Fish Tale Vicous Circle Amber, Fort George Red Tide Imperial Red Ale, Port Townsend Reel Amber, Rogue American Amber, Rogue Dry Hopped St. Rogue Red Ale, Rogue Santa's Private Reserve, Rusty Truck Fender Bender Amber Ale, Seaside North Coast Seaside Red, Three Magnets Munich Meridian SMASH, Top Rung 350 Red

American Blonde/Golden Ale: lightly to moderately-hopped, this straw-golden colored blonde beverage is a light-bodied and crisp beer often offered as a "cross-over" beer to newcomers to craft beer.

    7 Devils Lighthouse Session Ale, Astoria Da Bomb Blonde, Seaside Blonde, Bill's ASA's Premium Blonde, Chetco The Chetco Effect, Fishtale Blonde Ale, McMenamins Hills Goldstar, McMenamins Lighthouse Cascade Head Ale, O-Town Burfoot Easy Blonde, Pelican Surfers Summer Ale, Port Townsend Chet's Gold Golden Ale, Public Coast Blonde Ale, Rogue Oregon Golden Ale, Rusty Truck Beach Blonde Ale, Top Rung Hosechaser Blonde

American Dark Ale (aka Cascadian Dark Ale/Black IPA): A recently-developed American style, this dark brown to black colored beer combines roasty malt flavors with a strong hop presence.

Arch Rock Brewer's Select Series #2—Trident Black IPA, Defeat River Thor Cascadian Dark Ale, Fort George Grateful Death Zythos Black IPA, Fort George Next Adventure Black IPA, North Jetty Simquinox Hopped Up Dark Ale, Pelican Bad Santa, Fish Reel Ales Swordfish Double Cascadian Dark Ale, Rusty Truck Simcoe CDA, Three Magnets Black is the New Black Double IPA, Top Rung Good Jake CDA, Wolf Tree India Brown Ale

American Strong Ale: ales noted for their higher alcoholic content, usually above 7 percent ABV

Astoria Stone Cold Strong Ale. Buoy Winter Ale, Fathom and League Dark Edge Ale, Fort George Santa's Dinner Jacket, Hondo's Ho Ho Hondo's Winter Ale, Port Townsend Winter Ale, Rogue Imperial Youngers Special Bitter, Rogue Monk Madness

American Wheat Ale: an American version of *hefeweizen* that is frequently filtered.

101 Brewery Sidewinder White Wheat, McMenamins Lighthouse Whaler's Wheat

Barley Wine: high in alcoholic content (usually over 10 percent ABV), this has been called a "sipping beer." It is full-bodied and dark brown in color and has complex malt flavors that include caramel, toasty, and fruity notes.

Bill's Ole 1400 Barleywine, Fort George Balzac's Barleywine, Fort George Packy's Barleywine, McMenamins Lighthouse The Commodore's Reserve, Pelican Mother of All Storms, Pelican Stormwatchers Winterfest, Port Townsend Barley Wine, Reel Ales 102 Highly-Hopped Barley Wine, Rogue XS Old Custacean Barleywine, Rusty Truck Barley Wine, Three Magnets Old Skook Barleywine, Wolf Tree Bull of the Woods Barley Wine, Yachats Heceta Lightkeeper Barleywine

Belgian Blonde/Golden Ale: light to medium-bodied, gold to deep amber in color, this ale has a malty sweetness, spicy notes, and moderate hoppiness.

Pelican Ankle-Buster Ale, Rogue Beard Beer

Belgian Dark Ale: ranging in color from amber to garnet, this medium-bodied beer balances dry and spicy notes with rich malty sweetness.

Belgian India Pale Ale *see* **India pale ale**

Belgian Strong Ale: stronger in flavor and alcoholic content and fuller in body than Belgian Dark.

Pelican Golden Pelican, Pelican Le Pelican Brun

Berliner Weisse: crisp, low alcohol (usually under 5 percent ABV) wheat beer, with tart, sour, and citrusy notes.

Bier One Berliner Weisse, de Garde Bu Weisse, de Garde Imperial Bu Weisse, de Garde Imperial Hop Bu, Three Magnets Secret Sour

Bitter: The beer that is most often associated with an evening at an English pub, it has a balance between malt sweetness and hop bitterness, with earthy, nutty, and grainy flavors. Light-bodied and gold to copper in color, it is low in carbonation and in alcoholic content (often under 5 percent ABV). ESB (Extra Special Bitter) is more full-bodied and higher in alcoholic content than Bitter. Although it has more bitterness than Bitter, rich malty flavors dominate. Dark gold to copper in color, it is low in carbonation.

Astoria ESB, Barhop Predecessor ESB, Buoy Premium Bitter, McMenamins Lighthouse Boiler Bay ESB, Pelican Nestucca ESB, Rogue Youngers Special Bitter

Brown Ale: brown ale is noted for its rich malt flavors, including nutty, toffee, and chocolate notes. This medium-bodied beer is generally sweet, although moderate hopping prevents the sweetness from becoming cloying.

Barhop Summer Brown, Fort George Nut Brown Red Ale, McMenamins Lighthouse Sleepy Hollow Nut Brown, Misty Mountain Buckland Brown Ale, Pelican Dorymans Dark Ale, Port Townsend Browner's Brown Ale, Public Coast American Brown Nut Ale, Rogue Farms Fresh Roast Ale, Rogue Hazelnut Brown Nectar, Seaside 5 Mil Winter Ale, Three Magnets Estate Brown Ale, Three Magnets Brotherhood Brown

Cream Ale: straw to pale gold in color, this light-bodied ale is high in carbonation but low in hop bitterness and has a malty sweetness.

Buoy Cream Ale, McMenamins Wilhelm's Nitro Cream Ale, Pelican Kiwanda Cream Ale

Dark Mild: a popular session beer which is light to medium-bodied and gold to dark brown in color. Fairly low in alcohol (usually under 5 percent ABV) and in carbonation, it has almost no hop presence. Sweet chocolate and caramel malt flavors dominate.

Dubbel: a Belgian ale noted for its rich malty flavors and spicy notes. Dark amber to brown, it is lightly hopped. Generally sweet to the taste, with a light to moderate bitterness, it has a dry finish.

Propolis Achillea Farmhouse Dubbel with Yarrow, Hyssop, and Thyme; Propolis Wendas Farmhouse Dubbel with Wild Heather; Propolis Urtica Farmhouse Dubbel with Wild Nettles

Dunkelweizen: a wheat beer that uses dark malts and is sweeter than hefeweizen.

Fathom and League Dungeness Dunkie Weizen, Leavenworth Boulder Bend Dunkelweizen

English Strong Ale: amber to red in color, with malty and fruity flavors and a noticeable alcohol presence: O-Town Sails 'n' Gunpowder

Extra Special Bitter (ESB) *see* **Bitter**

Flanders oud bruin: this centuries-old Belgian style is light to medium in body and deep copper to brown in color. It is both sweet and spicy. The use of burnt sugar contributes to the sweetness, while the yeasts and such additives as pepper provide spicy notes.

Golden Ale *see* **American Blonde/Golden Ale**

Gose: pronounced gos-uh, this low-alcohol German wheat beer is crisp and tart, with salty notes.

de Garde Amarillo Hose, de Garde Citra Hose, de Garde Hose, de Garde Nelson Hose

Hefeweizen: from the German words for "yeast" and "wheat," this pale to amber colored ale has been called "liquid bread." Generally close to 50 percent of the malt used is wheat. Highly carbonated, it has virtually no hop character, but does have banana and clove notes. Because it is unfiltered, it has a hazy appearance.

Arch Rock Brewer's Select Series $5—Banana Belt, Astoria Volksweissen, Bill's Foggy Notion Weissbier, Cascadia Heffe, Hoh River Hawk Hefeweizen, Hondo's Old Yeller Wiezen, Leavenworth Whistling Pig Hefeweizen, Public Coast Uncle Fred's German Wheat, Rogue MoM Hefeweizen, Rusty Truck Hefeweizen, Seaside Muther Hefer-Weizen

India Pale Ale (IPA): this pale gold to amber ale is more heavily hopped than are pale ales. In English IPAs, the hop influence is moderated somewhat by the malts, which add bready, caramel notes. American IPAs are much more aggressively hopped, increasing the bitterness and also adding citrusy and floral notes. Double or Imperial IPAs are fuller-bodied, intensely hoppy, and higher in alcoholic content. Session IPA, a newer version of the style, is lower in alcoholic strength.

7 Devils Groundswell IPA, 7 Devils Symphonic ISA, Arch Rock Brewer's Select Series #3—Adipose IPA, Astoria Bitter Bitch Imperial IPA, Astoria Ichiban IPA, Astoria Solar Dog IPA, Barhop FnA/IPA, Bier One Brewing Smooth Hoperator IPA, Bill's Evil Twin IPA, Bill's The Stranger IPA, Blackbeard's Hop Fever, IPA, Buoy IPA, Buoy Kettle Demon IPA, Buoy Single Hop Centenial IPA, Buoy Single Hop Galaxy IPA, Chetco Chinooker IPA, Chetco Lilly Brew Single Hop IPA, Chetco Summer Salmon IPA, Chetco Thunder Rock IIPA, Chetco Thunder Rock IPA, Chetco Raymond's Fathead Red IPA, Chetco Willa Nelson IPA, Chetcoe MikeRoe IPA, Defeat River 1.21 Jigahop! IPA, Defeat River Beachhead ISA, Fish Tale Organic India Pale Ale, Fish Tale Organic Winterfish Ale, Fort George 3 Way IPA, Fort George Beta IPA 6.1, Fort George Omega Tex Double IPA, Fort George Overdub IPA, Fort George Roses on Roses XVIth Chapel Imperial IPA, Fort George Suicide Squeeze IPA, Fort George the Optimist IPA, Fort George Vortex IPA, Hoh River Hoppy Hoh Imperial IPA, Hoh River Hoh Frostbite IPA, Hoh Qweets IPA, Hondo's Double Dog IPA, Hondo's Triple Dog Dare Imperial IPA, Hondo's Dog Day IPA, McMenamins Lighthouse Over the Hop IPA, McMenamins Spar-tesian IPA, Misty Mountain Black Gate Black Rye IPA, Bier One Brewing Conte Blonde IPA, Wolf Tree Camille's Golden IPA, North Jetty Cape D IPA, North Jetty Lights Out Double IPA, North Jetty North Head IPA, Westport King Tide IPA, O-Town Budd Bay IPA, O-Town O-Face IPA, O-Town the Hoppy Reverend IPA, Pelican Belgian IPA, Pelican Imperial Pale Ale, Pelican Red Lantern IPA, Pelican Silverspot IPA, Pelican Umbrella, Port Townsend Hop Diggidy IPA, Port Townsend Imperial India Pale Ale, Port Townsend Glasskisser Imperial IPA, Public Coast Oswald IPA, Rogue Captain Sigs Deadliest Ale, Rogue Farms 4 Hop IPA, Rogue Farms 6 Hop IPA, Rogue Nation Brutal India Pale Ale, Rogue XS Imperial India Pale Ale, Rusty Truck Cruiser Session IPA, Rusty Truck Amarillo Wheat IPA, Rusty Truck McKay's Cascade Harvest Fresh Hop IPA, Rusty Truck Pedal to the Metal Double IPA, Rusty Truck Road Wrecker IPA, Seaside Lock Down Double IPA, Seaside Lock Up IPA, Three Magnets 2X (Imperial) IPA, Three Magnets 3 Mag Rain IPA, Three Magnets 3 Mag Sun IPA, Three Magnets Big Juice Double IPA, Three Magnets Session IPA, Top Rung Heavy Irons IPA, Top Rung Prying Irons IPA, Top Rung Shift Trade IPA, Top Rung Initiative ISA, Triceratops Sammy IPA, Triceratops Turok Brett IPA, Triceratops El Dorado Wet Hop IPA, Triceratops Citrasaurus Down

Double IPA, Triceratops Molly IPA, Triceratops Rhythm and Rye IPA, Wolf Tree Tail Hold IPA, Yachats Cone Picker Imperial IPA, Yachats Jenne's IPA

Irish Stout *see* **Stout**

Kolsch: originally brewed in Koln, Germany, this beer has been jokingly referred to as "the ale that wishes it were a lager," because of its light body, pale color, and high carbonation. It balances gentle hop and malt flavors and has a crisp mouth feel and a dry finish.

Fathom and League Krabben Kolsch, Westport Kaleidoscope Kolsch, Misty Mountain Kolsch, North Jetty Yellow Boots Kolsch, O-Town Kolsch Kobain, Yachats Up River Kolsch

Kristalweizen: a clear, filtered, straw-to-light-amber version of hefeweizen.

Lambic: this 400-year-old Belgian style ale is unusual in that its fermentation process is natural or spontaneous, using wild yeast that is floating in the air. It has been described as fruity, earthy, sour or tart, and very dry. Gold to amber in color, it is light-bodied and low in carbonation. Unmalted wheat is used in the brewing process. Sometimes brewers will blend old (aged) lambic with young limbic to create a beer called Gueuze, a dry, fruity, effervescent beer. In fruit lambics, whole fruits are added after the start of fermentation and the resulting mixture aged in oak or chestnut barrels. *Kriek* uses cherries; *Framboise,* raspberries, *Peche,* peaches, and *Cassis,* black currants.

de Garde The Archer (with grapes)

Oatmeal Stout *see* **Stout**

Pale Ale: this gold to amber ale, which was much paler than the popular brown ales and porters of the late eighteenth century, balances nutty, caramel malt notes with a noticeable hop bitterness. English style pale ale is more earthy in flavor as contrasted to West Coast style American pale ale, which has fuller hop bitterness, flavor, and aroma. Both are crisp and have a dry finish. Belgian pale ale is less bitter than the other two and is lighter-bodied and has some malty sweetness. Many brewers are now creating single hop pale ales to highlight the unique characteristics of specific varieties of hops.

7 Devils Advocate Pale Ale, 101Brewery Peckerpole Pale Ale, Barhop PA 7, Barhop Redneck Logger Pale, Bill's Duck Dive Pale Ale, Buoy Pale Ale, Cascadia Speakeasy SMASH, Chetco Logger Pale Ale, Defeat River Bravest Pale Ale, Dungeness Railroad Pale Ale, Fathom and League Olympic Peninsula Ale, Fish Tale Organic Wild Salmon Pale Ale, Fort George Sunrise Oatmeal Pale Ale, Fort George Tender Loving Empire NWPA, Fort George Vertigo Effect Pale Ale, Hoh River Pale Ale, Hondo's Dry Hopped Belgium Pale, Hondo's Pugtail Pale, Hondo's Runnin' Late Pale, Hondo's Pacifica Pale, McMenamins Lighthouse Hammerhead Pale Ale, Misty Mountain Double Pale Ale, O-town Brewtarsky (Belgian) Pale, Pelican Elemental Ale, Pelican Flock Wave Pale Ale, Pelican Seahops Pale Ale, Port Townsend S.H.I.P Single Hop Imagination Ale, Public Coast The People's Pale Ale, Rogue Farms OREgasmic Ale, Rogue Farms Single Malt Ale, Rogue Wasted Sea Star Purple Pale Ale, Rusty Truck All F(uggl)'d Up English Pale Ale, Seaside Simcoe Pale Ale, Three Magnets Best English Pale Ale, Three Magnets Eldorado and Amarillo Wet Hop Pale Ale, Three Magnets English Summer Ale, Three Magnets Galaxian

Pale Ale, Three Magnets Golden Mandarina SMASH, Three Magnets 10 Minute Pale Ale, Top Rung Chinook the Hop Pale, Top Rung Comet the Hop Pale, Top Rung Simcoe the Hop Pale, Top Rung Wet Line Fresh Hop Pale Ale, Top Rung Falconer's Flight 7Cs Pale Ale, Yachats Perpetua Xtra Pale Ale, Yachats X-Pale Experimental Hop Pale Ale

Porter: named after the late–eighteenth-century London workers for whom it was originally brewed, this brown to black-colored and full-bodied ale uses several malts to create a complex variety of flavors. Relatively low in alcohol, it is moderately bitter. Baltic porters have higher alcohol content.

7 Devils Blacklock Oat Porter, Arch Rock State of Jefferson Porter, Barhop Judge Porter, Bill's Ragsdale Porter, Blackbeard's Puffin Porter, Buoy Porter, Chetco Very Berry Porter, Chetco Save for Ted Robust Porter, Fishtale Mudshark Porter, Fort George Demeter's Porter, Fort George Panamax Porter, Fort George Vladimir Gluten, Hoh River Porter, Hondo's Dexter Joe's Mocha Porter, McMenamins Lighthouse Seaside Porter, North Jetty Semper Paratus Porter, O-Town Oridian's Hammer Baltic Porter, O-Town Priest Point Porter, Port Townsend Porter, Port Townsend Talking Moon Imperial Porter, Rogue Mocha Porter, Rusty Truck Taft Draft Toffee Porter, Three Magnets Smoked English Porter

Red Ale: a light to highly-hopped, medium-bodied, amber-copper colored beer, with toasted malt notes and a caramel sweetness.

Bill's Rudy's Irish Red, Bill's Oatmeal Imperial Red, Buoy NW Red Ale, Defeat River IRA, Hoh River Ruby Beach Red, Hondo's Red Dog India Red Ale, Misty Mountain Sea of Ruin Imperial Red Ale, Port Townsend Red Barchetta, Public Coast Irish Red, Public Coast NW Red, Fish Reel Ales Starfish Imperial Red Ale, Rogue Imperial Red, Rusty Truck Stupiphany Imperial Red Ale, Three Magnets Red Sauce IRA

Roggen: this German ale uses malted rye and is both spicy and sour, with a noticeable hop finish.

Fort George The Road to Rye, Port Townsend Grey Sky Rye, Three Magnets Rye Meridian

Saison/Farmhouse Ale: designed as a beer with which farm workers could quench their thirst during hot summer days in the fields, this Belgian-style ale is gold to amber in color, light to medium-bodied, and highly carbonated. It is spicy (often white pepper is used), moderately bitter, fruity, and sour or tart.

Buoy Imperial Rainbow Petit Saison, de Garde side Project Saison Desay, Fort George/The Commons/Plazm Farmhouse Ale, Fort George Beta Saison 1.0, Fort George Secret Saison, Misty Mountain Riverdale Saison, O-Town South Sound Saison, Pelican Saison du Pelican, Propolis Granum Herbal Saison Brett, Propolis Spruce Golden Saison, Propolis Beltane Golden Elderflower Saison Brett, Propolis Golden Herbal Saison, Propolis Zephyros Golden Elderflower Saison Brett, Propolis Borage Golden Saison Brewed with Borage Flowers, Propolis Melissa Golden Saison with Lemon Balm, Propolis Apricot Ostara Saison, Propolis Gardin Amber Saison Brett, Rusty Truck Serena Rye Saison, Three Magnets Autumnal Saison, Three Magnets Helsing Farmhouse Saison, Three Magnets Hoppy Small Saison, Three Magnets Karakterbier Brett Saison, Three Magnets Woofers Table Beer, Yachats 10 Mile Saison

Scotch Ale/Wee Heavy: this strong, dark, creamy, full-bodied ale is mahogany in color. It has caramel flavors and sometimes, because of the malts used, smoky notes.

Fathom and League Mastodon Scotch Ale, Fort George Wee Heavy Scotch Ale, Fort George Plaid Scotch Ale, Pelican MacPelican's Wee Heavy Ale, Port Townsend Peeping Peater Scotch Ale

Scottish Ale: designated as light, heavy or export depending on the alcoholic content, this ale is not as strong as Scotch Ale. Malt flavors dominate over hops.

North Jetty Leadbetter Red Scottish Ale, Pelican MacPelican's Scottish Ale

Stout: Dark brown to opaque black, it is noted for the roasted flavors imparted by the malted and unmalted barley. English stout is a somewhat sweet ale with caramel and chocolate flavors which are balanced by the hop bitterness. Irish stout is dryer than English versions and often has coffee and chocolate flavors. Designed to be a session beer, it is slightly lighter in body than English versions. Oatmeal stout, in which unmalted oatmeal is added in the brewing process, is very smooth in texture. Russian (Imperial Stout) usually has an alcoholic content above 10 percent ABV. It is bitterer than other stouts, and has much fuller malt flavors

7 Devils Carnie's Big Fig Stout, 7 Devils the Dark is Rising, 101 Brewery Look Out Stout, Arch Rock Brewer's Select Series # 4—He-Man Imperial Stout, Astoria Bad Ass Stout, Astoria Trolley Stop Stout, Bier One Brewing Max Stout, Bill's Allie Mae's Irish, Buoy Oatmeal Stout, Chetco Block & Tackle Stout, Dungeness Kelly's Stout, Fathom and League Alderwood Smoked Oatmeal Stout, Fathom and League Four Leaf Irish Style Stout, Fish Tale Smaug Stout (imperial), Fort George Accasbel's Dry Stout, Fort George Black Sands Imperial Stout, Fort George Cavatica (Imperial) Stout, Fort George Legion of Doom Stout, Fort George North the Eighth Imperial Stout, Fort George Shot in the Dark (imperial) Breakfast Stout, Fort George Summer Stout, Fort George The Three Wisemen (imperial) Stout, Fort George Viva La Stout, Fort George Voluptas Stout, Hondo's Hellbound Mocha Imperial Mocha Stout, Hondo's River Bar Imperial Stout, McMenamins Irish Stout, McMenamins Lighthouse Terminator Stout, North Jetty Discovery Coast LBCR Coffee Stout, O-Town Alki Chai Milk Stout, Pelican Irish Handcuffs, Pelican Sunami Stout, Port Townsend Strait Stout, Port Townsend Land's End Imperial Stout, Propolis Wyrt Farmhouse Stout, Public Coast Black Stack Stout, Rogue Imperial Stout, Rogue Shakespeare Oatmeal Stout, Luke-cifer Imperial Barrel Aged Double Stout, Rusty Truck Procrastinator Stout, Seaside Shorty's Oatmeal Stout, Seaside Stormcrow, Triceratops Hawthorne Coffee Milk Stout, Three Magnets Brimley Stout, Three Magnets Major Tompkins Imperial Stout, Top Rung My Dog Scout, Top Rung Pyrolysis Imperial Stout, Yachats Marbled Murrelet Dry Stout

Tripel: Although lighter in body than Dubbel, this Belgian Ale is stronger in alcoholic content (7 to 10 percent ABV). Bright yellow to gold, it has spicy and fruity notes and a sweetness that is balanced by a moderate hop bitterness.

Reel Ales Monkfish Belgian Style Tripel, Yachats Holdfast Tripel

Witbier: from the Belgian word for "white," this unfiltered wheat beer is pale and cloudy in appearance. Highly carbonated and crisp, it is low to medium-bodied and is often flavored with coriander and orange peel.

Arch Rock Brewer's Select Series #1—28 Finger Wit, Fort George Quick Wit, Hondo's CitWit, Pelican Winema Wit

Specialty Beers

In addition to creating a great variety of styles through their different uses of the four basic ingredients of beer (malts, hops, yeast, and water), brewers often use such additives as fruits, vegetables, herbs, spices, honey, chocolate and coffee to introduce nuances of flavor. In the following list, where the name (or type) of a beer does not indicate what additive is used, the additive is named in parentheses.

Fruit beers: (Note that Belgian fruit lambics are not included in this list.)
Arch Rock 100 Apricot Lager, Astoria Brewberry Wheat (marionberries), Astoria Strawberry Blonde, Bill's Blackberry Beauty (blackberries and marionberries), Bill's Cherry Porter, Blackbeard's Strawberry Blonde, Buoy Black Currant Weiss, Buoy Raspberry Chocolate Stout, Chetco Imperial Coconut Porter, Chetco Unite Pink Pale (raspberry), Cascadia Respect Your ELDERberry (porter), de Garde Apricot Bu (Berliner Weisse), de Garde Biere Noire (sour beer with black raspberries), de Garde Blackberry Whiskey Barrel Bu (Berliner Weisse), de Garde Cherry Raz Bu (Berliner Weisse), de Garde Imperial Boysenberry Bu (Berliner Weisse), de Garde Imperial Cranberry Bu (Berliner Weisse), de Garde Imperial Peach Bu (Berliner Weisse), de Garde Imperial Raspberry Bu (Berliner Weisse), de Garde Nectarine Premiere (Berliner Weisse), de Garde Special Rouge (sour/wild beer with cherries and raspberries), Fathom and League Pumpkiness Lager, Fort George Cherry Chocolate Stout, Fort George Divinity Framboise (raspberries), Fort George Drunkin Pumpkin, Fort George Eat a Peach, Fort George North the Fifth American Strong Ale (fruitcake mix), Fort George Pie (wheat) Beer (strawberry/rhubarb), Fort George Black Walnut Stout, Fort George South (raspberry), McMenamins Ruby (raspberry), North Jetty Starvation Alley Weisbier (cranberry). Rogue Farms Pumpkin Patch Ale, Rogue Voodoo Doughnut Mango Astronaut, Rogue Voodoo Doughnut Pretzel, Raspberry, and Chocolate Ale, Rusty Truck Cherry Chocoholic Baltic Porter, Rusty Truck Moonlight Ride Blackberry Ale, Three Magnets Syrah Barrel Red Currant Saison, Top Rung Raspberry Wheat, Top Rung Trashed Pumpkin Triceratops Strawberry Sour, Yachats Headland Huckleberry Wheat, Yachats Kwak-Wala Salal Sour Saison

Vegetable beers/herb and spice: Cascadia Butternut Squash Beer, Cascadia Chanterelle Beer, Cascadia Green Tea Saison, Dungeness Jalapeno IPA, Fort George Magnanimous IPA (fir tips), Fort George the Murky Pearl Oyster Stout, Fort George Truffle Shuffle Stout, Fort George Spank Stout (pesilla, jalapeño, habanera, Anaheim peppers), Fort George Spruce Bud Ale, Fort George Roscoe IPA (wild rice), Fort George Squashbuckler (Pumpkin), McMenamins Kris Kringle (cinnamon and ginger),Misty Mountain King Under the Pumpkin Russian Imperial Stout, Port Townsend Yoda's Green Tea Golden Ale, Rogue Juniper Pale Ale, Rogue Chipotle Ale, Rogue Sriracha Hot Stout, Three Magnets Just BEET it, Top Rung Flashover Red (hot peppers), Wolf Tree Spruce Tip Ale, Yachats Cetacea Szechuan Peppercorn Saison

Honey beers: 101 Brewery Hook Tender Honey Brown Ale, Rogue Farms Honey Kolsch, Seaside Honey Badger Blonde

Chocolate and coffee beers: (Note that while some malts can impart coffee and chocolate notes to a beer, only those beers which use coffee and chocolate are included in this list.)

Astoria Poop Deck Porter (coffee), Bill's Bruce's Chocolate Stout, Chetco Black Thunder Coffee Stout, Fort George Java the Hop (coffee IPA), Fort George Coffee Girl Stout, Fort George Working Girl Porter (coffee), Hondo's Chocolate Porter, O-Town Mount Olympus Brown (coffee), Rogue Chocolate Stout, Rogue Double Chocolate Stout, Seaside Black Dynamite Stout (chocolate)

Appendix C: Glossary of Beer and Brewing Terms

This appendix provides brief definitions of some essential terms relating to beer and brewing. More terms and fuller definitions can be found in Dan Rabin and Carl Forget's *A Dictionary of Beer and Brewing*, second edition (Boulder, CO: Brewers Publications, 2008), and *The Oxford Companion to Beer*, edited by Garrett Oliver (New York: Oxford University Press, 2012). Descriptions of specific beer styles can be found in Appendix B.

ABV: abbreviation for alcohol by volume.

ABW: abbreviation for alcohol by weight.

additive: an ingredient such as fruit, fruit purees or extracts or spices added to the wort during or after the boiling process to add flavors. One very unusual additive is found in Fish Brewing's Roister Oyster Stout, in which whole oysters are added during the boil.

adjunct: corn, rice or some unmalted cereal grains are sources of fermentable sugar and are sometimes substituted for malted grain in the brewing process. Use of adjuncts usually results in beers that are paler in color and lighter in body.

aftertaste: taste and feel on the tongue after a mouthful of beer has been swallowed.

alcohol by volume: Standard mainstream lagers are usually around 5 percent ABV. Many craft beers have higher alcohol by volume percentages, although these do not often exceed 10 percent ABV.

alcohol by weight: because alcohol weighs less than water, alcohol by weight percentages are lower than alcohol by volume percentages by approximately 20 percent.

ale: one of the two main categories of beer (the other is lager). Ales are brewed with top-fermenting yeast which rises to the top of the wort during fermentation. They are fermented at temperatures of between 60 and 68 degrees Fahrenheit and are often darker, more full-bodied and more robust in flavor than lagers.

all-grain beer: beer brewed using only malted grains. No malt extracts (syrup made from malt) or adjuncts (such as corn or rice) are included.

barley: when it is malted and mashed to produce fermentable sugars, this cereal grain is one of the four main ingredients of beer. Two-row barley is considered superior to six-row for brewing purposes.

barrel: a standard measurement by volume for beer, a barrel contains 31 gallons of beer—that's 55 six-packs of beer.

barrel-aged: beer that is aged in wooden barrels that previously contained such beverages as port wine, bourbon, and rum takes on flavors of those liquors, in addition to the flavors of the type of wood with which the barrels are made. Some brewers put barrel staves in conditioning tanks to add flavors.

beer: an alcoholic drink made with the fermented sugars from malted grains, usually barley, and flavored with hops.

body: sometimes referred to as mouth-feel, it is the tactile sensation—such as thickness or thinness of beer—in the mouth. Stout is more full-bodied than pilsner.

boutique brewery: synonym for cottage brewery.

Brettanomyces: a genus of yeast often used in traditional Belgian styles such as lambics and saisons to give the finished beer "funky" tastes and sourness. Frequently referred to as "Brett."

brewpub: a pub that brews its own beer mainly for consumption on the premises and that serves food prepared on the premises.

bright beer: beer which, after primary fermentation and filtration and before packaging or serving, is placed in a large tank for clarification, carbonation, and further maturation.

budget beer: low-priced beer, sometimes referred to by megabreweries as "value-priced beer," and by some people as "lawn mower beer." Frequently budget beers are brewed with large quantities of less expensive adjuncts (such as corn and rice) instead of malted barley. Many devoted craft beer drinkers drank budget beers as college students. Examples include Old Milwaukee and Busch.

CAMRA (Campaign for Real Ale): a consumer organization started in England in 1971 to protest the invasion of English pubs by megabrewers supplying mass-produced pale lagers. The organization fought for the preservation of "real ale": cask-conditioned, non-pasteurized beer.

carbonation: the dissolving of carbon dioxide, a by-product of the fermentation process, into beer, which creates a bubbling and foaming when a bottle is poured or a keg tapped. Beers such as pale lagers, designed to be served at lower temperatures, are more highly carbonated than those served at higher temperatures. Many drinkers of American pale lagers are surprised at how relatively "flat" some British ales seem.

collaboration beer: a beer brewed together by two or more breweries. In November 2015, Eclipse Brewery of Portland and Fort George Brewery of Astoria jointly created JH2IPA, named after their brewers John Harris and Jack Harris.

conditioning: a secondary fermentation in which yeast is added after beer has been transferred from fermenting tanks to kegs, casks or bottles.

contract brewery: a company without brewing facilities that hires another brewery to produce its recipes, but then markets and sells the product itself. The term is sometimes used to refer to the brewery that makes the product under contract for another company.

coolship: a large flat-bottomed uncovered tank filled with wort on which wild airborne yeast acts. de Garde of Tillamook uses coolships in its brewing process.

cottage brewery: term for a small craft brewery.

craft brewery: a smaller, independently owned brewery producing small batches of all-malt (containing no adjuncts) beer.

crossover beers: beers which are sufficiently similar to mainstream beers to give inexperienced drinkers an introduction to craft brewed products. Some brewers refer to these as "training wheels" beers. Blonde and golden ales are popular crossover styles.

crowler: a 32-ounce can which is individually filled and sealed at a brewpub or taproom.

draft beer: a beer, often unpasteurized, that is served directly from a keg or cask. The term "bottled (or canned) draft beer" used by some brewers is an oxymoron.

dry beer: beer brewed with yeasts that create a higher alcoholic content and which have less sugar in the finished product.

dry hopping: adding hops late in the brewing process to enhance flavor and aroma without increasing bitterness.

drinkability: a term often used in the advertising of megabrewers to describe a beverage that tastes good, is non-threatening, and makes the drinker want another.

esters: compounds formed during fermentation that give fruity aromas and tastes to beer.

extract: a syrupy or sometimes powdered concentration of wort, often used instead of malted grains by homebrewers.

fermentation: the action of yeast on the sugar in wort, producing carbon dioxide and alcohol. "Bottom-fermenting" yeasts are used for brewing lagers; "top-fermenting" yeasts for ales.

fire brewing: use of direct fire instead of steam or hot water to provide the heat to boil wort.

foam: the gathering of bubbles of carbon dioxide at the top of a glass or mug of beer. Beer judges often assess the quality of foam by its color, thickness, and retention period

gluten free beer: beers made without barley or wheat, which contain ingredients which can cause people with gluten intolerance to have serious adverse reactions. Rice, sorghum, and corn, which are sources of fermentable sugars, are frequently used as substitutes for barley and wheat.

green beer: newly fermented, unconditioned beer. Also a colored beer served in some taverns on March 17.

growler: a half-gallon refillable glass bottle used by many brewpubs to sell their beer for customers to take off premises. Quarter-gallon growlers are often called growlitos.

head: the foam collected at the top of a glass or mug of beer.

hops: the cone-shaped flowers of a climbing vine which are used to give beer bitterness and a variety of aromas and tastes. In the eighteenth and nineteenth centuries, hops were added as a preservative for ales shipped from England to India. Many varietals of hops used in brewing have been developed in the last 50 years. One of the most important, Cascade, is often an ingredient in India pale ales, the most popular style of the craft brewing "revolution" of the last four decades.

IBU: abbreviation for International Bitterness Unit.

ice beer: a lager conditioned at temperatures low enough to cause water to form ice crystals which are then removed to give the beer higher alcohol content.

Imperial: term sometimes given to beers with high alcohol content (usually above 7 percent ABV). These higher alcohol "big" beers are often labeled "Double."

International Bitterness Unit: unit of measurement, in parts per million, of the level of bitterness contributed to beer by hop compounds. The higher the number of units, the greater the bitterness. Most North American lagers are low in IBUs (15 or less), while India pale ales are high (often 60 IBUs or more).

kraeusening: the process of introducing a small amount fermenting wort to fully fermented beer, resulting in secondary fermentation and natural carbonation.

lace: often considered one of the important visual qualities of beer, lace refers to patterns of foam created on the inside of a glass as the beer level goes down.

lager: from the German word *lagern,* to store, lager beers are brewed with bottom-fermenting yeasts and then stored for conditioning for longer periods and at lower temperatures (around nine degrees Fahrenheit) than ales. Developed in Germany, lager beers became more widely brewed with the development of refrigeration and are now the most-consumed type of beer in the world. Many craft brewers do not include lagers in their portfolios as the length of the fermentation period ties up tanks for too long.

light beer: a beer that is low in calories and alcoholic content, usually 4 percent ABV.

light struck: term applied to beer that has developed an unpleasant, "skunky" taste because of exposure to sunlight. If you leave beer in a clear bottle or glass too long in the sun, it will soon turn skunky. In TV ads, beers in clear bottles placed on chairs on the beach look wonderful, but probably taste dreadful.

liquor: a brewers' term for the water used in making beer. Because the mineral content of water influences the taste of beer, it is important to have the appropriate liquor for the style of beer being brewed.

malt: grain (usually barley) that is soaked in water until germination begins and then heat-dried to convert the starches in it into soluble, fermentable sugars. The length and temperature of the procedure produces different types of malt that create different flavors and colors in beer.

malt extract: a syrup or powder sometimes used instead of malt in the brewing process.

mashing: the process of steeping ground malt in very warm to hot water to produce wort, which contains the soluble sugars to be converted into alcohol during the fermentation process.

microbrewery: a small brewery with an annual production of under 15,000 barrels of beer, most of which is sold off-premises in kegs, bottles, or cans.

mouth-feel: texture of beer (light to full-bodied, lightly to heavily carbonated), experienced in the mouth.

nanobrewery: a brewery using small brewing equipment, usually of one or two barrel capacity, and producing a limited volume of beer annually. Many restaurants have purchased nano-brewing systems so that they can add their own beers to those they have purchased from other breweries.

nitrogen: a gas which, when used instead of carbon dioxide to dispense draft beer, gives the beer a creamy texture. "Nitro beers," in which the beer from a tap or in cans or bottles have been infused with nitrogen, have a smooth, creamy mouth-feel. Nitro beers have become popular during the middle of the 2010s.

nitrogen infusion: the process of putting nitrogen into beer as it is dispensed into a pitcher or glass.

nose: the aroma of freshly poured beer.

open fermentation: putting boiled wort into large open containers so that it can attract wild, airborne yeasts to begin fermentation. de Garde Brewing uses this process.

organic beer: beer made from all or nearly all ingredients that have been certified as having been organically grown.

pasteurization: the brief exposure of beer to high heat to kill micro-organisms and to extend bottled beer's shelf life.

pitching: adding yeast to cooled wort in fermentation tanks to begin the process of fermentation.

real ale: unpasteurized, cask-conditioned beer served on draft.

regional brewery: a brewery producing from 15,000 barrels to 6 million barrels annually and distributing its product into several states. Fish Brewing of Olympia and Rogue Ales of Newport are classified as regional breweries.

Reinheitsgebot: the Bavarian Purity Law, enacted in 1516, which mandated that only barley malt (and later other malts), hops, water, and (after it had been identified) yeast could be used to brew beer. Although the German government repealed the law in 1987, many microbrewers advertise their adherence to the philosophy of the law.

rice: a grain which contains a very high percentage of starch that can be converted into fermentable sugar and is often used as an adjunct (substitute) for more expensive barley or wheat malts.

sacchrification: process of turning malt starches into fermentable sugars.

scurvy grass ale: according to *Dictionary of Beer and Brewing,* this was a combination of watercress and ale that was believed to stave off scurvy.

seasonal beers: beers, such as pumpkin beers, that are released at specific times of the year.

session beer: because of their low alcoholic levels and smooth mouth-feel several session beers can be consumed during an evening (a session) at a pub or tavern. Recently, many craft breweries have begun to make session IPAs.

shelf life: the amount of time that canned or bottled beer can be kept before beginning to spoil. For most craft beers, this is usually around three months. High alcohol beer styles such as barley wine may be kept for considerably longer periods.

SMASH: acronym for a beer brewed with a *single* *malt* *and* a *single* *hop*. Brewers enjoy creating small batches of these beers to explore different flavors created by the combination of the two ingredients.

special edition beers: usually limited, small batches of unusual or experimental styles of beer.

style: a group of beers that share many of the same characteristics of appearance, aroma, taste, and alcoholic content. (See Appendix B for discussions and examples of specific styles.)

taproom: a room, frequently located at a brewery, which is licensed to sell that brewery's beer, usually by the glass for consumption on the premises, but sometimes for take-away in growlers, bottles, or cans.

tulipai: the *Dictionary of Beer and Brewing* defines the term as "yellow water" and as a synonym for "tiswin," a beer once brewed by the Apaches.

wet hopping: the addition of freshly picked hops to wort during the fermentation process to add flavors and aromas to the beer. Wet hopped beer is available in the fall, shortly after the hop harvest.

wort: (pronounced "wert"): the solution containing fermentable sugars that is created during mashing of malt. The solution is boiled with hops, then cooled. Yeast then turns the sugar into alcohol and carbon dioxide.

yeast: the unicellular, microscopic organism that converts sugars in the wort into alcohol and carbon dioxide. Many breweries have proprietary yeasts developed for their exclusive use. An example is Pacman Yeast, which was developed for Rogue Ales.

zymology: the scientific study of the processes of fermentation.

Appendix D:
From Grain to Glass:
Brewing, Packaging, Drinking

The Big Four: Basic Ingredients

Water, malted grain, hops, and yeast.

For centuries, these have been the basic ingredients of beer. Because there are different types of each ingredient and the four can be combined in a variety of ways, they can be used to create dozens of different styles of beer.

Throughout the twentieth century, beer advertising frequently emphasized water to stress the purity and "crisp, clean" flavor of the beer. Olympia Brewery proclaimed "It's the water" and made much of the artesian wells that lay beneath the Tumwater, Washington, brewery. Hamm's Brewing of St. Paul, Minnesota, announced that it was brewed in the "Land of Sky Blue Waters." The list of ingredients on the labels of Rogue Ales' products includes "Free Range Water."

Water makes up over 90 percent of a glass or bottle of beer. Brewers call it "liquor" and five gallons of it are required for each gallon brewed. In addition to the water content of the product, it is used in the brewing process and in the vigorous cleaning of equipment. The relative hardness or softness of water influences the taste of the beverage and, before the twentieth century, certain styles emerged because of the composition of the water close to a brewery. The hard water of England's Burton-on-Trent contributed to the distinctive taste of the pale ales brewed there; the soft water in the Bohemian city of Plzen was an important element of its acclaimed pilsners. Now, scientific techniques enable brewers to alter tap water so that it possesses the qualities needed for whatever style they may be brewing. This process is often called "building water."

Centuries ago, beer was certainly safer to drink than the water that went into its production. In some ways that may still be true. Air and ground pollution certainly contaminate the sky blue lakes or the free range water. Moreover, the supposedly pristine waters of lakes, streams, and natural wells may have absorbed chemicals that, while not harmful, can adversely affect the taste of the beer brewed.

Malt, which supplies the fermentable sugars that become the alcohol in beer, is made when kernels of grain (usually barley, but sometimes wheat or rye) are steeped in water until they germinate: they are then dried, and roasted in kilns. During the process, insoluble starches are converted into the soluble starches and sugars essential to the brewing process. By using different strains of grain and kilning at different and varying temperatures, different kinds of malt are produced, each kind helping to create a style of beer with a distinctive color, flavor, and aroma. For example, Vienna malt, which is gold in color, adds nutty, toasty notes to beer. Chocolate malts create a flavor that seems slightly burnt. And amber malts evoke the flavors of toffee and bread. Some brewers replace a portion of the malts with such less expensive adjuncts as corn and rice, which also contain fermentable sugars.

Hops, the cone-shaped "flowers" of a vine related to cannabis, have lupulin glands which contain alpha acids that produce a bitterness that balances the sweeter malt tastes in beer, often create citrusy or floral aromas and flavors, and act as preservatives. In fact, in the nineteenth century when the British shipped beer to colonial officials in India, they used heavy doses of hops to help it survive the long sea journey. With over a hundred varieties of hops available, it is not surprising that the various hop extracts, powders, pellets, and whole flowers used in brewers' recipes (usually at a ratio of one part to over thirty parts of malt) have been called the spices of brewing. What are often referred to as the "C Hops"— Cascade, Centennial, Chinook—have been regularly used by craft brewers in their very popular pale and India pale ales. "The Noble Hops"—Hallertau, Saaz, and Tettnang, to name three—are used by brewers to create the crisp and delicate bitterness that characterize German and Bohemian style pilsners.

Some modern brewers complement or replace a portion of the hops in a recipe with herbs that, before the widespread use of hops began in the later Middle Ages, were used to contribute bitterness and flavor to beer. Some of the bittering and aroma ingredients being used include spruce tips, nettles, and clary sage. Propolis Brewing of Port Townsend, Washington, lists among the ingredients of some of its beers "bittering and aromatic root herbs."

Yeasts, one-celled micro-organisms, are essential to the brewing of beer. Without them there would be no beer, just a flat, malt-flavored, non-alcoholic beverage. Yeasts feed on the fermentable sugars derived from malt or adjuncts and produce alcohol and carbon dioxide as "waste materials." Medieval monks, who brewed what was to them liquid sustenance, referred to yeast as "Godisgood." Early brewers often depended on airborne, invisible strains of this divine gift to alight on their liquid and work its heavenly miracles. Some breweries, such as de Garde in Tillamook, still rely on natural fermentation brought about by wild yeasts. Yeast was first specifically identified in the seventeenth century; in the nineteenth century, the research of French scientist Louis Pasteur made possible the isolation and development of over a hundred strains of yeast that are used in brewing. In addition to producing alcohol, each strain of yeast contributes a different flavor to the beer. This is particularly the case in Belgian style beers, where the yeast contributes to the characteristically sour and funky tastes.

In addition to these four basics, brewers sometimes include such ingredients as spices, fruits or fruit extracts, honey, maple syrup, chili peppers, and pumpkins. Called additives, as distinct from adjuncts, these items do not generally influence the alcoholic content of beer, but contribute additional flavors to the basic ones created by the interactions of the water, malts, hops, and yeast. Some unusual additives have included bacon, peanut butter, and oysters. When beers are aged in wooden barrels, they often acquire subtle traces of the tastes of the rums, whiskeys, wines, or other alcoholic beverages that had been previously stored in the barrels.

Brewing and Brewing Equipment

Brewing begins after the brewer chooses or develops a recipe, gathers the appropriate ingredients, and, perhaps most important, makes sure that the brewing equipment is clean—very, very clean. Without completely sanitized equipment, the possibilities of creating bad, spoiled beer increase greatly.

The first step is **milling** chunks of malt into a fine grist which is easily mixed with heated (around 150 degrees Fahrenheit) water (referred to as hot liquor) when it is deposited in a large metal vessel called a **mash tun.** What results is a "porridge" or **mash** in which the malt's starches are turned into fermentable sugars. The mash is strained and the **wort** (which is pronounced *wert*), the liquid containing the fermentable sugars, transferred to a **brew kettle,** where it is boiled for between one and two hours. This process sterilizes the liquid and helps prevent contamination. During the boil, hops are added. When the boil is finished, the hop residue is removed and the liquid passed through a **heat exchange unit** to cool it to the appropriate temperature for adding yeast.

At this stage, the liquid is basically malt and hop-flavored water containing a lot of sugar. However, when it's transferred to a **fermentation tank** and the yeast is added, the wort gradually begins to turn into beer. Within eight to ten hours, the process of fermentation is well under way. For ales, which are made with top-fermenting yeast, the temperature in the fermentation tank is kept between 60 and 68 degrees Fahrenheit; for lagers, which use bottom-fermenting yeast, the tanks are kept at 48 degrees Fahrenheit. Some brewers begin fermentation by placing cooled wort in large open vessels called coolships, where the liquid can attract airborne yeasts. For ales, after a week to two, the now-alcoholic beverage is transferred to **conditioning or aging tanks** to mature. Fermentation for lagers runs between three and four weeks. Ales are conditioned for up to two weeks, lagers for six weeks or more. At this point, the beer is ready to be delivered from the tanks to taps in a brewpub, or to be packaged in kegs, bottles, or cans.

Packaging Beer

Until the early twentieth century, many people took a pitcher or small bucket to the local pub or tavern, where they had it filled with beer and took it back home. Late in the nineteenth century, when glass became cheaper to manufacture, beer began to be bottled, and after the Second World War, tin and later aluminum cans became the preferred containers for beer. Before the widespread availability of bottles, most beer was consumed away from the home. Afterward, consumption shifted to the home. Beer ads in the 1950s showed well-dressed adults enjoying a cool one in their living rooms. When breweries became major sponsors of weekend televised sports, much beer was consumed by armchair athletes sitting in front of the television. And then, as satellite and paid television became available late in the century, sports bars began to spring up, all of them with numerous television sets, each tuned to a different game, mounted on the walls. The consumption of beer outside the home was making a comeback.

When the craft brewing revolution began in the late 1970s, purists insisted that bottles were the only acceptable containers for beer. Cans, they said, gave beer a funny taste, and, perhaps more important to them, they felt that aluminum containers evoked un-genteel connotations of big-bellied men clutching cans of "value-priced," pale yellow, fizzy lagers as they sat on the hoods of their pickup trucks.

Over the past decade, however, the attitudes of craft beer brewers and fans to canned beer have changed. Many microbrewers have either switched from bottles to cans or have begun to package in both bottles and cans. Bottles are expensive to clean and to ship and can easily break or chip. Lightweight cans cool more quickly and, because they are airtight and keep light out, ensure a fresher, unspoiled product. They are popular with hikers and picnickers as they are easy to carry to and from recreational destinations.

At first, the major disadvantage for craft brewers considering switching from bottles to cans was the fact that canning machines were very expensive and cans, which had to be printed with the label for a specific product, had to be ordered in large quantities. Having made an investment in up to 100,000 cans, a brewer had to commit to making a large volume in the style indicated on the label. Bottles permitted the brewing of smaller quantities and different styles; all that was required was a different label on the bottle. During the last few years, smaller and less expensive canning machines have come on the market and a method developed that made it possible to have preprinted labels affixed to cans. In addition, there are now companies that own mobile canning facilities and travel to small breweries where they are able to can as many beers as the brewery or brewpub needs.

But if people still want beer fresh from the conditioning tanks, just the way their great-great-grandfathers got it, they may be able to head to a nearby microbrewery or brewpub. They won't have to bring a bucket or pitcher; they can just ask for a growler—a half-gallon, reusable, screw-top glass bottle—or a party pig—a heavy 6.5-liter plastic container that stands on four legs. With the growler they just unscrew the caps; with the pig they obey the instructions: "Push the snout and the beer comes out." Some breweries have equipped their taprooms with crowler fitting machines. A crowler is a 32-ounce aluminum can which is filled with the beer a customer orders and then sealed.

Beer Is Surrounded by Enemies

Beer has many enemies. They aren't legions of keg-smashing temperance zealots; they're light, air, heat, and time. Exposure to light (especially fluorescent light and sunlight) will cause a beer to become light struck and give it a "skunky" flavor. Clear glass bottles are not beer friendly. Brown bottles or (better yet) cans keep the harmful rays away from the liquid. Of course, sun can also warm the beer and make it taste insipid. If it is shelved in non-refrigerated areas at retail outlets or at home, or if it undergoes a series of temperature changes on the way from the store to home, its flavor can be altered for the worse.

Fresh air may be good for people, but it isn't good for beer. When oxygen interacts with it, the result is a stale, cardboard-tasting beverage. If there's too much space between the cap and the liquid level of the bottle or if the cap isn't fitted tightly, the enemy air may be working on the contents long before you decide to pop the cap.

The final enemy of beer is time. With the exception of some high-alcohol beers like barley wine, beer has a fairly short lifespan. After three or four months of sitting in the refrigerator or on store shelves, the beer in bottles or cans should be retired and sent down the sink to become a part of the water cycle. Check the best-before date on the label if there is one, and, if there isn't, check to see that no dust has gathered on the shoulders of the bottle or top of the can. A dusty beer is probably an old beer.

When you get home, put your beer quickly into the fridge (making sure that the light is out after the door closes!) and don't save it for a festive occasion that is too far in the future.

Enjoying Your Beer

Many people can remember mowing the lawn in the backyard or chopping firewood at the campground or cabin and opening a can of what has been called "lawn mower beer," the stuff that's priced way below the other beers, and chugging it back. It quenches the thirst and if it gets warm or is spilt, it doesn't matter, because, not only was it probably really cheap to begin with, but also, it didn't taste that great. But to enjoy fully a well-brewed lager or ale, don't just grab it ice cold from the refrigerator or the ice chest and gulp it from the bottle or can. In the last two decades, aficionados have developed a series of steps for enjoying beer that are as intricate as those obsessed over by wine lovers. Enjoying a glass of good beer is a wonderful sensory—some would say aesthetic—experience, involving sight, smell, taste, and tactile sensations.

The first thing is that the beer should be served at the proper temperature. Of course, it would be pretty inconvenient and expensive to have several mini-fridges each set at the appropriate serving temperature for a certain style of beer. In her book *Cheese and Beer*, Janet Fletcher offers a very practical method for making sure the temperature of the beer you are about to pour is just right. She suggests taking the bottle or can of beer out of the fridge and letting it warm for a certain period of time. Pale ales, IPAs, Kolschs, wheat beers, and pilsners should be served straight from the fridge. Amber and red ales, amber lagers, bocks, Oktoberfests, saisons, and sour ales should stand for 15 minutes. Belgian-style strong golden ale, dubbels, stouts and porters, and tripels should leave the fridge half an hour before they are opened and poured. And barley wine, Extra Special Bitter, and Imperial stouts have the longest waiting time—45 minutes.

When it's at the appropriate temperature, pour the beer carefully into a very clean, non-chilled glass. An improperly washed glass may contain traces of soap or other residue that can alter its taste. Glasses chilled in the freezer compartment of the fridge may have attracted condensed moisture and food odors, and, when beer is poured into them, the chill may lower the temperature below the recommended serving ranges. If you want to make sure the glass doesn't have any dust in it or has become too warm where it has been standing, fill it with cold tap water, swish the water around inside it, pour the water out, shake the glass to remove any drops, then pour. Do not dry the glass with a towel or paper towel. If you're trying more than one style of beer at a single setting, it's recommended that you use a new glass for each beer.

Different shapes of glasses have been developed to enhance the appearance, aroma and taste of specific styles. For example, the thin, tapered pilsner glass helps to support the delicate head and to release the carbonation bubbles of lagers. The goblet, resting on a thick stem and base, maintains the rich head of stronger Belgian ales. The weizen glass, tapered gracefully inward just above the base and then slightly outward, captures the aromas of wheat beers. A brandy snifter is just right for swirling, sniffing, and sipping such high-alcohol brews as barley wine.

There are two schools of thought on how to pour a glass of beer. However, both have the same goals: to avoid spillage, to create a head that's about an inch high, to capture the beer's aromas, and to release the appropriate amount of carbonation. One school advocates pouring the beer into the middle of an upright glass, pausing as often as necessary to prevent foam from overflowing. The other recommends initially pouring the beer into a tilted glass, then gradually raising the glass to a vertical position to complete the pour.

Once the pour is completed, it's time, not to start drinking, but to admire the beer in the glass. Notice its color, the texture of the head, and the bubbles coming from the bottom of the glass. Lift the glass to your nose and enjoy the subtle malt and hop aromas rising from the foam.

Now, it's time for the first taste—the most important one because the palate loses some of its sensitivity with succeeding sips. Take a hearty, rather than a delicate, sip—not an Adam's apple-wobbling, chug-a-lug, "gee, it's hot today" gulp, but enough so that the beer can slide over and along the sides of your tongue on its way to the back of the mouth. The first impressions may be of the malt flavors, usually sweet and, in the case of beers made with darker malts, tasting of coffee or chocolate. The bitterness of the hops usually comes later, counterbalancing the malt's sweetness and often contributing floral or fruity notes. Depending on the types of hops, malts, and yeasts used, a range of delicate flavors contrasting and complementing each other can be enjoyed in a sip of beer. And if the beer has additives—fruit, spice, or other things nice—taste them as well. They should be delicate and suggestive, not overwhelming.

As your sip is working its way across your mouth, you'll also experience what the beer experts call mouth-feel, the beer's texture. It will range from thin to full-bodied depending on the style and may be more or less effervescent depending on the level of carbonation. Lagers, especially mainstream ones, tend to be thin-bodied and highly carbonated, the darker ales more robust and frequently not so highly carbonated. Important though it is, the first taste won't tell you everything about the beer you are drinking. With later sips, different characteristics will become evident.

If you're having a beer tasting party, it's recommended that no more than five different styles be sampled; after that palate fatigue may set in. At a tasting party, provide each guest with a separate glass (small juice glasses, wine glasses, or special beer sampler glasses), or even small plastic glasses for each beer to be sampled. Each guest should also have a bottle of water and either some bread (such as slices from a white baguette) or plain, unsalted crackers. A cracker or piece of bread, along with a swig of water, will cleanse the palate between samplings.

For decades, much has been said about pairing wines and foods. Recently, beer connoisseurs have stated that beer is a more complex beverage than wine and can be paired with a great variety of foods. It's more than just a beer and a hot dog at the ball game or a beer and burger in the back yard. Some brewpubs and restaurants have beer cicerones trained to assist patrons in choosing the right beer or beers to accompany whatever menu selections they decide on. Restaurant and brewpubs also frequently put on special dinners, with a different beer complementing each course. Three excellent books on beer-food pairing are Janet Fletcher's *Cheese & Beer* (Kansas City: Andrews McMeel Publishing, 2013), Garrett Oliver's *The Brewmaster's Table: Discovering the Pleasures of Real Beer with Real Food* (New York: ECCO, 2005), and Julia Herz and Gwen Conley, *Beer Pairing* (Minneapolis: Voyageur Press, 2015).

Enjoy the full experience of the beer. And when you're finished, don't forget to wash and rinse your glass or glasses thoroughly. Remember: cleanliness may or may not be next to godliness, but full enjoyment of your next glass of beer depends on it.

Chapter Notes

Introduction

 1. www.brewersassociation.org/press-releases/this-year-in-beer-U-S-brewery-count-reaches-all-time-high-of-4,144.

 2. www.brewbound.com/news/anheuser-busch-inbev-to-acquire-breckenridge-brewery.

 3. These statistics are drawn from www.brewersassociation.org/statistics and *The New Brewer*, 32 (May/June 2015).

Chapter 1

 1. The website www.brewerygems.com/olympia.htm and Bill Yenne's *Great American Beers* (St. Paul, MN: MBI, 2004) are excellent sources of information about Olympia and other historic breweries.

 2. Heidi Behrends Cerniway's comments are drawn from a telephone interview conducted December 7, 2016.

 3. Well 80, a brewpub scheduled to open in downtown Olympia in 2017, is named after an artesian well under the building where the brewpub will be located. Plans are to use the well water for brewing.

 4. www.nwtravelmag.com/mcmenamin-brothers

Chapter 2

 1. www.grist.org/article/Horton-fishbrewingcompany.

 2. Telephone interview with Crayne Horton, December 12, 2016.

 3. *Pullman Daily News*, December 30, 1998, 48.

 4. Telephone interview with Lisa Vatske, December 12, 2015.

Chapter 5

 1. Jeff Burlingame, *Moon Olympic Peninsula* (Berkeley, CA: Avalon Travel, 2015), 74.

Bibliography

Books

Acitelli, Tom. *The Audacity of Hops: The History of America's Craft Beer Revolution*. Chicago: Chicago Review Press, 2013.

Burlingame, Jeff. *Moon Olympic Peninsula*. Berkeley, CA: Avalon Travel, 2015.

Cantwell, Dick, and Peter Bouckaert. *Wood & Beer: A Brewer's Guide*. Boulder, CO: Brewers Publications, 2016.

Fisher, Joe, and Dennis Fisher. *The Homebrewer's Garden*. North Adams, MA: Storey Publishing, 1998.

Fletcher, Janet. *Cheese & Beer*. Kansas City, MO: Andrews McMeel Publishing, 2013.

Herz, Julia, and Gwen Conley. *Beer Pairing: The Essential Guide from the Pairing Pros*. Minneapolis, MN: Voyageur Press, 2015.

Hieronymus, Stan. *For the Love of Hops*. Boulder, CO: Brewers Publications, 2012.

Joyce, Brett. *Rogue Farms: 1880–2012, Three Centuries, a Short History*. Newport, OR: Rogue Nation, 2012.

Mallett, John. *Malt: A Practical Guide from Field to Brewhouse*. Boulder, CO: Brewers Publications, 2014.

McRae, W.C., and Judy Jewell. *Moon Coastal Oregon*. Berkeley, CA: Avalon Travel, 2014.

Meier, Gary, and Gloria Meier. *Brewed in the Pacific Northwest: A History of Beer Making in Oregon and Washington*. Seattle: Fjord Press, 1991.

Morrison, Lisa M. *Craft Beers of the Pacific Northwest: A Beer Lover's Guide to Oregon, Washington, and British Columbia*. Portland, OR: Timber Press, 2011.

Mosher, Randy. *Tasting Beer: An Insider's Guide to the World's Greatest Drink*. North Adams: MA: Storey Publishing, 2009.

Ogle, Maureen. *Ambitious Brew: The Story of American Beer*. Orlando, FL: Harcourt, 2006.

Oliver, Garrett. *The Brewmaster's Table: Discovering the Pleasures of Real Beer with Real Food*. New York: HarperCollins, 2003.

_____, ed. *The Oxford Companion to Beer*. New York: Oxford University Press, 2012.

Palmer, John, and Colin Kaminski. *Water: A Comprehensive Guide for Brewers*. Boulder, CO: Brewers Publications, 2013.

Rabin, Dan, and Carl Forget. *Dictionary of Beer and Brewing*, second edition. Boulder, CO: Brewers Publications, 2008.

Shomler, Steven. *Portland Beer Stories: Behind the Scenes with the City's Craft Brewers*. Charleston, SC: The History Press, 2015.

Smith, Gregg. *Beer: A History of Suds and Civilization from Mesopotamia to Microbreweries*. New York: Avon Books, 1995.

Thompson, Logan. *Beer Lover's Washington: Best Breweries, Brewpubs & Beer Bars*. Guilford, CT: Globe Pequot Press, 2013.

Van Wieren, Dale P. *American Breweries II*. West Point, PA: Eastern Coast Breweriana Association, 1995.
White, Chris, with Jamil Zainasheff. *Yeast: The Practical Guide to Beer Fermentation*. Boulder, CO: Brewers Publications, 2010.
Yaeger, Brian. *Oregon Breweries*. Mechanicsburg, PA: Stackpole Books, 2014.
Yenne, Bill. *Great American Beers: Twelve Brands That Became Icons*. St. Paul, MN: MBI Publishing, 2004.

Periodicals

All About Beer (bi-monthly).
Craft Beer & Brewing (bi-monthly).
Northwest Brewing News (bi-monthly).
Oregon Beer Growler (monthly. Also on line at www.oregonbeergrowler.com).
The New Brewer (bi-monthly).

Websites

www.brewbound.com
www.brewersassociation.org
www.brewerygems.com
www.grist.org
www.nwtravelmag.com
www.washingtonbeerblog.com

Index